Fairness, Justice, and Language Assessment: The Role of Measurement

Published in this series

Fairness, Justice, and Language Assessment:

The Role of Measurement

TIM McNAMARA
UTE KNOCH
JASON FAN

OXFORD
UNIVERSITY PRESS

Great Clarendon Street, Oxford, OX2 6DP, United Kingdom

Oxford University Press is a department of the University of Oxford.
It furthers the University's objective of excellence in research, scholarship,
and education by publishing worldwide. Oxford is a registered trade
mark of Oxford University Press in the UK and in certain other countries

ISBN: 978 0 19 401708 4

Printed in China

This book is printed on paper from certified and well-managed sources

ACKNOWLEDGEMENTS

*The authors and publisher are grateful to those who have given permission to reproduce the following extracts and
adaptations of copyright material*: p.12 Extract from *Common European Framework of Reference for Languages:
Learning, Teaching, Assessment* by Council of Europe. Copyright © Council of Europe. Reproduced by
permission of Council of Europe. p.14 Extract from *Michigan English Language Assessment Battery Technical
Manual 2003* by J.S. Johnson. Copyright © 2003. Reproduced by permission of Cambridge Michigan
Language Assessment LLC ("Michigan Language Assessment"). p.35 Extract from *A User's Guide to
Winsteps Ministep Rasch-Model Computer Programs* by J.M. Linacre 2016. Copyright © 2017 by J.M. Linacre.
Reproduced by permission. p.45 Extract from 'Reasonable mean-square fit values' by B.D. Wright,
J.M. Linacre, J.E. Gustafson, and P. Martin-Loff from *Rasch Measurement Transactions*. Copyright © 1994.
Reproduced by permission of the Institute for Objective Measurement, Inc. p.46 From *Applying the
Rasch Model: Fundamental Measurement in the Human Sciences*. Copyright © 2015. Taylor and Francis
Group LLC Books. Reprinted with permission. p.50 Extract from 'Dichotomous Infit and Outfit Mean-
Square Fit Statistics' by B.D. Wright and J.M. Linacre from *Rasch Measurement Transactions*. Copyright
© 1994. Reproduced by permission of the Institute for Objective Measurement, Inc. p.66 Extract from
'Polytomous Mean-Square Fit Statistics' by R.M. Smith from *Rasch Measurement Transactions*. Copyright
© 1996. Reproduced by permission of the Institute for Objective Measurement, Inc. pp.92–3 Extract
from *Measuring Second Language Performance (Applied Linguistics and Language Study)* by Tim McNamara.
Copyright © 1996. Reproduced by permission. p.94 From *Diagnostic writing assessment: the development
and validation of a rating scale* by U. Knoch, Jan 1, 2009. © Peter Lang GmbH, Internationaler Verlag
der Wissenschaften. p.164 Extract from L. Mossenson, P. Hill, & G. Masters (1987). Tests of reading
comprehension. Melbourne: Australian Council for Educational Research. Reproduced by permission.
p.170 Figure from *The Common European Framework of Reference for Languages (CEFR)* published by
Eaquals. www.eaquals.org. Reproduced by permission. p.180 Extract from 'Dimensionality and
construct validity of language tests' by G. Henning from *Language Testing*, 6 January 1992. Copyright
© SAGE Publications. Reproduced by permission. pp.186–7 Extract from 'Using G-theory and many-
facet Rasch measurement in the development of performance assessments of the ESL speaking skills
of immigrants' by B.K. Lynch and T. F. McNamara from *Language Testing*, 4 January, 1998. Copyright
© SAGE Publications. Reproduced by permission.

Sources: www.fina.org

*Although every effort has been made to trace and contact copyright holders before publication, this has not been
possible in some cases. We apologize for any apparent infringement of copyright and if notified, the publisher will be
pleased to rectify any errors or omissions at the earliest opportunity.*

Acknowledgements

This book has a long history. It is an extensive re-writing, expanding, and updating of *Measuring Second Language Performance* (McNamara, 1996), which has long been out of print. It would not have happened without the energy and co-authorship of my younger colleagues at the Language Testing Research Centre (LTRC) in Melbourne, Ute Knoch and Jason Fan, to whom I am extremely grateful. This project is a further fruit of the extraordinary collegial atmosphere of the LTRC, and I acknowledge the support and fellowship of colleagues there over nearly thirty years.

All academic writing involves many minds beyond those of the immediate authors. Terry Quinn drew my attention to the political and ethical character of language testing, a view already articulated by my role models in language testing: Bernard Spolsky, Elana Shohamy, and Alan Davies. For the specific formulation 'fairness' vs 'justice', I am indebted to Henry Widdowson, who suggested this very Widdowsonian contrast following a presentation at the University of Vienna. I am grateful to Kerry Ryan and Kellie Frost for their role in clarifying this distinction. Irwin Kirsch and Bob Mislevy at ETS helped my understanding of the role of measurement in ensuring test fairness. And I am deeply indebted to those fellow Australians who have coached me in Rasch measurement over the years: Geoff Masters, Ray Adams, Patrick Griffin, Margaret Wu, and Mark Wilson.

We would like to thank Sophie Rogers, Antoinette Meehan, and Penny Hands at OUP for their support throughout the process of preparing the manuscript. Thanks also to Anne Burns for her suggestions about the framing of the book, and to Dan Douglas for his comments on the final manuscript.

Tim McNamara

It has been such a pleasure working with Tim and Jason on this project—I have learned a lot in the process. I would like to thank my colleagues at the LTRC for their support over the years, and Cathie Elder for her never-ending wisdom and patience in answering all my questions, as well as for her support during my sabbatical.

Ute Knoch

Thanks to Tim and Ute for their inspiration and encouragement, which have made this writing project an amazing journey for me. Thanks also to Jin Yan for nurturing my initial interest in language assessment when I was a graduate student at Shanghai Jiao Tong University, and Trevor Bond for convincing me of the power of Rasch measurement and for coaching me in Rasch techniques. I joined Tim and Ute as co-author when I was a visiting scholar at the LTRC, and thank Ute and other colleagues there for their warm collegial support during my visit.

Jason Fan

Contents

I

Introduction

Language testing and assessment is a central area of applied linguistics, and language tests are of great and increasing consequence in contemporary society. Tests and assessments act as gatekeeping devices in educational, employment and immigration contexts, and can easily be misused. Yet language testing is little understood by people outside the charmed circle of its practitioners, and even those inside the circle typically aren't equipped by their training to understand the social and policy roles that language tests play. This book examines the technical measurement expertise (specifically within the Rasch tradition) that is needed for the study of the development and improvement of tests and other assessment instruments, and situates it within the context of the social role of language tests. It places at the centre of its concerns the responsibility of language testing practice to make decisions that are just. It argues that there are two distinct aspects of this issue: one is internal to the test, for which, following the distinction proposed in McNamara & Ryan (2011), we use the term *fairness*, and one is external to the test, i.e. the contexts in which it may be used, for which we use the term *justice*. This book discusses and illustrates the distinction; in particular, it focuses on ways in which tests can be made *fairer* by understanding and maximizing their technical quality, and by interrogating the validity of their assumptions using Rasch techniques. But in order to understand why this kind of interrogation and concern for quality matter, we need to understand their role in making tests more just.

The quality of tests

One of the most significant roles of language tests today is as part of the internationalization of education. Why are language tests needed in this context? The language education of international students is big business, not only in English-speaking countries such as the US, the UK, Canada, New Zealand, and Australia, but increasingly in European universities that offer graduate courses taught in English rather than in the national language of the country concerned. When the Australian universities decided to enter the international education market in a major way in the late 1980s, they realized that a major handicap they faced was the lack of a means of establishing the communicative readiness of prospective international students to participate successfully in the educational courses on offer. As a result, Australia joined the UK in the revision of the existing British test used for the purpose, the English Language Testing Service (ELTS), and the resulting International English Language Testing System (IELTS), introduced in 1989, was and remains a joint British–Australian endeavour.

The reason for this initiative shows us something about the function of language tests in the internationalization of education. As part of the selection and admission process, educational institutions need information about potential candidates' readiness to study through the medium of English. Institutions are not usually in a position to meet each applicant in person in the country in which they reside. Instead, they do it by proxy, relying on others who are in a position to do so to form an opinion. This task is carried out by testing organizations, who arrange for samples to be gathered of the applicant's communicative performance on tasks claimed to be relevant to the decisions to be made about them. These samples are then judged against criteria also claimed to be relevant, and a report sent to the institution considering acceptance. This process of gathering information about the applicant's relevant skills in communication, both written and spoken, is necessarily rather impersonal, and is currently conducted on an industrial scale. Two of the most widely used tests used for this purpose, the International English Language Testing System (IELTS), owned and operated jointly by Cambridge Assessment, the British Council and IDP Australia (an organization representing Australian Universities), and the internet-based Test of English as a Foreign Language (TOEFL iBT), currently test millions of candidates a year.

The industrial scale of operation of these language tests raises two kinds of issues about the defensibility of their use. These are considered from the point of view of test candidates who are international university applicants, given that the tests fulfil a gatekeeping role. First, there is the question of the relevance and the quality of the information that the test supplies about the applicant, i.e. claims about the applicant's readiness to cope with the communicative tasks they will face on entry to the university. If the tasks that they are asked to do fail adequately to represent what will be required of them in the university setting, either by asking too much of them, or too little, then the information available in test scores may be misleading. For example, a survey of the writing experiences of first-year undergraduates in courses at an Australian university revealed that there were fundamental differences between the writing tasks they were asked to perform at university and the kinds of writing tasks contained in IELTS (Moore & Morton, 2005). The IELTS writing tasks did not resemble the genres or conditions of writing of academic writing tasks, but were more akin to writing in 'public non-academic genres such as the letter to the editor or the newspaper editorial' (p. 64).

Alternatively, the tasks may underrepresent what is required, by being too short, by being decontextualized, or by not allowing for the role of specific subject-matter knowledge, which may assist in writing tasks in specific subject areas, and so on (McNamara, Morton, Storch, & Thompson, 2018). Another study identified differences between the writing done by recent graduates in their first employment, and those required in IELTS; this is an issue given that IELTS can be an exit requirement on graduation for students in certain cases (Moore, Morton, Hall, & Wallis, 2015). For example, IELTS writers are typically required to take the role of customer, while in the workplace they would be on the other side of the transaction, with resulting differences in goals and pragmatic requirements.

The second issue that may trigger misleading conclusions lies in the way in which performances are evaluated. For example, it has been known for over 150 years, since studies were carried out into the written entrance examinations for Oxford and Cambridge universities, that the chance of a borderline person being accepted for admission is typically as much a question of who reads the paper as who writes it (Linacre, 1989). Judges (or *raters* as they are usually known in research on language testing and assessment) may differ widely in their judgements. An applicant rejected for admission to an international university or a candidate who fails to be awarded a scholarship on the basis of a language test score may rightly feel resentful if they understand that the decision made about their abilities might have been different had another rater been involved. Research on the assessment of spoken and written performances has shown clearly that the reported score should be thought of as representing an amalgam of a number of factors, of which the ability of the candidate is only one. Other factors such as the specific topic or task, the method of testing, the rater, and so on, will all influence the score to some extent.

In order to understand the extent to which the score is a useful indicator of the candidate's ability, we need to be able to estimate how much influence factors such as task, rater, and test method have on scores, and to reduce their impact as far as possible so that we get a clearer measure of the relevant abilities of the candidate. In order to do this, a number of useful analytic methods are available, and this book is intended to introduce the most useful of these for communicative assessments of spoken and written language, i.e. Rasch measurement. The point of learning about such methods is not simply for their own sake: understanding such methods puts us in a stronger position to guarantee the reasonableness and defensibility of the language assessments used in making important life decisions about people.

The fairness and justice of tests: an example

The question of whether a language test is just does not arise only in educational contexts. Language tests also control access to employment where an ability to communicate is one of the required professional competencies. One test, whose quality two of the authors of this book have been involved in investigating and improving for many years, is the Occupational English Test (OET) (Elder, 2016). This test is used to assess the readiness of internationally trained health professionals who speak English as a second language to operate in their professional capacity in the English-medium health workplace. The test is in four parts, one for each skill (speaking, listening, reading, and writing); the speaking test is scored by trained judges from an audio recording of an interaction with a trained interlocutor. It is currently used in the UK, Ireland, Australia, New Zealand, and Singapore for the registration of health professionals trained abroad. It forms part of a series of assessments of qualifications and professional skills which must be successfully completed before the person is allowed to practise professionally without supervision in the new country.

Candidates who have not succeeded in a test sometimes write to the organization administering the test expressing their frustration with their result, and questioning the defensibility of the conclusions of the test. Below is an example of the kind of complaint that is sometimes received. An international student of nursing had failed to meet the language requirement for registration, even though he had passed his nursing examinations and had successfully completed a clinical placement:

> I am writing to question the way of correcting the mark for speaking from a recording. I heard that 2 linguists or more than 2 will listen and mark in regard to fair and correction.
>   However, there is problem and possible wrongly marking just by listening a recording. None qualify nurses of my clinical placement have problem understand my english and I am confident talk to them, but i couldnt get the pass grade in speaking but I tried three times. I have remembered my performance after each time, and. I can't understand why I failing.

The writer reasonably enough raises issues about the method by which he was assessed: a lot is at stake for him. He complains that his speaking score does not represent fairly how well he manages oral communication with colleagues in the workplace: 'None qualify nurses of my clinical placement have problem understand my english and I am confident talk to them'. Of course we have no other evidence, apart from this assertion, that he does succeed, and note that he does not say anything about his communication with patients, which is the focus of the tasks on the speaking test. Nevertheless, the issue he raises goes to the heart of the responsibility of those involved in testing and assessment: do the impressions they report about the abilities and skills of people on the basis of performance in tests that they have designed correspond to the actual performance of people in the workplace? This is an example of a fundamental issue of the *validity* of assessments, an issue we will discuss in detail in Chapter 2.

In this case, the test score represents a judgement that the candidate is not yet ready to manage the communicative demands of the workplace. What methods can testers use to ensure that, as far as possible, the interpretations about test takers' abilities represented by the test score are defensible? The field of psychometrics, or the theory and practice of the measurement of human cognitive abilities, exists to investigate the validity of inferences from test scores. This is principally done by means of studies designed to investigate threats to the meaningfulness and defensibility of such inferences. There are myriad threats of this kind given the inevitable impersonality and artificiality of the procedures used to sample communicative performance in large-scale tests, and the relative brevity of the sample used to judge the candidate's communicative ability. Note, for example, that performance in the Occupational English Test, as in all stand-alone tests, is not sampled directly from the workplace, but from a simulation of the communicative tasks that are held to be typical of the workplace. There is much, then, to investigate in terms of satisfying ourselves that the conclusions drawn about the candidate from the test are reasonable and defensible.

The candidate himself refers to two further such issues: 'I am writing to question the way of correcting the mark for speaking from a recording. I heard that 2 linguists or more than 2 will listen and mark in regard to fair and correction.' The issues he raises are (1) the possible bias introduced by the fact that the assessment is made from an audio recording and not by someone who is able to see the candidate speaking and (2) the possible bias introduced by variation in standards among different judges.

Both of these issues are potentially made more serious because of the logistics of test administration, and the need to minimize the cost of assessments to candidates. On logistics, because the OET, like any other international test, has to be available all over the world, and because the candidature is not large, given the specialized nature of the test, it is not practically or financially feasible to train judges to do the rating of the spoken and written performances on location. Nor is it economically viable for video recordings of the performance to be made—because of the extra personnel and equipment required. Instead, performances are audio-recorded and the recordings are then judged by judges (raters) who were not present at the interaction. On the question of rater bias, each spoken performance on the OET is scored independently by two raters, and their scoring patterns (of leniency/severity and self-consistency) are analysed using the statistical techniques that this book introduces. Scores are adjusted for the relative leniency or severity of the rater, and inconsistent ratings are sent to a third rater. In this way, the analysis of rater behaviour compensates for the potential variation among raters. This analytic work is made possible by the fact that all the performances are double-rated, allowing comparisons across raters and candidates.

Another way for nursing candidates to satisfy the requirement of communicative competence for the clinical workplace is to pass a general proficiency test not specific to the workplace, such as IELTS. This raises different issues of the defensibility of test scores. With IELTS, the potential problem of rating from audio recordings is avoided in most cases because ratings are made directly by the examiner, who interacts face to face with the candidate. It is possible to design research to systematically compare these two approaches to rating—via audio recording, or directly by an interlocutor/examiner. This can be done by getting a number of candidates to take the same test under two conditions: once where the performance is rated from a recording, and once where it is rated by raters who are present. To what extent do inferences about candidates' ability depend on which of the two conditions they are rated under? Again, scores from each condition, and the behaviour of raters under each condition, can be analysed using the techniques to be introduced in this book. In this way we have a surer basis for addressing the complaints about the lack of fairness made by candidates such as the nurse who wrote this letter. The nurse may be right that the method negatively affects the impression of his performance; or it may be that the study shows that the impact of the method is relatively slight, and that a similar conclusion would have been reached with a 'live' rating.

A further issue of fairness is alluded to when the letter writer notes that his performance in the Speaking test assessment is rated twice, in the interests of being 'fair and correct'. Would the test have been substantially less 'fair and correct' if only one judge had listened to his performance, as happens in many tests, including widely used tests such as IELTS? A potential biasing effect here, as we have seen, is the influence on scores of who the rater happens to be. A single rating leaves the candidate relatively at risk; indeed, it can be shown that the chances of a borderline candidate getting a different score (either higher or lower) is approximately 40%—a substantial amount. An understanding of the precise risk of rating designs involving a single rater (compared with designs involving two or more raters, as in the OET) can be achieved by carefully designed studies of agreement between judges rating the same sets of performances. Comparison across raters, and studies of the self-consistency of raters, is then possible. How to design and implement such a study is one of the topics of this book.

There is, then, an enormous, even daunting, variety of threats to the meaningfulness of the inferences from test scores in language assessments, and the research techniques and research findings that we will present in this book will illustrate both the nature of the specific issue of fairness involved, and how measurement expertise can help make tests fairer by identifying and mitigating such threats.

But the question of whether or not the use of a test is just is not exhausted by simply investigating and improving test quality, important as that is. In addition to the question of the capacity of the test to generate information about individual candidates that is useful for making decisions about them, there is the broader question of the use of tests for decision-making purposes in the first place.

In a second letter of complaint, the international nurse raised further issues of fairness:

> I am one of the nurses wanting to be a registered nurse of Australia. But I cannot register only because of the barrier of the OET, despite successful nursing exams and clinical placement ...
>
> I understand communicating in English necessary and important but, professionalism, attitude and personal way towards the needy people is important than actual test when you concern about how well they can be cared ... the person's inside nursing skills is more than significant.
>
> I fail in writing and speaking twice, and I still trying to pass with great pressure due to visa problem. Why losing good nurses only because not passing English test? Have you ever thought just how they feel when they work hard and passed most part of the training, but cannot register only because they failed one part of the OET? I believe that it is cruel and unfair! ...

Here, the issue is the relevance of language proficiency altogether in judgements of a nurse's overall competence. It is perfectly reasonable to ask about the relationship between language proficiency and other aspects of professional skill—what the writer calls 'professionalism, attitude and personal way'. Are they part of the relevant communicative skill, and can they be evaluated by language professionals? This is a question of the appropriate *construct* of the language and communication test. A major study (Elder, 2016) using Rasch techniques as part of a wider range of research approaches, including qualitative ones, addressed this question and concluded that there were ways in which the construct to be tested in the OET sub-test of speaking could be safely extended to include the kinds of professional skills described by the letter writer, which could be consistently assessed by language-trained raters. The recommendations of this study are about to be implemented in the test, thus addressing one of the letter writer's criticisms.

Other criticisms are less easy to address. The letter writer is frustrated at the blocks to his own career, unreasonable in his view; he has satisfied most of the requirements for professional registration: why should he now be blocked because of claimed weaknesses in communication skill (claims which he disputes)? The registration authorities tend to take a more conservative view, insisting that the rights of patients to treatment by health professionals who can understand them and who can be understood must be guaranteed. Whose rights will then prevail? What level of communication skill is enough? Minimum standards of communication skill that are required for a particular professional setting can in fact be established through standard-setting research, some of it involving the techniques presented in this book. This was done in the case of the revised OET speaking sub-test (Pill & McNamara, 2016; see also Chapter 6). But while policies about minimum standards can be informed by the kind of research techniques introduced in this book, policy-makers often respond not to the findings of such research, but to external political pressures. A case in point is a decision made in 2016 to require a more demanding standard of communicative skill for nurses wishing to work in the UK, which led to a large number of applicants failing to get registration. Employers of nurses then lobbied the government to relax the new rules, given the extreme shortage of nurses in the National Health Service. While debate on such policy issues can be informed by validation research, as in the case of the studies we have mentioned here, there is no guarantee that it will play a primary role in determining the policy outcome. Both in the UK and Australia, policies on minimum standards have often changed in response to labour shortages or labour surpluses. There will also be disagreements about the substance of the construct being measured. What weight should be given to communicative skill in the broader evaluation of professional readiness? What does this skill consist of? Decisions about all such matters take us beyond technical questions of test quality into the broader question of the values informing policy, and hence of what we call the *justice* of tests.

Conclusion

How just, if at all, is language testing practice? This is not a new question. It was raised nearly forty years ago by Bernard Spolsky (1981), and with renewed vigour following the ethical approach to validity pioneered by the American educational measurement theorist Samuel Messick, to be discussed in detail in the following chapter (Messick, 1989). The reader is referred to the extensive discussions in Davies (1997, 2004), Kane (2010), Kunnan (2000, 2004, 2010), Shohamy (2000, 2001, 2006), Spolsky (1981), and Xi (2010), among others, which have sought to clarify the responsibilities of language testers for the tests they are involved in developing. We will not rehearse these arguments here; discussions can be found in Frost (2018) and in McNamara & Ryan (2011). In this book, we will adopt the terminology proposed by McNamara and Ryan (2011) to distinguish two differing aspects of the overall justification for the use of tests: on the one hand their internal quality, which we call the *fairness* of the test, and on the other the defensibility of the policies and values implicit in their use, which we call the *justice* of the test. We will elaborate this distinction and its relationship to research on the validity of tests underpinned by Rasch measurement techniques in the following chapter.

    This introductory chapter has argued that the primary subject matter of this book, a guide to the use of the techniques of Rasch measurement in language testing research, is not merely a matter of psychometrics or measurement per se. Instead, crucially, such techniques underpin the justification for the use of language tests, particularly the defensibility of test quality. In the following chapter we will discuss the validity of language tests and its relation to test fairness and test justice in the sense of those terms proposed here. We will give examples of how these complex issues arise in the development of tests, their implementation, and their maintenance. In subsequent chapters we will systematically introduce the reader to the uses of Rasch measurement in language testing. We will present in an accessible way the conceptual bases for the different kinds of analysis required in test validation, and show how each kind of analysis can be implemented using real language data samples. We will also explain, with examples from the companion website (www.oup.com/elt/teacher/fjla), how to use the two most popular programs available to implement Rasch analysis: Winsteps and FACETS. Throughout the book, we will try to indicate what fairness issues are at stake in the examples we give. This will allow us to keep our eye firmly on the 'so what?' question of how approaches to language testing research can contribute to making tests both fair and just.

2

Validity, justice, and fairness

Introduction

This chapter will discuss the notion of validity in language testing and its relationship to the distinction we are proposing between the *fairness* of tests (their internal quality) and the *justice* of tests (to what extent the uses to which they are put are defensible). We will then consider the way in which Rasch measurement can be used as a tool in researching and improving test fairness in particular. Rasch measurement has found a natural home in language testing, as its ability to investigate the qualities of performance assessments of speaking and writing, central to the teaching of language as and for communication, is unrivalled. The potential of Rasch measurement to support the justice of tests will also be explored.

Validity: what is at stake in language tests?

Most large-scale language tests are primarily administrative instruments, serving bureaucratic purposes. They are ambitious, claiming to gather evidence sufficient to form a useful picture of communicative skills of the person presenting for the test, and doing this in a professional, if impersonal, way, efficiently, and affordably for clients using the test. Just like procedures that are used to gather evidence in other domains such as medicine and the law, the procedures used to gather and interpret evidence in language tests are fallible, and research is needed to investigate their quality and usefulness. The guiding framework for this investigation is the theory of validity.

The primary source of thinking about validity in language testing is still the classic discussion of the topic in the work of Samuel Messick (1989). What is distinctive about Messick's work is that he focused not primarily on the processes of test design and development, but on the assumed meaning of the scores and the nature of the decisions that are based on score meaning. In other words, he anchored his discussion of validity in the contexts in which tests are used rather than in the laboratory of test design. He takes a moral approach to validity: for Messick, the defensibility of test score inferences is a question of the rights of those who are subjected to tests; it is not simply a technical question.

Messick's famous definition of validity reads as follows:

> Validity is an integrated evaluative judgement of the degree to which empirical evidence and theoretical rationales support the adequacy and appropriateness of inferences and actions based on test scores or other modes of assessment.
> (Messick, 1989, p. 13)

This difficult formulation needs unpacking. It is easiest if we take the sentence from the end. 'Other modes of assessment': these might be observation of performance in the workplace or in class, for example. 'Inferences and actions' refers to the two fundamental features of assessments. The first is that we use the evidence gathered in a test to reach conclusions (that is, make inferences) about the abilities of candidates in settings beyond the test, the settings that the test is targeting. For example, take the procedures most countries adopt to assess whether someone is safe to drive a car. This often has two components: a knowledge-based test (of the road rules, for example) and a performance test (a short period of driving in normal traffic conditions, together with a demonstration of specific manoeuvres such as reverse parking). On the basis of the evidence of these two tests, an *inference* is made about the person's ability to handle a car in circumstances beyond the test, i.e. that they are (or are not) sufficiently safe and competent to handle further driving experiences without supervision. Based on that inference, an *action* follows—for example, the issuing of a driver's licence.

Returning to Messick's formulation: he then asks, 'How adequate are those inferences and how appropriate are those actions?' This opens up a hugely complex area, which is the central area of concern for language testing research. It applies particularly to borderline decisions about individual test takers: those who narrowly 'pass', or who narrowly 'fail' to reach some standard relevant for a decision—for example, university admission in the case of tests such as IELTS or TOEFL iBT, or the case of the nurse seeking registration in an English-speaking country described in Chapter 1. How can we feel confident that the categorization of the individual in terms of the reporting possibilities available (a level on a scale such as IELTS, for example—as a '5' rather than a '6') is defensible, and would not be reversed if different evidence had been gathered, or it had been interpreted differently, or scored by another rater? The score is a kind of shorthand for the inference that has been made about the person on the basis of their test performance. It is not just a factual or mathematical statement about the nature of the test performance, but represents an interpretation of what the performance is held to indicate—the general inference about the person's communicative abilities. Note that the verbal descriptors that go with scores on a scale such as IELTS, or on the Common European Framework of Reference (Council of Europe, 2001) refer to general capacities or abilities. The specific content of the test tasks is not reported, as it is the generalization that counts. For example, the Global Scale of the Common Reference Levels of the CEFR defines its third highest (B2) of six levels as follows:

> Can understand the main ideas of complex text on both concrete and abstract topics, including technical discussions in his/her field of specialisation. Can interact with a degree of fluency and spontaneity that makes regular interaction with native speakers quite possible without strain for either party. Can produce clear, detailed text on a wide range of subjects and explain a viewpoint on a topical issue giving the advantages and disadvantages of various options.
> (Council of Europe, 2001, p. 24)

Similarly, IELTS Band 6 is defined in the following terms:

> Competent user: The test taker has an effective command of the language despite some inaccuracies, inappropriate usage and misunderstandings. They can use and understand fairly complex language, particularly in familiar situations.
> (IELTS, 2018)

Such statements represent inferences about the abilities of candidates on the basis of their test performances. The terms in which the statements are phrased represent the *construct* of the test, that is, the dimensions of ability that the test claims to be able to identify in candidate performances.

Returning finally to Messick's definition of validity, he asks: 'What is the empirical evidence for the inferences we make? What theoretical rationale links candidate test performance to the inferences about the candidates that the test is making?' The question of 'empirical evidence' opens up a vast area of validity research and constitutes the primary subject matter of this book. What kind of empirical evidence does Messick have in mind? Here he is talking about research on the validation of tests, which involves assuming from the outset that the inferences that we make about candidates may not be right. That is, we may be doing an injustice to candidates by mis-classifying them in terms of scores and reporting scales; this might result in actions being taken (for example, their being denied access to educational opportunity or a desired work setting) that are unfair. Messick puts the onus on those responsible for developing tests to defend the inferences and decisions they are making about people, noting that they should not simply assume their correctness by virtue of the very existence of the test instrument. Taking this responsibility involves researching the threats to the meaningfulness of test scores. Let us again take the example of the nurse from Chapter 1: we need to be sure, in relation to the test that denied his access to registration in Australia, that, for example, (1) its tasks were relevant to the domain in which he wished to work, (2) he had adequate opportunity to show his level of communicative skill, (3) other judges would have interpreted the evidence of his performance in the same way, (4) had the evidence been gathered differently or if different evidence had been gathered, then a similar decision would have been reached, and so on. There are many ways in which tests can be fallible and hence unjust, and the task of test validation research is to conceptualize and systematically investigate these ways.

Messick sees two main kinds of threat to the meaningfulness of test score inferences, which he calls *construct under-representation* and *construct-irrelevant variance*. We can easily recognize these threats in language assessment data. Canagarajah (2018) gives examples of non-native-speaker teaching assistants in an American university whose spoken proficiency in English as measured by standardized tests is low, but whose subject-matter knowledge and teaching skills (including boardwork) make it possible for them to communicate successfully with their students. Research on academic writing emphasizes the gap between the complex reality of the compositional process in academic settings and the highly artificial nature of writing tasks in most tests of English for academic purposes (McNamara et al., 2018), and is an example of construct under-representation. Test validation research of the kind introduced in this book can help address these issues, as we will see. One issue that has been explored using Rasch techniques (as part of a larger suite of methods) is the need to ensure that the criteria used to evaluate test performance reflect the actual criteria that are relevant in real-world communicative settings (Elder, 2016; Elder et al., 2017).

Research on the extent and impact of construct-irrelevant variance is also something that will feature heavily in this book. For example, Rasch measurement is particularly well suited to investigating the effect of the rating process on inferences about candidates. Research has long demonstrated that judgements of complex human performance vary considerably. This is widely recognized: selection panels for jobs typically do not involve a single person, but multiple individuals, all with slightly different perspectives, and consensus is sought before a decision is made. Similarly, in the Olympic Games some performances—for example, diving, gymnastics, and so on—are judged by experts. Here are the current rules for judging diving in international competitions, according to the governing body of the sport:

> In the individual and team events, when seven (7) judges are used, the secretaries shall cancel the two (2) highest and the two (2) lowest judges' awards. When more than two (2) awards are equal only two of the equal awards shall be cancelled. If only five (5) judges are used, the secretaries shall cancel the highest and the lowest award. ...
>
> The secretaries shall independently add the remaining awards and multiply this total by the degree of difficulty for the dive to determine the score of the dive.
>
> (Fédération Internationale de Natation, 2017, p. 13)

Given the complexity of features that must be judged, and the inevitable variability in perception of a weighting of those features, multiple judges are used, and the judgements that are the outliers are discarded. Judgements of other complex human performances such as speaking and writing in a second language are similarly complex and variable. This variability in the opinions of judges can be a source of unfairness, as the outcome of the assessment will, to a certain extent, depend on which particular judge was involved in the judgement; another judge might have given a different score. These differences between judges can, in other words, lead to variations in scores that are not a reflection of differences in the *ability* (the 'construct') being measured, and hence fall under the heading of what Messick calls 'construct-irrelevant variance', a source of invalidity of score inferences.

How variable is human judgement of the productive skills of writing and speaking? This has been studied for over 150 years. Consider Table 2.1 (Johnson, 2003) to get an idea of the typical variability found in judgements of the productive skills in language tests by highly trained and professional judges.

The table presents data from 14 raters (Raters A–N) judging performance on writing tasks of the Michigan English Language Assessment Battery (MELAB), a test of English for Academic Purposes developed by the English Language Institute, University of Michigan. The data were collected over the period 1991–1998. In each cell there are two figures. The bottom one, in brackets, showed how many essays were read by the raters in the pair (both raters in each pair rated the same essays, so it was possible to compare their scores). The top line in each cell summarizes the degree of agreement in the scores given for each pair of raters, using Pearson's correlation coefficient. (This is a statistical measure, on a scale of 0 to 1, about how predictable the set of scores from the second judge is for the same papers, given the scores of the first judge.) The higher the correlation value, the more predictable the second set of scores is. The term 'predictable' here means that the judges are in agreement about the relative ordering of the papers, from best to worst (though not in terms of the absolute scores given, so that judges could be consistent with one another in their ranking, but one judge could be consistently harsher than the other). The range of correlations is between 0.59 and 0.93, with about two-thirds of the correlations (44) at 0.8 or above and one-third (26) at 0.79 or below. In other words, there is a very great range, even among highly trained, experienced, and professional raters.

To help us interpret what this means, Table 2.2 (see page 16) shows how much of the overall pattern of scores of one rater is reflected in the overall pattern of scores of the other rater at various levels of strength of the correlation. The average correlation reported for this set of scores is 0.81. As the table shows, at this level, only about two-thirds of the pattern of scores of one rater is reflected in the pattern of scores of the second rater (i.e. there is still a great deal of variability). If the score awarded to candidates was the average of the scores of the two judges, and that average was compared with the average of another pair of judges for the same papers, the correlation would increase to 0.90, about as high a level as can be achieved in practice, and the lowest correlation would be 0.73—not ideal, but a great deal better than 0.59 (Johnson, 2003).

What this data shows us in general is the great variability in scores of judges even under ideal conditions, and the threat to the fairness of assessment that this represents. The threat is particularly important when there is a single judge as in many important international tests such as IELTS. It is precisely

Rater	A	B	C	D	E	F	G	H	I	J	K	L	M
B	.84 (n=836)												
C	.80 (n=1046)	.81 (n=325)											
D	.88 (n=313)	.87 (n=254)	.78 (n=196)										
E	.86 (n=118)	.88 (n=378)	-	-									
F	.79 (n=415)	.82 (n=519)	-	-	.80 (n=110)								
G	.86 (n=349)	.79 (n=78)	.68 (n=145)	.93 (n=21)	.87 (n=25)	.70 (n=75)							
H	.89 (n=10)	.85 (n=222)	-	-	.87 (n=25)	.81 (n=108)	-						
I	.77 (n=637)	.75 (n=281)	.76 (n=350)	.77 (n=48)	-	-	.88 (n=156)	-					
J	.79 (n=1245)	.77 (n=377)	.76 (n=901)	.82 (n=403)	-	-	.82 (n=154)	-	.72 (n=420)				
K	.82 (n=445)	.85 (n=593)	.82 (n=191)	.79 (n=11)	.76 (n=44)	.82 (n=420)	.80 (n=95)	.79 (n=64)	.84 (n=293)	.82 (n=158)			
L	.87 (n=1320)	.85 (n=494)	.80 (n=428)	.84 (n=123)	.75 (n=39)	.83 (n=428)	.86 (n=344)	.91 (n=70)	.77 (n=277)	.79 (n=827)	.82 (n=454)		
M	.85 (n=442)	.73 (n=205)	.59 (n=216)	.85 (n=33)	.85 (n=85)	.75 (n=137)	.88 (n=145)	.86 (n=15)	.77 (n=163)	.77 (n=295)	.74 (n=126)	.88 (n=492)	
N	.88 (n=51)	.68 (n=12)	-	-	-	-	-	-	-	-	.91 (n=51)	.91 (n=12)	.93 (n=29)

Table 2.1: MELAB Composition interrater correlation coefficients (Johnson, 2003)

Correlation coefficient	Shared variance in scores	Unshared variance in scores
0.95	90%	10%
0.90	81%	19%
0.80	64%	36%
0.77	59%	41%
0.70	49%	51%
0.60	36%	64%

Table 2.2: Interpreting correlation coefficients

this 'construct-irrelevant variance' that the techniques of Rasch measurement to be introduced in this book are designed to investigate—and to remedy as far as possible. Remember throughout that what may appear as a technical matter involving statistics such as correlations is in fact a matter of fairness.

While the analysis of data from communicative tests involving human judgements of speaking and writing is a crucial area of research on the validity of language tests, there are many other issues of test quality that arise in other contexts. For example, objectively scored language tests of every kind, such as tests of reading, listening, and vocabulary, are also susceptible to similar threats to validity that may compromise the quality of the inferences they yield. The techniques of Rasch analysis involving what is known as the basic Rasch model, to be introduced in the following chapter, are useful in detecting sources of invalidity in such tests. Do all the items in a test form a coherent construct? Do the separate parts of a listening test represent different kinds of listening, which should be reported separately, or can they be reported as a single score? What margin of error is associated with the classification of candidates at different grade levels, particularly candidates whose scores fall near grade level boundaries? Can a test be shown to be biased in favour of one gender or another, for example, by its selection of topics, or the kinds of response formats it uses? Are two forms of a test of equivalent difficulty, or if not, can we develop a way of making sure candidates are not unfairly disadvantaged by being required to take one form or another? These and many other questions of fairness can be addressed using the techniques of Rasch measurement to be introduced in this book.

So far in this chapter, we have considered issues of *fairness* that are internal to the quality of the test. But as we will see, Messick, in his famous discussion of validity, urged us to go beyond this, to consider the social dimension of assessment, the social values implied in test constructs, and the social consequences of test use. This takes us to issues of *justice*, external to the test, to which we now turn.

The social role of language tests

Many discussions of the validity of language tests restrict themselves to the kind of issues of fairness and test quality we have discussed so far in this chapter. That is, they restrict themselves to essentially psychometric (measurement) matters, with a purely cognitive focus (conceptualizing the issues in terms of knowledge and ability located in the individual). But Messick (1989) firmly located the business of assessment in a social space. He did this in two ways: first, by insisting that all test constructs embody social values, which need to be defended as part of test validation; and second, by alerting us to the intended and unintended consequences of test use.

The values implicit in language test constructs are not always obvious, and one aim of current research in language testing, under the heading of Critical Language Testing (Shohamy, 2001), is to reveal and evaluate the values embedded in test constructs. These can often be shown to be related to struggles for power and control among social groups. An example is the policy of the International Civil Aviation Organization (ICAO), a United Nations agency responsible for coordinating international policy on civil aviation, requiring pilots and air traffic controllers involved in international aviation to be able to demonstrate a minimum level of proficiency in English in order for them to be licensed. (Note that ICAO has no real power to enforce this policy, leaving it up to the civil aviation authorities of member countries, but there is a moral pressure to conform to it.) The International Language Testing Association (ILTA) has offered to assist ICAO in vetting the quality of the tests used. A review by Alderson (2010) had suggested that many of the tests do not meet acceptable standards of fairness: they are poorly designed, not properly trialled and validated, may not focus on relevant oral communication skills, and so on. Another factor is ICAO policy, which forbids the test developers from mixing technical expertise with language issues. However, as the research we are about to report shows, experienced pilots and air traffic controllers know that technical knowledge is an inextricable part of language use. (A similar issue arises in the testing of English for health professionals, where clinical competence cannot by law be assessed by language assessors—reasonably enough, on the face of it; but it is clear that language proficiency and clinical knowledge are difficult to disentangle. For a discussion of this issue in that context, see Elder, 2016.)

There has been considerable research on the validity issues involved in the development of fair tests of aviation communication (Read & Knoch, 2009). Many of the fairness issues arising, and the methods for investigating them, are the subject of this book: how to identify the impact of the particular tasks set in the tests, how to understand and control for variability among the judges of performance, the effect of background factors on their judgements (native-speaker status, experience of aviation, etc.), and so on. In other words, the measurement techniques we will introduce are there to help us understand and address features of the design and implementation of the assessment that have nothing to do with the candidate's ability, yet may have a bearing on the outcomes for individual candidates. Such techniques help us to identify features that are a potential threat to test fairness. This work is very important, as the extent of such threats can often only be revealed by the careful investigative work that we will be introducing here. Most people put their faith in tests—an issue that Elana Shohamy (2001) has emphasized—when there really is no basis for that faith, if the properties of the tests in question are fully understood.

What, then, are we to make of the policy of various national aviation authorities, notably those in South Korea and Japan, to subvert the ICAO requirements through various means, to ensure that no aviation personnel in their national systems fail the test? In the case of South Korea, this was done by publicizing the detailed content of the test online before the administration of the test so that candidates could prepare for it, and by allowing repeated attempts by people who did not pass on the first attempt. This behaviour would appear to be reckless if the test had the responsibility that it claimed for ensuring the safety of passengers and air crew. Clearly, the aviation authorities in these two countries, and possibly many others, lacked faith in the policy mandating the test in the first place. Why would this be so?

Kim (2012; see also Kim & Elder, 2015) investigated this issue. Routine recordings of air traffic communication (between air traffic controllers and international pilots) at Incheon airport near Seoul, the main international airport in South Korea, were analysed and instances of 'near misses'—potentially dangerous situations which were averted—were identified. South Korean pilots and air traffic controllers were then used as informants to interpret the transcripts of the recordings. What had gone wrong? What had caused the accidents? It was found that language proficiency was rarely an issue; mostly it was inexperience, or wordiness, or failing to conform to the strict routines of communication prescribed by ICAO for everyday communication situations in aviation. Pilots and air traffic controllers are trained in what is called radiotelephony (which requires the use of set phrases), and in techniques involving exact repetition by participants in a communication of what has been heard, in order to demonstrate turn-by-turn comprehension of each part of a message before proceeding. In contexts where the situation requires more than the use of set phrases, there is joint responsibility for the success of the communication between more and less proficient speakers. It was found that native speakers or highly proficient non-native speakers were often the most responsible for the failure of the communication, not the other way around. Those most at risk of losing their jobs from the ICAO policy were the older, most experienced pilots and air traffic controllers, who were in fact highly unlikely to be responsible for dangerous miscommunication. Although the level of their English language proficiency in many cases made it unlikely that they would succeed in the English language tests mandated by ICAO, they more than compensated for this relative lack by their years of experience and their ability to recognize and remedy dangerous situations almost instantly, and were, in fact, extremely safe. It was these older and very experienced aviation personnel that the test put most at risk of losing their jobs. On the other hand, it exempted on principle native speakers from further testing; these were the very ones that the research found to be frequently flouting the rigorous conventions of aviation communication, which are intended to guarantee safety. In other words, the policy itself was the problem, not the tests used to implement it. It is perhaps no accident that the policy committee of ICAO, which introduced the policy, was dominated by representatives from English-speaking nations. The very construct of the test represents the values and the privileges of native speakers at the expense of non-native speakers, when in fact, as the research showed, nativeness or non-nativeness has little do with safety in this aviation context. Instead, cooperative communicative behaviour and depth of professional experience are keys to the avoidance of communication breakdown.

The issues discussed here, then, involve the mandate for the test itself, the social and policy context in which the test finds its rationale. We restrict the term 'justice' to issues of this external, policy-related kind, to distinguish it from internal issues of test quality, which, as we have said, we refer to as test 'fairness'. This distinction is intended to help us understand that even a test that was as fair as it could be made to be, carefully designed, validated, its areas of weakness identified and remedied as far as was humanly possible, might still involve issues of justice in the very fact that it is used at all, for example, as serving a misguided or discriminatory policy. This issue occurs more frequently than we would like to admit in situations where tests are used as instruments of policy—as, increasingly, they are.

We are now in a better position to evaluate, in a potentially different way, the objections made about professional registration that we considered in the introductory chapter. It is legitimate to ask whose values and interests are involved in policies requiring a demonstration of proficiency in English as part of professional registration. In the case of health communication, one obvious answer is that the well-being of patients depends on the quality of health professional communication with patients and with professional colleagues in the clinical setting. This seems a reasonable basis for defending the justice of the language proficiency requirement for registration in the health domain. But it is more complicated than that. For example, what role does language proficiency alone play in successful performance of clinical communication tasks? And how much communicative ability is enough? Where should we set the bar? We have seen in the example from international aviation that it is easy to overstate the importance of proficiency, when successful professional work depends on a composite of skills, of which language proficiency is only one. And in the clinical context, Cameron and Williams (1997) report on a study of a Thai nursing trainee in the United States whose proficiency is low but who manages interaction successfully with patients and her supervisor. Factors such as inferencing, communication strategies, and professional competence underlie the success of her communication, and these are factors that are often not evaluated in spoken language tests. As Hymes (1972) points out, communicative competence involves not only cognitive abilities other than language, such as professional knowledge and insight, but also non-cognitive aspects of performance: temperament, emotional empathy, confidence, patience, warmth, and so on. Hymes termed these additional cognitive and non-cognitive factors 'ability for use', which may well have a compensatory function when language proficiency appears limited. Given that successful task performance is a function of the interaction of multiple aspects of competence, we need to be clear about what minimum language proficiency is required in particular settings. Decisions about 'how much is enough' can be supported by expertise from the technical field known as standard setting. Standard setting involves judgements from domain experts and, like all judgements, they will display variability from judge to judge and from occasion to occasion. The statistical techniques to be introduced in this book can play a role in standard setting (Hsieh, 2013; Pill & McNamara, 2016) and thus in making testing policy itself fairer.

However, technical expertise is not always called on even in standard setting: often, decisions about standards to be reached are not based on studies designed to determine the minimum standard of competence actually required for performance in a particular setting, but exist as a policy lever in the hands of those in authority, to control immigration flows, or to respond to employment conditions. Examples abound. Impossibly difficult language tests were used to exclude refugee doctors from practice after the Second World War in Australia, a situation which remained until the early 1980s. Frost (2018; see also McNamara, Khan, & Frost, 2014) traces the experiences of a group of temporary residents in Australia as they try to meet the requirements for permanent residency. One of the criteria required for permanent residency is proficiency in English, on the grounds that language competence is necessary to secure employment, and for proper integration. However, the level of proficiency required is not determined by a careful study of the level needed for these purposes, but is used as a lever to control numbers of new permanent residents, in response to political pressures that have little to do with rational reasons for requiring certain levels of English. The informants in the study have worked successfully professionally and have successfully studied for higher degrees in Australia, and yet struggle to meet the increased language requirement, demonstrating its lack of connection to the actual communication needs of prospective permanent residents such as these.

Frost's study is part of a larger examination over the last two decades of the defensibility of language proficiency requirements in immigration and citizenship (Extra, Spotti, & Van Avermaet, 2009; Hogan-Brun, Mar-Molinero, & Stevenson, 2009). Extramiana, Pulinx, and Van Avermaet (2014) have analysed which levels of proficiency in the national language, using the CEFR, are required for residency and citizenship in various European countries. The survey shows great variability, with required levels highest in countries where anti-immigrant parties are prominent politically. Given that the CEFR is a universal, functional scale, that is, it describes functional levels of communicative ability independently of any particular language, then the required levels, if they truly reflect the level that is needed for functional effectiveness in the society the immigrant is about to enter, ought to be the same. The fact that they are not shows that the demand for proficiency is based not on a well-motivated understanding of functional need for the language as demonstrated by research, including standard-setting research, but on the political situation in the country involved. The question of the justice of the levels required in particular settings is thus closely related to the values at play in the political debates about immigration, and is not merely a question of the technical quality of the tests used to implement the policies that prevail. Messick (1989), in his discussion of values and consequences in testing, appears to believe that the values embodied in tests are in the hands of test developers, who are therefore responsible for them; but critical language testing has shown that this is far from the case, as tests, particularly language tests, are made by policymakers to serve a range of social and political functions in contemporary society over which language testers have no control.

Summary

We have argued in this chapter that we can understand the question of the fairness and justice of language tests only in relation to discussions of test validity. We are guided here principally by the profound understanding of test validation represented by the work of Messick (1989) in particular, the implications of which have been interpreted for language testing by Bachman (1990), Bachman and Palmer (1996, 2010), Chapelle (2008), McNamara and Roever (2006), and Kane (2006) in educational measurement more generally. Test score validation depends heavily on the ability to investigate the quality of tests and the inferences about individuals drawn from them. This aspect of test score validation, internal to the test itself, addresses questions of *fairness*, to use the distinction proposed in McNamara & Ryan (2011). The uses of tests, which are determined externally to the tests themselves, and independently of them, through policy, involve questions of what we call *justice*, using the same distinction. Language testing expertise of the kind that this book is intended to develop may play some role in revealing aspects of the justice of tests in this latter sense, as in the example of its use in standard setting (Pill & McNamara, 2016); but understanding the impact of language-testing policy on the lives of individuals and on the societies in which they live is more often revealed through case studies, ethnographies, discourse analysis, policy and document analysis, and other qualitative methods that are not the subject of this book. We would argue, however, that the potential extent of *unfairness* in language testing practice is vast, and can usually only be revealed by careful technical and statistical analysis. Thus, though this book focuses on developing in the reader an understanding of measurement techniques—Rasch measurement in particular—and an ability to use them in the validation of language tests, it does so in the service of improving the fairness of language tests, at bottom a social question of rights and equity. This theme is emphasized throughout the book. But for now we will turn to an introduction to basic concepts in Rasch measurement, which we will begin in the following chapter.

3

The basic Rasch model

Introduction

In Chapter 2 we outlined some of the test-internal issues of fairness that can be investigated with Rasch measurement. In this chapter we will look in detail at some of the basic concepts and tools of Rasch measurement. In the earlier chapters, the examples focused mainly on issues of fairness in relation to performance assessments; however, more objectively scored tests (for example, those assessing listening and reading) should also be subjected to fairness investigations. In this chapter we will focus on the basic Rasch model, which is used to analyse dichotomously scored test data, i.e. data that attracts correct or incorrect answers for each item and is therefore scored as either 'o' or '1'. We typically use test items that are scored in this way to assess listening, reading, vocabulary, and grammar. So, what fairness-related issues can we investigate in dichotomously scored tests? We can explore whether the test items (questions) are well designed and able to provide us with valuable information about the students. We can estimate whether the test items are pitched at the correct difficulty level and whether the test as a whole is able to provide us with precise information about the students' ability. We can also gain an understanding of whether the test instrument we have designed is able to measure students well and reliably both as a group and individually, or whether all or some students are unfairly disadvantaged by our test procedures. While some parts of the chapter are designed to introduce statistical concepts, we will explain the relevance of these to test fairness throughout the chapter.

In this chapter we will present the basic concepts and procedures of Rasch measurement in a way that should be clear and accessible for the non-expert. No previous statistical or mathematical knowledge is expected. We will begin by explaining the basic differences between classical test theory and Rasch measurement by using a relatively simple data set. This will be used to demonstrate patterning in the data. From this, the key Rasch concept of expressing the ability of test takers and the difficulty of test items in terms of the probability of success will be introduced. We will then describe several different key concepts of the output of the Rasch analysis, including:

- item–person (Wright) maps (including the expression of probability in terms of a measure known as the logit)
- person ability
- item difficulty
- fit statistics (person and item fit)
- item–person summary statistics
- test reliability

The analysis of test data in classical test theory

Before gaining an understanding of Rasch measurement, it is useful to examine how test data is analysed in classical test theory. We will then show the advantages of Rasch measurement in flagging issues of fairness relating to our testing instruments. In classical test theory, impressions of ability are dependent on the ability levels of the cohort in which you are tested; if you happen to be tested among a relatively strong group, you will be seen to be less able than if you are tested in a relatively low-ability group, and vice versa.

So how is test data modelled in classical test theory? Henning (1987) provides a simple and clear summary of the procedures for language testers. In general terms, a classical analysis of test scores provides information on the following aspects:

- information about the quality of each test item: *item difficulty* and *item discrimination*
- information on the quality of the test as a whole: *test reliability*
- information about the candidate: *person ability*.

Item difficulty (or more correctly, *item facility*, or the ease of answering the item correctly) in the case of a dichotomously scored item is presented in terms of the proportion (p) of candidates getting an item correct. The difficulty of items will thus inevitably depend on the ability of the group that is used in trialling the item.

Item discrimination is handled in terms of whether an item successfully distinguishes between those who do well and those who do poorly on the test overall. The basic assumption underpinning the item discrimination index is that stronger students should do better on an item than weaker students. In other words, we would require of an item of moderate difficulty that it be answered correctly by a substantially higher proportion of those scoring well on the test overall than of those scoring poorly overall. An item that is answered correctly by those whose overall score on the test is low but not answered correctly by those with overall high scores is considered to be an unsatisfactory item. This is because the item is not helping to define the ability of test takers in a way that is consistent with the other items.

An important quality of a test in traditional analysis is its overall *reliability*, estimated in terms of a *reliability coefficient* such as KR-20 or Cronbach's alpha; this is a function or summary of the discrimination of individual items. The higher the item discrimination indices of the individual items in a test, the better the overall test reliability. Test reliability is also boosted by longer tests (i.e. more items in a test) as well as trial cohorts with heterogeneous ability levels.

Person ability in the traditional approach is represented by total scores on the test. However, ability is thus dependent on the difficulty of the test for the group; an easier or more difficult set of items would result in different total scores.

As can be seen by the above description of test analyses in classical test theory, there are a number of limitations to this approach: item difficulty is directly dependent on the trial population, and person ability is directly related to the difficulty of the items. In the following sections, we examine how Rasch measurement can overcome these limitations.

Beyond raw scores: the basics of Rasch measurement

Rasch measurement takes the characteristics of the initial trial population into account in forming its estimates of features of items such as item difficulty. (The technical term for these features is *item parameter*; difficulty is one parameter, and consistency, expressed by discrimination in classical test theory, is another.) Rasch analysis of test data is more complex and more sophisticated than the traditional procedures outlined above. In traditional analyses, the value of each item difficulty parameter directly reflects the abilities of the trial group. (Facility values represent the proportion of candidates in the trial group who got the item correct.) These values are unstable because of the inevitable variability in trial groups; they are likely to be different, sometimes radically so, if the items are trialled on another group and a new analysis is done. We need to take account of the relative abilities of the trial group so that we can get a picture of how difficult the items would be for other candidates than those represented in the trial group. Similarly, given that every test represents a particular selection of potential test items, ability estimates in traditional analyses are limited by the particular characteristics of the test items chosen—their difficulty, for example.

Rasch measurement theory offers attractive solutions to these practical problems of measurement. It enables estimates of candidates' underlying ability to be made by analysing the candidates' performance on a set of items, identifying what the chances are of a candidate at a given ability level answering an item correctly, and then establishing how well the items were matched to the candidates' ability level. How this works in more detail is described later in this chapter. Thus the candidate ability estimates (known as *measures*) are not simply dependent on the items that were taken; we have avoided the trap of assuming that ability is transparently visible from raw scores. Similarly, the underlying difficulty of items can be estimated from the responses of a set of candidates by taking into account the ability of the candidates and the degree to which there was a match between the ability of the trial group and the difficulty of the items. Central to this approach is the way in which candidate ability is related to item difficulty: this is done by estimating from the data the chances or probability of a candidate of a given ability achieving a certain score on an item of given difficulty. The Rasch model proposes a simple mathematical relationship between ability and difficulty, and expresses this relationship as the probability of a certain response.

The difference between the classical test theory analysis of raw scores (counts of how many items a candidate got right) and item facility values (simple counts of how many candidates got an item right) on the one hand, and Rasch estimates of underlying ability and difficulty on the other, is similar to that between descriptive and inferential statistics. With descriptive statistics, a sample is taken and the characteristics of the sample are described, but no inferences are drawn about the characteristics of the population from which the sample is taken; no claim as to the representativeness of the sample is made. With inferential statistics, the characteristics of the sample are used to make estimates of the population from which it has been taken, with appropriate margins of error for these estimates. For example, if you wanted to estimate the degree of pollution of the water in San Francisco Bay, it would obviously be impractical to analyse all the water in the bay. Instead, samples from a number of sites might be drawn and analysed; the characteristics of the samples could then be described with descriptive statistics—the mean concentration of pollutants in repeated analyses, for example. These characteristics of the samples would then be used to draw inferences about the quality of the water in the bay as a whole, with an estimate of the margin of error in these inferences; inferential statistics would be used in this process. We can compare traditional and Rasch analyses in the same way.

In the case of traditional analysis, the characteristics of a particular group of test takers on a particular group of items, and the characteristics of those items for that particular group of test takers, are described and summarized. But we have no way of knowing whether these descriptions of person ability and item difficulty would be maintained for the persons over different items and for the items if they were tried out on different subjects. Rasch analyses make generalizations from the performance of a particular sample of subjects on a particular sample of items to enable us to estimate the ability of candidates in relation to the entire universe of such items and the difficulty of the items for the entire population of prospective test takers.

This property of Rasch measurement has sometimes been misrepresented by unfortunate and misleading slogans such as 'person-free item estimates' and 'item-free ability estimates', which seem to run counter to common sense. Of course, all estimates of item characteristics, including Rasch estimates, are based on responses of particular candidates to particular items, and will ultimately be limited by the quality of the data on which they are based. Small data sets and test items tried out on groups for whom they are ill-matched will provide crude, scarcely usable estimates of underlying ability and difficulty; Rasch measurement provides no magic solutions to problems of poor or inadequate data. But Rasch measurement reports on the quality of the data on which its estimates are based and, if it is poor, it will flag the estimates as potentially being in error.

The basic concepts of Rasch measurement may seem unfamiliar and difficult to grasp at first, but will become clearer in the context of an actual data analysis. In the remainder of this chapter we will examine these concepts and procedures in some detail. We will do so by focusing on a small data set of dichotomously scored (i.e. correct or incorrect) reading test items.

Observing patterning in test data

Rasch measurement is an attempt to model the relationship between various facets or aspects of the test situation. Two facets common to all testing situations are the ability of each candidate and the difficulty of the test items. The Rasch model in its basic version proposes that, where orderliness and patterning are found in test data, there will be a simple relationship between these two facets, such that the probability of a correct answer on an item is related to the difference between the ability of the candidate and the difficulty of the item. The patterning that the model expects is understandable in a common-sense way: the more able the candidate, the higher his or her chance should be of getting the answer correct. Orderliness (and hence, predictability) in the data is often apparent simply by 'eyeballing' the data, provided we set the data out in a way that enables us to see the kinds of relationship of interest. Let us look at an example.

The data in Table 3.1 is from the trial of a reading test. Although the whole reading test was made up of three passages with 56 items and was taken by 80 students, we selected a subset of data: 20 students responding to one reading passage with 12 items. Some of the items were dichotomously scored (i.e. correct or incorrect) multiple-choice items, while others were scored dichotomously by raters using a detailed marking guide. Instead of entering the results of the multiple-choice items using the actual choices the candidates selected during the test (i.e. a, b, c, or d), the data for all items was entered as either 1 (correct) or 0 (incorrect). Missing responses by students were entered as 0 (incorrect).[1]

Eyeballing and detecting any patterns in the data in this format is difficult. To help us identify patterns in the data, it is useful to make two simple

	Items												
Candidate ID	1	2	3	4	5	6	7	8	9	10	11	12	Total score
1	1	1	1	0	0	1	1	0	1	1	0	1	8
2	0	0	0	0	0	0	0	0	0	0	0	0	0
3	0	0	1	0	1	1	1	1	1	1	0	1	8
4	0	1	1	0	0	1	0	1	1	0	0	1	6
5	1	0	1	0	0	0	0	0	0	0	0	0	2
6	1	1	1	1	1	1	1	1	1	1	1	1	12
7	1	1	1	0	1	1	1	1	1	0	0	1	9
8	0	1	1	0	0	1	0	1	1	0	0	0	5
9	1	0	1	0	0	0	0	1	1	0	0	0	4
10	1	1	1	0	1	1	0	0	1	0	0	0	6
11	1	1	1	0	0	0	1	1	1	0	0	1	7
12	1	0	1	1	1	1	1	1	1	1	0	1	10
13	1	0	1	1	0	1	1	1	0	1	0	1	8
14	1	1	1	0	1	1	1	1	0	0	0	1	8
15	0	1	1	1	0	1	1	1	1	0	0	1	8
16	0	1	1	0	0	0	0	0	1	0	0	1	4
17	0	1	0	0	1	0	0	1	1	1	0	0	5
18	0	0	0	0	0	0	0	1	0	0	0	0	1
19	0	1	1	1	0	1	0	1	1	0	0	1	7
20	1	0	1	0	1	1	0	1	0	0	0	1	6
Item total correct	11	12	17	5	8	13	9	15	14	6	1	13	

Table 3.1: Unordered raw data from reading test

re-organizations: (1) sorting the candidates in order of total score, and (2) sorting the items in order of total correct (see Table 3.2).

In Table 3.2, more able candidates are at the top of the table and weaker candidates are at the bottom. Easier items are on the right and harder items on the left. We therefore find more os (incorrect answers) in the bottom left-hand sector of the table and more 1s (correct answers) in the top right-hand sector of the table. In between, we find an area of messiness. This is an area where recently learned abilities that are not yet fully mastered fall. Let us inspect the table a little more closely. We have one test taker, Candidate 6, who answered all items correctly and one test taker, Candidate 2, who

Candidate ID	Items												Total score
	11	4	10	5	7	1	2	6	12	9	8	3	
6	1	1	1	1	1	1	1	1	1	1	1	1	12
12	0	1	1	1	1	1	0	1	1	1	1	1	10
7	0	0	0	1	1	1	1	1	1	1	1	1	9
13	0	1	1	0	1	1	0	1	1	0	1	1	8
14	0	0	0	1	1	1	1	1	1	0	1	1	8
3	0	0	1	1	1	0	0	1	1	1	1	1	8
15	0	1	0	0	1	0	1	1	1	1	1	1	8
1	0	0	1	0	1	1	1	1	1	1	0	1	8
11	0	0	0	0	1	1	1	0	1	1	1	1	7
19	0	1	0	0	0	0	1	1	1	1	1	1	7
20	0	0	0	1	0	1	0	1	1	0	1	1	6
4	0	0	0	0	0	0	1	1	1	1	1	1	6
10	0	0	0	1	0	1	1	1	0	1	0	1	6
17	0	0	1	1	0	0	1	0	0	1	1	0	5
8	0	0	0	0	0	0	1	1	0	1	1	1	5
9	0	0	0	0	0	1	0	0	0	1	1	1	4
16	0	0	0	0	0	0	1	0	1	1	0	1	4
5	0	0	0	0	0	1	0	0	0	0	0	1	2
18	0	0	0	0	0	0	0	0	0	0	1	0	1
2	0	0	0	0	0	0	0	0	0	0	0	0	0
Item total correct	1	5	6	8	9	11	12	13	13	14	15	17	

Table 3.2: Raw data from reading test—rearranged[2]

answered all items incorrectly. Our reading test seems to be separating the candidates into a range of levels. Item 11 is very difficult—only Candidate 6 answered it correctly. Candidate 7, one of the more able students, shows a predictable response pattern. He scored os on the three hardest items and answered all other items correctly. Similarly, Candidate 4, who answered half the items correctly, answered all the easier items correctly, but was not able to answer the more difficult items on the left of the table. We can see similar predictability when eyeballing the results for the items. Item 11 (the most difficult item) was only answered correctly by the most able student, Candidate 6. Item 7, which is an item of medium difficulty, was answered correctly by the top nine students, while all other test takers got the answer wrong.

Importantly, real test data is not always neat and tidy, as can be seen from Table 3.2. For example, we would probably have predicted that Candidates 13 and 14 (two relatively able candidates) would answer Item 9, the third easiest item, correctly. Similarly, Candidate 17 who only received an overall score of 5 out of 12, answered items 10 and 5, both relatively difficult, correctly. Candidate 5's correct answer of Item 1 is equally unpredictable, as it seems too difficult for someone who only answered one other (easy) item correctly. It is possible that this item was answered by guessing (or cheating). Candidate 12's incorrect answer of Item 2 might be due to a lapse in concentration.

The eyeballing of data (when possible in smaller data sets like this one) can give us some information, for example about items that need revising, unexpected candidate behaviour, or item coverage. For our data set, we need to develop some easier or some harder items to adequately measure Candidates 2 and 6, as the items we have are not able to provide us with much information about these test takers. We do not want to delete these test takers from the data set, but we know that we do not have enough information based on this reading test to estimate their ability.

There are, however, several things we cannot easily learn from eyeballing the data. One of the problems of using raw scores (such as the total scores in Table 3.2) becomes obvious when we look at our data set. When we use raw scores, we often mistakenly judge the distances between score points to be equal. Raw scores just give us an indication of the ordering of candidates. What we need is a more precise way of determining how much more able, say, Candidate 15 is than Candidate 11, or how much more difficult Item 11 is than Item 4. Let us have a closer look at Candidates 8 and 17. Both received a raw score of 5, but achieved this in different ways. Candidate 8 answered five easier items correctly, while two of Candidate 17's five correct answers were on difficult items. Does a raw score of five have the same meaning for these two candidates? It could be argued that Candidate 17 has more ability on the construct measured than Candidate 8, but it is also not clear why they then struggled to answer easier items. One possible explanation could be that the item format had an effect; maybe Candidate 8 struggles with answering multiple-choice items generally.

Similarly, we have no way of comparing items and candidates directly to tell us what probability a candidate has of answering a particular item correctly. We could take an informed guess, but that is all. The Rasch model can help us with these problems, as we will see later in this chapter.

Conducting a simple Rasch analysis

There are a number of statistical software programs for conducting a Rasch analysis. In this book we have chosen two: Winsteps and FACETS. We have chosen these because they have been widely used by researchers in language assessment and because of the user-friendly manuals that are available. There are many other possible programs, some of which are freely available; the analyses conducted in this book can also be completed with any of these. The analyses in Chapters 3 and 4 have mostly been conducted in Winsteps, while the analyses in Chapter 5 were conducted in FACETS.

Due to space limitations in this book, we provide detailed instructions and screenshots of how to conduct the analyses shown in this and subsequent chapters on the companion website (www.oup.com/elt/teacher/fjla). We hope that readers, after reading each chapter, will try out the analyses themselves and conduct similar analyses of their own data. On the website we detail how data files are created and how the analyses are best conducted. We also provide a list of activities that can be completed using the data files provided. All activities are accompanied by detailed screenshots and instructions. We hope that in this way the program and the output will be accessible to all readers.

A simple description of what happens during a Rasch analysis

Item difficulty and person ability are jointly estimated in Rasch analysis, using a mathematical procedure known as 'maximum likelihood estimation'. Put in relatively simple terms, this procedure aims to develop estimates of ability and item difficulty in terms of probabilities of expected responses to items by persons. The analysis begins with a provisional working hypothesis about the ability of persons (based on their total raw scores), and the difficulty of items (based on the number of people who got them right; that is, their facility values in traditional terms). It thus begins with working estimates of person ability and item difficulty, which are seen as determining the probability of a person of the estimated ability getting an item of the estimated level of difficulty right or wrong. Using the mathematical relationship between ability and difficulty proposed in the model, predictions are made as to the most likely outcome (right or wrong; that is, 1 or 0) for each cell in the matrix, given the ability of the candidate overall and the difficulty of the item as experienced by the other candidates. The model thus generates a hypothesized (predicted) score set for each individual in the cohort, and this is compared with the actual (observed) score set for that individual, to see how close the two are. If the discrepancy between the two is greater than a certain preset level of accuracy of prediction (usually a fairly stringent level; typically, the total score for each candidate must be predicted to within half a score point of its actual value), then the estimated item difficulties are revised, and are used as the basis for a recalculation of the ability estimates. These in turn may be used to generate new item estimates; the new person ability and item difficulty estimates are used to generate a new predicted data matrix, which is compared with the observed data, the extent of discrepancy noted, and further adjustments made accordingly if the preset level of accuracy of prediction has not been met. The process is essentially recursive until the required level of accuracy of prediction is met; at that point the calculations stop and the ability and difficulty estimates given are the ones finally reported.[3]

It is worth mentioning some technical terms for what we have described here, as they appear in the programs used for this kind of analysis and feature in research and test development reports. The estimates of person ability are termed *measures*, to distinguish them from (raw) scores; the point is that measures are on an objective measurement scale, the scale constructed in the analysis. We explain this objective measurement scale, the logit scale, in more detail on pages 32–34. The estimation procedure is known as *calibration*. Each successive, recursive cycle of estimation is known as an *iteration*. When the required level of accuracy has been reached, the program is said to have *converged*, and the level of accuracy required is expressed in terms of *convergence criteria*.

To summarize the key features of the Rasch approach:

- It estimates ability by considering data from an individual in the context of data from the whole data matrix, that is, the responses of all candidates to all items.
- It relates person ability and item difficulty by estimating the likelihood of responses of particular persons to particular items.
- The difficulty of an item is expressed conventionally as the probability that a person of a given ability will have a 50% chance of getting the item right (although this level may be altered in particular testing contexts, for example if you expect mastery of most of the items by individual test takers).
- Similarly, a person's ability is defined as the probability of that person having a 50% chance of getting an item of a given difficulty right.

Understanding the results of a simple Rasch analysis

The aim in the remainder of this chapter is to discuss some of the key pieces of output provided by a simple Rasch analysis, and to show how these are useful for exploration in relation to test fairness. We aim to make this output accessible to readers without providing too much technical information. The following key aspects of a simple Rasch analysis will be discussed:

- item/person map (Wright map)
- person ability
- item difficulty
- fit statistics
- item and person summary statistics
- reliability

Item/person map (Wright map)

Most Rasch-based programs produce a visual map matching up the ability of the test takers with the difficulty of the items in a test. Such maps have been given various terms in the literature, for example, item/person maps, variable maps, item-ability maps or Wright maps (named after the American psychometrician Ben Wright, who drew attention to the significance of Rasch's work for educational measurement, and was the co-author of two seminal books about Rasch measurement (Wright & Masters, 1982; Wright & Stone, 1979). These maps are produced by expressing the abilities of the test takers and the difficulty of items on a scale expressing the probability of success, the *logit* scale (pronounced 'loh-jit'; stress on the first syllable), so that a relationship between item difficulty and person ability can be seen. This means we can compare item difficulty and person ability for a particular group of test takers and test items to see how well matched they are. The mapping of item difficulty and person ability on the same scale is one of the most useful properties of a Rasch analysis. For example, comparison of the range of ability of the group with the range of item difficulty enables us to see whether a test is too easy or too difficult for a particular group. To get a better understanding of item/person maps, let us look at such a map produced for the reading data matrix we considered earlier.

Three features can be seen in Figure 3.1: (1) A scale of numbers running from 3 to −3 in the left-hand column. This is the *logit scale* (or log-odds scale); it is used to express the probability or 'odds' of success in a mathematically useful way. As the concept of the logit is almost certainly new to most readers, this will be described in more detail below. (2) The twelve items we entered into the analysis can be seen in the right-hand column. These are ordered from the most difficult at the top of the logit scale to the easiest at the bottom. (3) In the column between the logit scale and the items are the test takers from the test trial of our reading test, indicated by their ID numbers. Candidates with more reading ability are located at the top of our figure, and those with less reading ability are located at the bottom. As the items and candidates are pictured in relation to the same scale—the logit scale—we can now make direct comparisons. To make these comparisons, however, we need to understand the concept of the common logit scale. So let us consider that first.

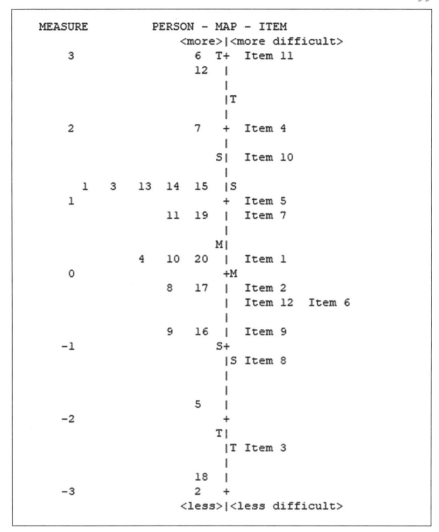

```
MEASURE              PERSON - MAP - ITEM
                     <more>|<more difficult>
    3                    6  T+   Item 11
                        12  |
                            |
                            |T
                            |
    2                    7  +    Item 4
                            |
                        S|      Item 10
                            |
     1   3  13  14  15   |S
    1                    +    Item 5
                   11  19  |    Item 7
                            |
                        M|
        4  10  20        |    Item 1
    0                    +M
         8  17           |    Item 2
                            |    Item 12   Item 6
                            |
         9  16           |    Item 9
   -1                    S+
                        |S Item 8
                            |
                            |
            5            |
   -2                    +
                       T|
                        |T Item 3
                            |
           18  |
   -3         2  +
                     <less>|<less difficult>
```

Figure 3.1: Wright map: reading data

Logit scale

The probabilities or odds of a particular response in Rasch measurement are not expressed in the same way as they are in electoral prospects or betting (5 to 1, 1 in 5, and the like) or weather forecasting (a 30% chance of rain) but in a form that is more tractable mathematically: the odds are expressed as a logarithm ('log' for short) of the naturally occurring constant *e*.[4] We thus speak of the 'log odds' of a response, rather than the odds of the response, and the units on the measurement scale constructed in this way are called 'log odds units' or logits. The logit scale has the advantage that it is an interval scale, that is, it can tell us not only that one item is more difficult than another, but also precisely how much more difficult it is.

Similarly, we can make claims about precisely how much more able a candidate is than another. This is helpful as it gives us a clear indication of differences in ability between candidates, which cannot be seen merely by looking at raw scores.

The logit scale is likely to be an unfamiliar measurement scale; as with any measurement scale it may take some time for a person to get a 'feel' for it, just as, if you move to a culture with a relatively unfamiliar measurement scale for, say, distance, or temperature, it may take some time to become accustomed to what a kilometre is, or a mile, or what degrees Celsius, Fahrenheit, or Kelvin mean. The key thing to remember is that logits express the probability, or odds, of success.

By convention, the average difficulty of items in a test is set at zero logits. Items of above-average difficulty will thus be positive in sign, and those of below-average difficulty negative in sign. Ability estimates in turn are related to item difficulty estimates, and by convention, a person of an ability expressed as 0 logits would have a 50% chance of getting right an item of average difficulty. Candidates more able than that will have positive logit values; candidates less able than that will have negative logit values. Remember that ability estimates are a function of how able a person is (that is, his or her chances of success) in relation to *particular items*. To give you a 'feel' for the logit scale, the following relationships between item difficulty and person ability are expressed on the scale. If a person and an item are well matched, that is, they are at the same location on the logit scale, the person has a 50% chance of success on it. If the difficulty of the item is 1 logit less than the person's ability level, the chances of success rise to approximately 75%; if it is 2 logits less, the chances are closer to 90%. On the other hand, if the item is 1 logit more difficult than the person's ability level, the chance of success falls to approximately 25%, and to about 10% in the case of a 2-logit gap. Table 3.3 (from Linacre, 2016) provides information on the correspondence between expressions of probability in terms of logits and expressions of probability in terms of percentage success. Note that the conversions in this table are only applicable to dichotomously scored items.

Examining the Wright map in more detail

After gaining a better understanding of the meaning of the logit scale, let us return to the item/person map of our reading test data (see Table 3.1). There are several observations we can make from a Wright map:

- We can make some basic 'descriptive' observations about the cohort of students who took the test (for example, which students are the most able, which the least) and about the items in the test (for example, which items are the most difficult, etc.)
- Item coverage: we can get a visual understanding of whether we have sufficient items covering the range of ability levels of our students.
- We can look at individual test takers and make an estimation of their probability of success on certain items.

Logit difference between ability measure and item calibration	Probability of success on a dichotomous item (%)	Logit difference between ability measure and item calibration	Probability of success on a dichotomous item (%)
5.0	99	−5.0	1
4.6	99	−4.6	1
4.0	98	−4.0	2
3.0	95	−3.0	5
2.2	90	−2.2	10
2.0	88	−2.0	12
1.4	80	−1.4	20
1.1	75	−1.1	25
1.0	73	−1.0	27
0.8	70	−0.8	30
0.5	62	−0.5	38
0.4	60	−0.4	40
0.2	55	−0.2	45
0.1	52	−0.1	48
0	50	−0	50

Table 3.3: Logit-to-probability conversion table (from Linacre, 2016)

- We can see whether the difficulty of items matches the test developers' intentions. For example, many tests are designed to start with easier items and then get progressively harder. The Wright map can give us an indication of whether our predictions of item difficulty are correct.
- The relative locations of items and candidates can give us an indication of how well our test matches the ability of the test takers.

Let us examine each of these points above in our data set.

Descriptive observations

In the data set we analysed, Candidate 6 is the most able (i.e. Candidate 6 displays the most ability in the trait we are trying to measure, which is reading). Candidate 2 is the least able in our data set. Item 11 is the most difficult item and Item 3 is the easiest.

Item coverage

The trial data set we are using here for illustrative purposes is only very small. We can see that the items are spread out in difficulty, but not as far as the candidate spread. This is particularly the case at the lower end of the table, where there are no items matching Candidates 2, 18 and 5. Only Item 3 can be found in that vicinity, not sufficient to give us enough data to confidently estimate the abilities of these three least able candidates relative to one another. We can also see several other 'gaps' in the spread of our items. There is a large gap between Items 8 and 3, a further gap between Items 1 and 7, and a gap between Items 5 and 10, in an area where five candidates, nearly a quarter of our trial population, are located. Furthermore, there is also a large gap in item coverage at the top of the scale, between Items 4 and 11. These gaps are an issue of fairness: candidates whose ability is not well matched by items may not have their ability as precisely estimated as candidates matched well by a number of items. This may matter if the pass/fail line is near these candidates' ability.

In larger data sets it can also often be the case that many items of equal difficulty can be found not to match many or any candidates. These items are in some ways redundant as they are not providing us with any additional information about test takers. This information can help test developers revise their test. Redundant items can be taken out of a test and extra items targeting specific difficulty levels can be written to match more closely the abilities of the test takers, although this is not always an easy task.

Probability of individual test takers answering certain items correctly

Let us try to apply the information learned from Table 3.3 to our data. Many of the items match up perfectly with candidates on the logit scale. For example, Candidate 7 and Item 4 are at the same position on the scale, meaning that there is a 50% probability of Candidate 7 answering Item 4 correctly. Similarly, Candidates 11 and 19 have a 50% probability of answering Item 7 correctly. Candidate 6, located approximately one logit higher on the scale has a 73% probability of answering Item 4 correctly. Candidate 5, however, who is located approximately 4 logits lower on the scale, has only a 2% probability of answering Item 4 correctly.

Item difficulty

Test developers can also check whether their intention for specific items matches reality. For example, many language tests are designed to start with some easier items and to end with more difficult items. For our test, the idea was to have two easier items at the beginning. However, this expectation has not been met, as Items 1 and 2 are in the middle of all items in terms of difficulty. The information from the trial can be used to revise the items if necessary.

Relative locations of items and candidates

The items of our test are reasonably well matched to our candidates. Two other scenarios are also possible (see Figure 3.2). On the left, we can see a situation where the test as a whole is too easy for the test takers. In this case, there is not much information available for the Rasch program to

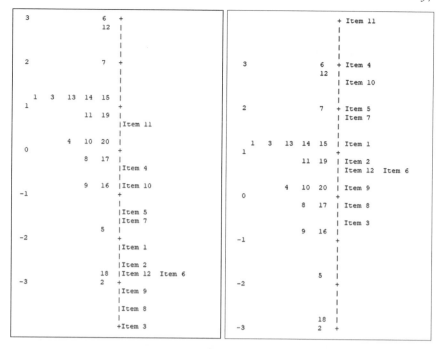

Figure 3.2: Sample Wright maps with (a) too many easy items on the left and (b) too many difficult items on the right

estimate the abilities of the higher-ability test takers. The items not matching any candidates at the bottom do not add any information to the measurement and are relatively redundant. The opposite is the case on the right-hand side of the figure. Here, most of the items are too difficult. Many items at the top of the figure are not matched to any test takers and, because there are no easy items, the Rasch program will not be able to accurately measure the ability of the three least able test takers. Note that the default setting of most Rasch software is that the average item difficulty is set at zero logit and the candidates are mapped in relationship to the item difficulties (though this setting can be altered if required). As described earlier in this chapter, providing test takers with a test that is either too easy or too difficult, and therefore not well matched to their ability levels, may also be unfair, in particular in high-stakes situations, where the inferences drawn and the decisions made based on the test scores are important for the test takers.

Person ability

Apart from the Wright map that we examined in detail above, Rasch programs also provide detailed output on a number of aspects in table format. First, we will consider the output in relation to person ability. Table 3.4

presents an extract of the person table for the results of our reading trial data set. We will consider the other elements in this table later in this chapter.

The table identifies the candidate in the column headed 'Person', the person's raw score total ('Total score') and the number of questions the person attempted ('Total count'). In the case of our data set, all test takers attempted all questions. For a Rasch analysis, not all cells in a data set need to be complete; it is possible to analyse data with missing responses, a point we will consider in more detail in Chapter 7. The table also reports the estimate of the candidate's ability measure ('Measure') in logits and the standard error associated with this measure ('Model S.E.'). At the bottom of the table, the mean and standard deviation of the set of estimates can be found. Winsteps (and other Rasch software programs) can provide this table in a number of ways: candidates can be ordered by entry number, by their estimated ability (i.e. 'Measure' in Table 3.4), in fit order (this will be considered below), or alphabetically.

PERSON	TOTAL SCORE	TOTAL COUNT	MEASURE	MODEL S.E.
6	12	12	4.18	1.86
12	10	12	2.83	1.10
7	9	12	1.91	.86
1	8	12	1.27	.76
3	8	12	1.27	.76
13	8	12	1.27	.76
14	8	12	1.27	.76
15	8	12	1.27	.76
11	7	12	.73	.72
19	7	12	.73	.72
4	6	12	.24	.69
10	6	12	.24	.69
20	6	12	.24	.69
8	5	12	-.24	.69
17	5	12	-.24	.69
9	4	12	-.72	.71
16	4	12	-.72	.71
5	2	12	-1.90	.86
18	1	12	-2.84	1.11
2	0	12	-4.20	1.87
MEAN	6.2	12.0	.33	.89
P.SD	2.9	.0	1.83	.35

Table 3.4: Person table (extract)

Let us take a closer look at the column detailing the standard error. Note that in this case, the error terms are relatively large because of the small data matrix[5]; the analysis is cautious about inferring underlying measures on the basis of relatively poor data. It can also be seen that the standard error is higher for test takers with very high or very low ability. The reason for this is that there is less data for the program to estimate their ability (as there are fewer items matched to their ability level) and therefore the software is less certain that the estimation of these measures is accurate. While such high standard errors are unusual in real test data, it is important to remember that test takers associated with high standard errors for their measures may be less precisely estimated, which is a threat to fairness.

Item difficulty

Item difficulties for the items in the trial are reported in Table 3.5. The item is identified in the column headed 'Item'; the columns headed 'Total score' and 'Total count' refer to the number of persons getting the item right (the total score) and the number of persons attempting the item (the total count)—from which we can derive the facility value of the item in traditional analysis; the estimate of the difficulty of the item is in the column headed 'Measure' and the error associated with this estimate is also given ('Model S.E.'). As was the case with the standard error (SE) reported for the test takers, the standard errors for the items of our trial data are large, mainly due to the fact that we have such a small sample size. The standard errors are larger for the hardest and

ITEM	TOTAL SCORE	TOTAL COUNT	MEASURE	MODEL S.E.
Item 11	1	20	5.09	1.85
Item 4	5	20	2.00	.62
Item 10	6	20	1.64	.58
Item 5	8	20	1.01	.55
Item 7	9	20	.72	.54
Item 1	11	20	.14	.55
Item 2	12	20	-.16	.56
Item 6	13	20	-.48	.58
Item 12	13	20	-.48	.58
Item 9	14	20	-.83	.61
Item 8	15	20	-1.23	.66
Item 3	17	20	-2.33	.85
MEAN	10.3	20.0	.42	.71
S.D.	4.5	.0	1.83	.35

Table 3.5: Item table (extract)

easiest items, because few (or no) test takers are matched exactly in terms of ability. This is particularly the case for Item 11, the most difficult item, which is only matched to one candidate. The error term for this item is therefore very large, indicating that the estimation of the exact measure is difficult and contains some uncertainty. The easiest remedy for the large standard errors in our data would be to collect data from more test takers, in particular from test takers that are well matched to such items. The more information the Winsteps program has when estimating standard errors, the smaller the standard errors will be.

Fit statistics

In this section we will consider the extent to which the pattern of responses observed for individual items and test takers conforms to the general pattern displayed in the matrix as a whole (and therefore what the Rasch program expects), or goes against it. As indicated on page 30, a Rasch analysis proceeds by comparing expected and observed responses by individual candidates to particular items, and successively refines the predictions until there is a sufficiently close match between the expected and observed data. Once the analysis is complete and best estimates of person abilities and item difficulties have been arrived at, the program is in a position to summarize for each person and item the extent of fit between prediction and observation. In other words, the fit for each *row* (person) and each *column* (item) in the data matrix is calculated and reported. We are thus routinely provided with a set of statistics known as *fit statistics* in Rasch analyses. We will consider three aspects of fit (for both items and for test takers):

- Appropriate fit: the pattern for individual items and test takers, allowing for normal variability, fits the overall pattern.
- Misfit: the pattern for individual items and test takers does not correspond to the overall pattern in that it is less predictable.
- Overfit: the patterns for individual items or test takers is too predictable—it displays too little variability.

Confusingly, the output of a Rasch analysis produces four sets of fit statistics for each candidate and item entered into the analysis. Before considering carefully the differences between these, let us understand the basic concept of fit by looking at the raw data matrix for our reading test trial. Although produced in the same way, we will consider the meaning of fit statistics separately for items and candidates.

Item fit

The best way to understand the concept of fit is by looking at the raw data in Table 3.2 (see page 28). The data matrix of our reading trial data includes items in all three categories of fit listed above. We will consider each of these categories in more detail below.

Items showing appropriate fit

Consider first the column of responses in the matrix associated with Item 5 (moderately easy, answered correctly by eight candidates) and Item 4 (moderately difficult, answered correctly five times) reproduced in Table 3.6 for convenience. For Item 5, as we move down the column, initially (i.e. with the highest-scoring candidates overall), 1 is the most probable response; as candidates' total scores decrease, so does the likelihood that they will score a 0, and we get a mixed pattern of success and failure on the item; finally, 0s predominate, suggesting that, for the lowest-scoring candidates, the probability of scoring a 0 is greater than that of scoring a 1 on this item. For Item 4, the zone in which 0 is the most likely response begins higher up the column; that is, higher-scoring candidates have a good chance of getting this item wrong. In each case, the pattern of 0s and 1s is not perfectly predictable; that is, there are irregularities in the patterning. For Item 4, for example, the third-highest-scoring candidate overall got the item wrong, breaking the solid sequence of 1s in that part of the ability range. In other words, it is probable but not absolutely certain that high-scoring candidates overall will get such an item right. Overall,

Candidate ID	Item 4	Item 5	Total score
6	1	1	12
12	1	1	10
7	0	1	9
13	1	0	8
14	0	1	8
3	0	1	8
15	1	0	8
1	0	0	8
11	0	0	7
19	1	0	7
20	0	1	6
4	0	0	6
10	0	1	6
17	0	1	5
8	0	0	5
9	0	0	4
16	0	0	4
5	0	0	2
18	0	0	1
2	0	0	0
Item total correct	5	8	

Table 3.6: Items showing appropriate fit

however, these two items display good fit because although there is some unpredictability in the patterning, this is not more than would be expected in a typical data set. A Rasch analysis can help us identify when patterning is within or outside predictable patterns, something that may be very difficult to do with large data sets, in particular for less experienced researchers.

Item misfit

Table 3.7 shows an extract of the table to illustrate the response patterns for Items 2 and 8 only. We may contrast the orderliness of response to the two items discussed above with the lack of orderliness in responses to Item 2, which was answered correctly by 12 test takers, making it an item of medium difficulty. We see that there is a mixed pattern of successes and failures all the way down the range of ability, as indicated by total overall scores; one's chances of success or failure on this item seem independent of ability. Of the six highest-scoring candidates, three answered correctly, three incorrectly; of the ten lowest-scoring candidates, five answered the item correctly. For Item 8, the second-easiest item,

Candidate ID	Item 2	Item 8	Total score
6	1	1	12
12	0	1	10
7	1	1	9
13	0	1	8
14	1	1	8
3	0	1	8
15	1	1	8
1	1	0	8
11	1	1	7
19	1	1	7
20	0	1	6
4	1	1	6
10	1	0	6
17	1	1	5
8	1	1	5
9	0	1	4
16	1	0	4
5	0	0	2
18	0	1	1
2	0	0	0
Item total correct	12	15	

Table 3.7: Misfitting items

this randomness is mostly obvious in the lower section of the table, where some of the lower-scoring candidates answered the item unexpectedly correctly.

In summary, Items 2 and 8 elicited a pattern of responses that did not fit the general pattern or responses in the matrix, and can thus be classified as relatively *misfitting* items.

Item overfit

Item 7 (Table 3.8) showed a different pattern again. In this case, there is a deterministic rather than probabilistic relationship between total score and chances of success on the item: all those scoring below a certain point got the item wrong, whereas all those scoring above that point got the item correct. It seems as if this item is an 'all-or-nothing' item: at a certain point along the ability continuum, one's chances of a correct response to this item change from 0% to 100%.

Such a deterministic pattern does not fit the expectations of the Rasch model, which expects a more complex pattern of responses—that is, that there should be a little less orderliness in the data. This is an important aspect

Candidate ID	Item 7	Total score
6	1	12
12	1	10
7	1	9
13	1	8
14	1	8
3	1	8
15	1	8
1	1	8
11	1	7
19	0	7
20	0	6
4	0	6
10	0	6
17	0	5
8	0	5
9	0	4
16	0	4
5	0	2
18	0	1
2	0	0
Item total correct	9	

Table 3.8: Overfitting item

of Rasch analysis, where a certain degree of disorderliness is expected. For example, it calculates the chances of an individual of a given ability getting an item of a given difficulty correct. Let us say that there is a 70% chance of such an individual getting such an item correct. We will therefore not be surprised if the individual in question does get the item correct. However, occasionally we shall expect that individuals with this level of ability will not get such items correct. While we would not expect this to happen for any particular item (because the balance of probability says that the individual will get a correct response), we expect it to happen on a certain number of items; that is, we expect occasional violations of our expectations—30% of the time in the case mentioned. Let us contrast this with an item where we expect individuals of a certain ability to have a 20% chance of getting it correct. Again, we expect some individuals at this level to get the item correct, and others to get it incorrect, but we expect on the whole that 80% of individuals will answer incorrectly. Thus, we expect that occasionally an individual of lower ability will get a relatively difficult item correct, or an individual of higher ability will get a relatively easy item incorrect. If these results occur less frequently than the probabilistic model anticipates, then this form of model-data overfit is identified through the fit statistics.

Understanding item-fit statistics

Table 3.9 presents the five items we discussed in the previous sections with one of the fit statistics presented in Rasch output, the infit mean-square value. We can see that the two misfitting items (Items 8 and 2) have infit mean-square values of just above 1.3, the items with good fit (Items 4 and 5) have mean-square values close to 1, and the overfitting item (Item 7) has a mean-square value of much lower than 1. So how are these values interpreted?

Mean-square values have an expected value of 1, but can range from 0 to positive infinity (i.e. they are always positive); individual values will be above or below 1, according to whether the observed values show greater variation by being less predictable (resulting in values *greater* than 1) or less variation by being more predictable (resulting in values *less* than 1) than might normally

Item	more able.................... Candidates ....less able																					Infit meansq
8 (misfit)	1	1	1	1	1	1	1	0	1	1	1	1	0	1	1	1	0	0	1	0	1.35
2 (misfit)	1	0	1	0	1	0	1	1	1	1	0	1	1	1	1	0	1	0	0	0	1.334
5	1	1	1	0	1	1	0	0	0	0	1	0	1	1	0	0	0	0	0	0	1.05
4	1	1	0	1	0	0	1	0	0	1	0	0	0	0	0	0	0	0	0	0	.89
7 (overfit)	1	1	1	1	1	1	1	1	1	0	0	0	0	0	0	0	0	0	0	0	.55

Table 3.9: Raw data for five items with mean-square values

be expected. According to Bond and Fox (2015), an infit or outfit 'mean-square value of 1 + x indicates 100x% more variation between the observed and the model-predicted response patterns than would be expected if the data and the model were perfectly compatible' (p. 269). For example, an infit value of 1.45 indicates 45% more variation in the data than predicted. Similarly, a fit value of 1 – x indicates x% less variability compared to the model predicted variation. So a fit value (either infit or outfit) of 0.67 indicates 33% less variation than predicted.

How far away from the mean of 1 can we expect such values to vary before statistically *significant* problems of fit are indicated? A useful rule of thumb, provided by McNamara (1996), is that values in the range of approximately 0.75 to 1.3 are acceptable.[6] Values greater than 1.3 show significant misfit— that is, lack of predictability; values below 0.75 show significant overfit. Table 3.10, from Wright et al. (1994), shows reasonable ranges for mean-square statistics for a range of different assessment situations.

The complete Winsteps output table for our items can be seen in Table 3.11. In this case, the output is analysed in terms of fit order, with the most misfitting items at the top of the table, items with good fit in the middle rows, and items showing overfit in the lower part of the table.

We can see four columns relating to item fit. We have already encountered the infit mean-square value and learned how to interpret this. This is the most

Type of test	Range
Multiple-choice test (high stakes)	0.8 – 1.2
Multiple-choice test (run of the mill)	0.7 – 1.3
Rating scale (Likert/survey)	0.6 – 1.4
Clinical observations	0.5 – 1.7
Judged (where agreement encouraged)	0.4 – 1.2

Table 3.10: Suggested acceptable ranges for item mean-square statistics (from Wright, Linacre, Gustafsson, & Martin-Loff, 1994, p. 370)

```
-------------------------------------------------------------------------------
|ENTRY   TOTAL  TOTAL            MODEL|  INFIT   |  OUTFIT  |PTMEASUR-AL|EXACT MATCH|        |
|NUMBER  SCORE  COUNT  MEASURE  S.E. |MNSQ ZSTD|MNSQ ZSTD|CORR.  EXP. | OBS%  EXP%| ITEM   |
|-------------------------------------+----------+----------+-----------+-----------+--------|
|    2     12     20    -.16     .56|1.33  1.3|2.08  2.2|A .37   .56| 61.1  73.2| Item 2  |
|    8     15     20   -1.23     .66|1.35  1.0|1.45   .8|B .44   .58| 77.8  83.0| Item 8  |
|    1     11     20     .14     .55|1.28  1.2|1.36  1.0|C .42   .55| 66.7  71.4| Item 1  |
|    9     14     20    -.83     .61|1.18   .6|1.34   .7|D .49   .58| 83.3  79.0| Item 9  |
|    5      7     19    1.01     .55|1.05   .3| .92   .0|E .44   .46| 66.7  70.9| Item 5  |
|   10      6     20    1.64     .58| .96  -.1| .88   .1|F .51   .50| 72.2  75.9| Item 10|
|    4      5     20    2.00     .62| .89  -.3| .65  -.2|e .54   .48| 83.3  79.9| Item 4  |
|    3     17     20   -2.32     .85| .85  -.1| .57   .0|d .64   .59| 94.4  90.1| Item 3  |
|   12     13     20    -.48     .58| .70 -1.1| .53 -1.1|c .70   .57| 77.8  75.8| Item 12|
|    6     13     20    -.48     .58| .68 -1.2| .56 -1.0|b .70   .57| 88.9  75.8| Item 6  |
|    7      9     20     .72     .54| .55 -2.5| .47 -1.4|a .72   .53| 94.4  70.3| Item 7  |
|-------------------------------------+----------+----------+-----------+-----------+--------|
| MEAN  10.3   19.9     .42     .71| .98  -.1| .98      .1|           | 78.8  76.8|        |
| P.SD   4.5    .3     1.83     .35| .27  1.1| .49     1.0|           | 10.8   5.7|        |
-------------------------------------------------------------------------------
```

Table 3.11: Item statistics table

common fit index used in language-assessment-related research and test analyses. In Winsteps, and most other Rasch programs, the fit statistics are presented in two groups of two indices: *infit* and *outfit* statistics, each expressed in two alternative ways, as *mean square* or *ZStd*. Briefly, the infit statistics are the ones usually considered the most informative, as they focus on the degree of fit in the most typical observations in the matrix (ignoring outliers, or extreme observations). The outfit statistics, on the other hand, include every single observation, even extremely unpredictable single observations (outliers); such single observations may have a disproportionate influence on the summary statistic for fit. The infit statistics do not include such extreme values, and hence provide a more sensitive picture of the fit in the set of observations of greatest interest.

Fit values expressed in terms of the ZStd will vary around a mean of zero, and will be positive or negative according to whether the observed values show greater variation (resulting in a positive value of ZStd) or less variation (resulting in a negative value of ZStd) than might normally be expected. Values of ZStd outside the range +2 to −2 are said to indicate a significant departure from the expectations of the model. Values larger than +2 indicate significant misfit; values below −2 indicate significant overfit. Usually the mean square and the ZStd statistics will give the same indication of misfit or overfit. Where differences occur, this is usually related to sample size. With small sample sizes, as here, the values tend to be a little less reliable; with very large sample sizes (say, over 400), the ZStd values will be inflated and may lie outside the acceptable range by chance, and will not necessarily indicate a significant problem of fit; the mean-square statistic, on the other hand, is more likely to be acceptable with larger sample sizes, which is a conundrum that cannot be resolved. Table 3.12, adapted from Bond & Fox (2015), summarizes the different possible response patterns.

Let us look at the mean-square item-fit values in Table 3.11. We find that items 2 and 8 show misfit, which corresponds to our analysis of the raw data above. Note that the outfit mean square of Item 2 is significantly higher than the infit mean square, indicating that this value is due to an outlier in the data. The most overfitting item is Item 7 (mean square 0.55), which confirmed our expectations from eyeballing the data matrix.

Table 3.11 also shows a further column, the point-biserial correlation ('Pt measure correlation'). The point-biserial correlation coefficient is used to estimate the degree of relationship between a dichotomous variable and an interval variable. In this case, the program correlates the item score (in this case, a dichotomy) with the rest scores, that is, the total scores excluding the

Mean squares	ZStd (or t)	Variation	Fit type
> 1.3	> 2.0	Too much	Misfit
< 0.7	< −2.0	Too little	Overfit

Table 3.12: Interpretation of fit statistics (from Bond & Fox, 2015, p. 270)

scores on the item in question. According to Wright (1992), this correlation is based on raw scores and therefore an index from classical test theory, and are usually directly related to the fit statistics. If an item is found to be noisy (i.e. not following expectations) or misfitting, the point-biserial correlation is usually low. On the other hand, if an item is muted or overfitting, the correlation coefficient is usually high. Because this value is based on raw scores, we cannot say whether a value is acceptable or not; we can only judge whether it is bigger or smaller than we are used to. This makes it a misfit statistic of unknown size, according to Wright. If the point-biserial is negative, however, this indicates that the item contradicts the construct we are attempting to test.

Interpreting item fit

Both misfit and overfit are interpreted differently and have different implications for measurement.

Misfitting items can be interpreted as indicating one of several things. First, they may signal poorly written items; in this sense the interpretation is similar to that of poorly discriminating items in traditional analysis.[7] Such items may need revision; perhaps the multiple-choice distractors are at fault or the answer key needs revising. Secondly, they may indicate that an item is perfectly good in itself, but that it does not form part of a set of items that together define a single measurement trait. Two or more measurement traits may have been confounded in the construction of the test, and in this case it does not make sense to simply add up the scores on the items on the test and report them as a single score; that would be like adding apples and oranges—the things being added are not alike. Instead, two separate scores should be reported, one for each group of items.

Imagine you gave a class of people a test of reading competence. The items would be designed to test their abilities of skimming, scanning, inferring meaning, etc., but you decided to add one item in which test takers would be asked to translate a word in the reading text. It could be expected that the translating task would behave differently to the other items. This is because it is measuring a different ability from the other 'reading ability' items. We would expect this item to be misfitting. Misfitting items are simply those where an individual's performance on one item could not be predicted from the individual's performance on others. The item may be perfectly acceptable in itself; it just forms part of another set. We will return to this issue in Chapter 7.

Misfitting items degrade the quality of our measurement. Because of that, we should investigate the reasons for this misfit and aim to improve the items for subsequent test administrations or delete them from our test. Misfitting items should be removed before scores are reported to test takers. If this type of analysis is not conducted and such items are not identified and removed or revised, the results of the assessment may not be fair to the students, in particular those scoring close to decision-making points where their answers to one or more misfitting items may have determined which classification they are grouped into.

The question of overfitting items is rather different. These items are redundant because they give us no information that the other items do not already provide; the pattern of response to these items is too predictable from the overall pattern of response to other items. Worse, they may signal items that have a dependency on other items built into them; for example, if you can only get Item 7 correct if you get Item 6 correct (because understanding the point of Item 7 depends on your having first understood the answer to Item 6), then there will be too little variability in responses to Item 7 – the variability is constrained by the response to the previous item. Item 7 is not making an *independent* contribution to the measurement trait being measured by the test, and may therefore need to be revised or removed. Overfit usually has no real practical implications. As mentioned above, these items do not add much additional information in terms of estimating the item measures, but they do not cause any harm to our measurement either. In terms of technical implications, a large number of overfitting items might inflate the test reliability, although they may not be providing much extra information about test takers.

Wright (1991) provides some useful guidelines on why items may be identified as misfitting or overfitting and how test developers/researchers could deal with these items.

Person fit

Unlike traditional analysis, Rasch analysis enables us to investigate the coherence of an individual's responses as part of a set of responses from a larger group of individuals, and allows us to ask: Can the ability of this individual be defined in the same terms as the ability of others in the group? Do these responses 'fit' the overall pattern?

We will return to the reading-data matrix, and consider the response patterns of individual candidates; a selection of these is presented in Table 3.13. We have also included the associated mean-square values, which are interpreted in the same manner as the infit mean-square values for items we discussed on pages 44–47.

Let us examine the matrix of responses for Candidate 14, who received an overall score of 8 out of 12. Looking across the row of responses for this candidate, we see a pattern of os (the hardest three items) and then a string of successes for the remaining (easier) items, with one exception. According to our analysis, this candidate fits the data well. This candidate has an infit mean-square value of .89, which is close to the mean of zero.

This is, however, not the case for Candidate 13. This candidate does not show an immediately obvious pattern in his responses. Two of the three hardest items are answered correctly, as are two of the three easiest items. Similarly, Candidate 17, who only scored five out of twelve correctly, missed two of the four easiest items in our test, but was able to answer correctly two harder items instead. Candidates 13 and 17, therefore, are shown to be misfitting because their responses are outside what is predicted to be normal by the Rasch program. The infit mean-square values for these two candidates are significantly higher than the mean of 1, with 1.63 and 1.68 respectively.

Let us contrast these two candidates with Candidates 4 and 7. Table 3.13 shows that neither of these candidates' responses include anything unexpected. They both answered the easier items correctly and the harder items incorrectly. These candidates are flagged as overfitting in our analysis. Their responses are slightly too predictable, more predictable than one would expect in a real data set. The infit mean-square values for these two candidates are 0.51 and 0.54 respectively, much lower than the ideal mean of 1.

The orderliness or otherwise of a candidate's responses are summarized for us in terms of person-fit statistics, as with item-fit statistics. The person-fit statistics for the reading data are reproduced in Table 3.14. As before, we are

Candidate ID	harder .... Items .... easier												Infit mnsq	
	11	4	10	5	7	1	2	6	12	9	8	3		Total score
17 (misfit)	0	0	1	1	0	0	1	0	0	1	1	0	1.68	5
13 (misfit)	0	1	1	0	1	1	0	1	1	0	1	1	1.63	8
14	0	0	0	1	1	1	1	1	1	0	1	1	.89	8
7 (overfit)	0	0	0	1	1	1	1	1	1	1	1	1	.54	9
4 (overfit)	0	0	0	0	0	0	1	1	1	1	1	1	.51	6

Table 3.13: Raw data from reading test with infit mean-square values (extract)

```
|ENTRY  TOTAL  TOTAL            MODEL|  INFIT  |  OUTFIT  |PTMEASUR-AL|EXACT MATCH|         |
|NUMBER SCORE  COUNT  MEASURE   S.E. |MNSQ  ZSTD|MNSQ  ZSTD|CORR.  EXP.| OBS%  EXP%| PERSON|
|------------------------------------+----------+----------+-----------+-----------+-------|
|   17      5     12    -.24     .69|1.68  2.1|2.16   2.2|A  .16   .49| 45.5  70.6| 17   |
|   12     10     12    2.83    1.10|1.32   .6|1.93   1.0|B  .50   .65| 90.9  90.8| 12   |
|   13      8     12    1.26     .76|1.63  1.5|1.68   1.0|C  .33   .58| 54.5  77.4| 13   |
|    1      8     12    1.26     .76|1.11   .4|1.54    .9|D  .50   .58| 72.7  77.4| 1    |
|    3      8     12    1.26     .76|1.19   .6|1.01    .3|E  .52   .58| 72.7  77.4| 3    |
|   10      6     12     .24     .69|1.13   .5|1.10    .4|F  .47   .53| 72.7  71.9| 10   |
|   18      1     12   -2.84    1.11|1.08   .4|  .56    .1|G  .27   .26| 90.9  90.8| 18   |
|   14      8     12    1.26     .76| .89  -.2|1.06    .3|H  .60   .58| 90.9  77.4| 14   |
|   15      8     12    1.26     .76|1.01   .2|  .78   -.1|I  .60   .58| 72.7  77.4| 15   |
|   20      6     12     .24     .69|1.00   .1|  .89   -.1|i  .54   .53| 72.7  71.9| 20   |
|    5      2     12   -1.90     .86| .90   .0|  .91   -.3|h  .37   .35| 90.9  83.5| 5    |
|   19      7     12     .72     .71| .91  -.2|  .81   -.2|g  .60   .56| 72.7  73.8| 19   |
|   16      4     12    -.72     .71| .87  -.4|  .69   -.5|f  .53   .46| 72.7  72.3| 16   |
|    9      4     12    -.72     .71| .75  -.8|  .62   -.7|e  .57   .46| 90.9  72.3| 9    |
|   11      7     12     .72     .71| .75  -.7|  .68   -.5|d  .66   .56| 90.9  73.8| 11   |
|    8      5     12    -.24     .69| .63 -1.4|  .53  -1.2|c  .66   .49| 81.8  70.6| 8    |
|    7      9     12    1.91     .85| .54 -1.0|  .32   -.6|b  .79   .61| 90.9  82.0| 7    |
|    4      6     12     .24     .69| .51 -1.9|  .45  -1.5|a  .73   .53| 90.9  71.9| 4    |
|------------------------------------+----------+----------+-----------+-----------+-------|
| MEAN    6.2   11.9     .32     .89| .99   .0|  .98    .1|             | 78.8  76.8|      |
| P.SD    2.8    .2     1.80     .34| .32  1.0|  .51    .8|             | 13.2   6.1|      |
```

Table 3.14: Person statistics table

offered four sets of fit statistics. We have already encountered the infit mean-square statistics that are most commonly used in language assessment research in our discussion of five sample items above. The advice given about the choice of infit versus outfit statistics in the section on item fit is appropriate here, too (infit statistics are more informative in most cases). Outfit statistics are influenced by outlying data, while infit statistics focus only on the inlying observations, and therefore the more typical observations. ZStd statistics again vary around a mean of zero and can be positive or negative depending on whether the observed values show more variation than expected (positive ZStd) or less variation (negative ZStd). Values above +2 and below −2 indicate a departure from the expectations of the model.

It is clear from the table, as we would predict from an inspection of the data matrix, that Candidates 13 and 17 are misfitting candidates. The interpretation of this misfit is complex. It is advisable to go back to the actual responses of the individual to see which ones are causing the disturbance in the pattern, and to consider an explanation in terms of failure of mastery of a particular area, failure of attention in the test-taking process, failure of engagement with easier items, loss of concentration, guessing, anxiety, poor test-item construction, and the like. This inspection might be aided by Table 3.15, extracted and adapted from Linacre & Wright (1994), which provides sample candidate response patterns that can be used to diagnose candidate behaviour.

In general, a pattern of misfitting responses by an individual suggests that the individual's abilities are not being measured appropriately by this particular test instrument, which is an issue of fairness. Although the term 'misfitting individual' is sometimes used to describe this situation, it is important to stress that the direction of misfit is of the instrument to the person, and not the person to the instrument. There is a certain danger that this technical term may be taken (and mis-taken) metaphorically.

Person misfit is a major issue in test development. A test that produces significant levels of person misfit (greater than 2% of candidates) suggests that it is unworkable as a measurement procedure if the number of candidates exceeds a certain level, and will need revision to reduce the level of person misfit. The ability to provide an analysis of person misfit is an advantage of

Response to items Easy..............hard	Diagnosis of pattern	Outfit mean square	Infit mean square
011|1111110000|000	carelessness/sleeping	very high	approx. 1
111|1111000000|001	lucky guessing	very high	approx. 1
111|1000011110|000	special knowledge	approx. 1	above 1
111|1110********|***	plodding	low	?

*Note: the asterisks indicate items that have not been attempted by the test taker.

Table 3.15: Person response patterns and their implications for person fit (extract from Linacre & Wright, 1994, p. 360)

Rasch analysis over traditional analysis, which focuses on item characteristics and lacks a ready means of determining candidates that have not been well measured. Rasch analysis therefore provides us with this powerful tool to identify possible problems with our measurement instrument and any potential threats to fairness.

Item and person summary statistics

A summary of the item statistics can be found at the bottom of the item statistics table (see Table 3.11). The mean of the item measures is set by convention at 0 logits. The standard deviation of the measures can give us an indication of how the items are spread around the mean (we can, of course, see this visually in the Wright map). As mentioned above, the mean infit and outfit mean-square statistics are modelled to have a mean of 1. The actual mean is close to 1; in the case of our data, it is .98. The standard deviation (SD) of the mean-square values shows the spread in the data. In the case of the infit mean-square values, the SD is .27, while it is much larger for the outfit mean square (.49). The reason for this is that outliers are included in the outfit statistics. The ZStd fit scores (which are a transformation of the mean-square values so that they are distributed like Z) have a mean of close to 0 and a SD of 1.

The person summary statistics can be found at the bottom of the person statistics table (Table 3.14). The mean infit mean square is modelled to be 1 (or very close to 1, as is the case with our data where the mean infit mean-square value is .99). The mean outfit mean-square value is .98. The standard deviations of the Z- or t-statistic for the infit (1.0) and outfit (0.8) show that the vast majority of our test takers will be within the acceptable range of −2 to +2.

Reliability

In contrast to classical test theory, a simple Rasch analysis produces two reliability indices: a person reliability index and an item reliability index. Each of these supplies us with different information. The fact that both use the term 'reliability' can be confusing, because only one of them (person reliability) is similar to reliability as determined within classical test theory. Item reliability should not be confused with overall reliability measures such as KR-21 or Cronbach's alpha in classical test theory.

The person reliability index provides us with an estimate of how confident we can be with the ordering of the test takers. That is, if we were to give the same test takers a parallel set of test items (i.e. a similar test), would the test takers be ordered in the same way? The person reliability index is on a scale from 0 to 1 and is very similar to Cronbach's alpha (or 'test' reliability) in classical test theory.

The item reliability index has no equivalent in classical test theory. It provides us with an estimate of the replicability of the item locations along the logit scale, and is therefore concerned with the reliability of the item difficulty estimates. That is, if we were to give other test takers the same items, would the items be ordered in the same way along the continuum (i.e. would this result in similar item difficulty estimates)? The item reliability index is also on a scale from 0 to 1, with 1 being the highest. For both person and item reliability, we aim for an index of 0.8 or over. Linacre (1997a) provides a useful guide on target values for person (or test) reliability. The test reliability gives an indication of how well a test can discriminate between the test takers in a sample. A reliability of 0.9 can reliably distinguish between three to four levels, a reliability of 0.8 can distinguish between two to three levels and a reliability of 0.5 can distinguish between one or two ability levels.

To understand person and item reliability better, it is important to discuss what factors can boost or lower reliability. To increase person reliability (or test reliability), we need to include test takers with a wider ability range in our sample. We can also achieve a higher test reliability by increasing the number of items on a test. Figure 3.3 shows what person reliability can be expected in relation to the number of items in a test. This figure was created by Margaret Wu using simulated data (Margaret Wu, personal communication, March, 2011). The figure models the test reliability for different test lengths and shows that, with few items in a test, it is very difficult to achieve high reliability indices.

It is also possible to increase test reliability by having more categories per item (i.e. not simply relying on dichotomous items—this will be discussed further in Chapter 4). Note that simply adding more test takers to our sample will not boost reliability unless they are from a wider ability range than those tested before. The final way to boost person reliability is by having items that are well targeted at the test takers taking the test.

To boost item reliability, we need to increase the number of test takers in our sample or have items in our test with a large range of item difficulties. Note that item reliability is largely independent of test length. It is also important

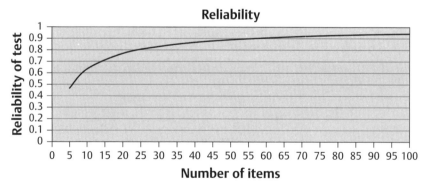

Figure 3.3: Influence of the number of test items on test reliability (from Margaret Wu, personal communication, March, 2011)

to note that if many test takers have not answered items, this can substantially lower the overall reliability. We will return to the topic of missing data in Chapter 7. Reliability is another index that we can use to examine the fairness of our test instrument as a whole.

Analysing multiple-choice data using the simple Rasch model

As mentioned earlier in this chapter, Rasch analysis programs such as Winsteps can help us gain a better understanding of how multiple-choice items, including the distractors, function. A simple analysis, like the one we conducted earlier in this chapter, where data was entered as either 0 (incorrect) or 1 (correct), only provides us with a partial picture of these items. To illustrate how a Rasch analysis can help us identify problems with the distractors in our data, we draw on a data set of 23 multiple-choice reading items designed for adult L2 learners. The test was trialled on a sample of 184 representative test takers. A first look at the reliability statistics for the test shows us that the Cronbach's alpha is .78. Table 3.16 shows the item measurement table we encountered for dichotomously scored items in sections earlier in this chapter.

The table shows that there is one item (Item 4) with high fit values of 1.63 and 1.70 respectively (i.e. misfit). This item also produced a negative pt biserial correlation of $-.12$, which indicates that test takers with higher ability on the test as a whole scored lower on this item. Let us now examine an

ENTRY NUMBER	TOTAL SCORE	TOTAL COUNT	MEASURE	MODEL S.E.	INFIT MNSQ	INFIT ZSTD	OUTFIT MNSQ	OUTFIT ZSTD	PTMEASUR-AL CORR.	PTMEASUR-AL EXP.	EXACT MATCH OBS%	EXACT MATCH EXP%	ITEM
1	82	184	.35	.16	1.00	.1	1.03	.4	.42	.43	70.7	69.4	Q1
2	43	184	1.52	.19	.98	-.2	.95	-.3	.41	.39	80.4	78.9	Q2
3	91	184	.11	.16	.91	-1.4	.87	-1.5	.51	.43	72.3	69.2	Q3
4	60	184	.97	.17	1.63	7.0	1.70	4.8	-.12	.42	57.1	72.2	Q4
5	36	184	1.79	.20	1.09	.8	1.16	.8	.29	.37	81.0	81.9	Q5
6	76	184	.51	.17	.97	-.4	.95	-.5	.45	.43	72.8	69.6	Q6
7	70	184	.68	.17	.96	-.6	.92	-.8	.47	.42	70.7	70.1	Q7
8	118	184	-.63	.17	.86	-2.1	.79	-1.9	.53	.41	76.1	70.5	Q8
9	120	184	-.69	.17	.96	-.5	.93	-.6	.44	.41	70.7	71.0	Q9
10	98	184	-.08	.16	1.03	.5	1.00	.0	.41	.43	66.8	69.2	Q10
11	115	184	-.55	.17	1.05	.7	1.02	.3	.38	.41	69.0	69.8	Q11
12	122	184	-.75	.17	1.08	1.2	1.16	1.3	.32	.40	69.0	71.5	Q12
13	74	184	.57	.17	.87	-2.1	.84	-1.7	.54	.43	76.1	69.8	Q13
14	93	184	.05	.16	.97	-.4	1.00	.0	.45	.43	68.5	69.1	Q14
15	81	184	.37	.16	.93	-1.1	.87	-1.4	.50	.43	72.3	69.4	Q15
16	113	184	-.49	.17	.84	-2.6	.78	-2.2	.56	.41	78.3	69.5	Q16
17	118	184	-.63	.17	1.03	.4	.99	-.1	.39	.41	69.6	70.5	Q17
18	112	184	-.46	.17	.92	-1.1	.88	-1.1	.48	.42	73.4	69.4	Q18
19	108	184	-.35	.17	.94	-1.0	.87	-1.3	.48	.42	70.1	69.2	Q19
20	119	184	-.66	.17	.85	-2.2	.77	-2.0	.54	.41	75.5	70.8	Q20
21	113	184	-.49	.17	1.11	1.6	1.08	.8	.33	.41	64.1	69.5	Q21
22	87	184	.21	.16	1.03	.6	1.08	.9	.39	.43	70.1	69.3	Q22
23	141	184	-1.35	.19	1.07	.8	1.12	.7	.29	.36	78.3	78.0	Q23
MEAN	95.2	184.0	.00	.17	1.00	-.1	.99	-.2			71.9	71.2	
P.SD	26.3	.0	.75	.01	.15	1.9	.19	1.5			5.3	3.4	

Table 3.16: Item measurement report: multiple-choice reading test

additional piece of information that we have for multiple-choice items. An extract of this additional table is shown in Table 3.17.

We have chosen an extract of the first five items of our multiple-choice test. For each item, we can see the data codes. In this case, the four multiple-choice options have been represented as 1, 2, 3, and 4. The key (i.e. the correct answer) is indicated in the column 'score value' with a 1. There is one item, Item 5, where one student also scored a zero, because he or she did not attempt the item. In the 'Data count' and '%' columns we can see how many students selected each option, and the students' average ability measure is indicated in the 'Mean ability' column. Let us now focus on Item 4, the item that was shown to be misfitting in Table 3.16. For some reason, the mean ability of test takers who chose the correct answer, 1, was lower than those who chose distractor option 4. This is indicated by an asterisk (*) in the table and also flagged by high mean-square values next to those distractor options.

Test developers who find problems such as these in their data have two options; they can either (1) review distractor number 4 and revise it to make it less attractive to high-ability test takers or (2) delete the item altogether as this is distorting the measurement, which is unfair to high-ability candidates in particular.

```
-----------------------------------------------------------------------------------------
|ENTRY   DATA  SCORE |   DATA     |    ABILITY      S.E.  INFT OUTF PTMA |       |
|NUMBER  CODE  VALUE | COUNT   %  |  MEAN   P.SD  MEAN  MNSQ MNSQ CORR.| ITEM |
|--------------------+------------+-----------------------------------------------+------|
|   1     4      0   |   45   24  |  -.42     .86   .13    .9   .8  -.27 |Q1    |
|         2      0   |   42   23  |  -.31     .81   .13    .9   .9  -.21 |      |
|         1      0   |   15    8  |   .04     .72   .19   1.2  1.2  -.01 |      |
|         3      1   |   82   45  |   .58    1.08   .12   1.1  1.1   .42 |      |
|                    |            |                                     |      |
|   2     3      0   |   25   14  |  -.42    1.07   .22   1.1   .9  -.19 |Q2    |
|         1      0   |   57   31  |  -.22     .93   .12   1.0   .9  -.20 |      |
|         4      0   |   59   32  |   .04     .85   .11    .9  1.0  -.03 |      |
|         2      1   |   43   23  |   .86    1.00   .15   1.0   .9   .41 |      |
|                    |            |                                     |      |
|   3     2      0   |    7    4  |  -.61     .80   .33    .8   .7  -.13 |Q3    |
|         4      0   |   16    9  |  -.53     .88   .23    .9   .8  -.18 |      |
|         3      0   |   70   38  |  -.40     .81   .10    .9   .8  -.37 |      |
|         1      1   |   91   49  |   .63     .97   .10    .9   .9   .51 |      |
|                    |            |                                     |      |
|   4     3      0   |   15    8  |  -.68     .95   .26    .8   .7  -.22 |Q4    |
|         2      0   |   16    9  |  -.68     .86   .22    .7   .6  -.23 |      |
|         4      0   |   93   51  |   .46    1.15   .12   1.8  2.3   .36 |      |
|         1      1   |   60   33  |  -.09*    .59   .08   1.8  1.6  -.12 |      |
|                    |            |                                     |      |
|   5     1      0   |   38   21  |  -.39     .84   .14    .6   .6  -.23 |Q5    |
|         3      0   |   24   13  |  -.04     .96   .20   1.0  1.0  -.05 |      |
|         2      0   |   85   46  |   .08    1.04   .11   1.3  1.3  -.01 |      |
|         0      0   |    1    1  |   .48     .00          .7  1.1   .03 |      |
|         4      1   |   36   20  |   .70    1.02   .17   1.1  1.2   .29 |      |
-----------------------------------------------------------------------------------------
```

Table 3.17 Multiple-choice distractor analysis: reading test

Summary

In this chapter we have introduced a number of key concepts in Rasch analysis through examining the pattern of responses of a group of trial subjects on a reading test. We have shown that a search for patterns in the data in order to make the responses (of individual candidates, and of candidates as a group) to particular items predictable is the basis of Rasch modelling. To the extent that the data are rendered predictable because they conform to the measurement model, we are in a position to infer that the relationship we have demonstrated between person ability and item difficulty for this particular group of subjects and items is likely to be true for these items with other subjects who are similar in language background, age, and other relevant characteristics; and for these persons with other items of similar type. We are thus able to make powerful general statements about person ability and item difficulty, which make possible extremely useful practical consequences, such as much simpler comparison of different test forms, the measurement of growth in ability over time, and the development of computer-based adaptive tests (where items with the same difficulty can be stored in item banks), among other things. We have shown that the degree of predictability of the pattern of responses for particular candidates and for particular items is also routinely reported in Rasch analyses by means of fit statistics. These form the basis for item revision, or for judgements about the suitability of the test for individual learners.

In Chapter 4 we will consider analysing data that attracts more than two score points, as well as Likert scale questionnaire data. For this purpose, we will introduce two more Rasch models: the rating scale model and the partial credit model. Each of these will be described in detail in the following chapter.

Activities on the website

The reading data file used in this chapter is provided on the companion website (www.oup.com/elt/teacher/fjla), with some activities for readers who are interested in exploring the topics presented in this chapter further.

Notes

1 Although Rasch analysis can analyse data sets with missing data, for the sake of simplicity we have chosen to recode missing data as 0 (incorrect). We will discuss data sets with missing data in Chapter 7.
2 Winsteps is able to create this rearranged data set for us. This can be found under an output table called 'Scalogram'.
3 The data does not always converge, i.e. the level of accuracy is not always met. Refer to Linacre (1989) for more information.
4 A logarithm is an *index* that has a *base*. The base can be any number, but the numbers 10 and 2 are frequently used as bases. The number 100 can be expressed as a logarithm of 10: using 10 as the base, 100 is the

equivalent of 10^2. The index or logarithm is 2; so we can say that the logarithm of 100 is 2—or more correctly, the logarithm to the base 10 of 100 is 2. Traditionally, logarithms were expressed to the base 10 in the majority of cases, so the default or unmarked logarithm base was 10, and so 'to the base 10' could be omitted. Similarly, 4 is 2^2, so that the index is 2 and the base is 2; the logarithm of 4 to the base 2 is 2. In the same way, 8 is 2^3, so that the logarithm of 8 to the base 2 is 3. e is a naturally occurring constant; another, more familiar, naturally occurring constant is π (*pi*), which is the ratio of the circumference to the diameter of a circle. Logarithms to the base e are called natural logarithms, and the logarithm itself may be referred to as an exponent.

5 The larger the number of persons and/or items, the smaller will be the error; recommended n sizes for candidates are 100 or more, depending on the level of accuracy required, but estimates on smaller sample sizes may be useful for certain purposes if the size of the error term is not an imperative consideration.

6 More accurately, for n sizes of 30 or more, the range is the mean ± twice the standard deviation of the mean-square statistic, reported at the bottom of the table of fit values in the output. In this case, where the standard deviation is 0.27, the relevant range is $0.98 \pm (2 \times 0.27) = 0.44 - 1.52$. The standard deviation is large in this case, partly because of the small number of observations. The interpretation of fit values in this particular analysis is made a little more difficult because of the small amount of data available to the analysis, but it serves our purposes in explaining the basic issues in understanding fit.

7 The fact that item misfit captures similar information to item discrimination indices is not surprising, given that they both indicate patterns of response to particular items that are at odds with the pattern of responses of the same individuals to the other items in the test.

4

Beyond simple right or wrong answers: the Andrich rating scale model and the partial credit model

Introduction

Many items in language tests go beyond simple right or wrong answers. For example, reading and listening tests often include short-answer questions that attract more than one score point. In certain contexts, scorers work with detailed marking guides to score short answers. They may at times interpret these scoring guides differently, which may pose a threat to fairness. We therefore need additional tools beyond the simple Rasch model explored in Chapter 3 to analyse such items and to uncover any threats to test fairness. Questionnaire research and semantic differential scales (scales that are set up with opposite terms at the end of each scale, for example, 'Vocabulary: strong → weak') are also more commonly used in language assessment and language assessment research, and the validity and fairness of such tools is often not sufficiently examined. Rasch measurement provides us with additional tools to help us analyse these types of data, and this will be the focus of this chapter.

In this chapter we will look at two extensions of the basic Rasch model: the Andrich rating scale model (Andrich, 1978) and the partial credit model (Masters, 1982).[1] We will examine the types of data that are usually analysed using these two models, and discuss how the models differ from each other and from the basic Rasch model we encountered in Chapter 3. In the first part of the chapter we will present an analysis using the partial credit model and examine how the output differs from the basic Rasch model. We will then explore in detail how the rating scale model differs from the partial credit model and the criteria to use when deciding between the two models. The final section of the chapter focuses on analysing questionnaire data using the rating scale model—a type of analysis not commonly used in the area of language assessment and applied linguistics research.

Data types typically analysed

The data that we typically subject to an analysis using either the rating scale model (RSM) or the partial credit model (PCM) is data in which each item attracts more than a simple right or wrong answer. Let us examine these types of task in more detail.

First, in comprehension tasks (either listening or reading), use is frequently made of *constructed response* formats. Items in short-answer question format require the candidate to provide a brief answer (a few words) to questions on the listening or reading passage. In this case, *partial credit* may be allowed for partially satisfactory answers; responses may thus be scored 0, 1, or 2, or perhaps 0, 1, 2, or 3, depending on the scope of the response.

Another type of scoring involves a more *extended response* on the part of the candidate, for example in a speaking or writing task. In this case, more complex judgements of the quality of the response may be required of raters, and the coding of the rater responses will lead to a type of data loosely referred to as rating scale data.[2] Typically, in the assessment of speaking and writing, the performance of candidates may be rated either on a rating scale, or using Likert or semantic differential procedures. Likert scales provide options describing each scale point. Most commonly, in a survey, for example, the scale points are described in terms of 'strongly agree', 'agree', and so on, but other descriptions such as 'very competent', 'competent', 'adequate', 'inadequate', or 'emerging' may also be used. Semantic differential scales, on the other hand, provide raters with a scale where individual scale points are not described, but rather, opposite adjectives are provided at either end of the scale. In the case of such rating scales, scores for a particular performance (or aspect of a single performance) can typically have values between 1 and 5 or between 1 and 9. Such scales can be holistic (where the skill is assessed once and as a whole) or analytic (where the performance is judged repeatedly, each time on a separate criterion). Criteria judged might be fluency, appropriateness, or intelligibility (in the assessment of speaking) or organization (in the assessment of writing). It is possible to analyse rating scale data with either the Andrich rating scale model or the partial credit model. In both cases, however, the influence of the rater is ignored. The analysis of rating scale data in which the influence of the rater is taken into account will be described in Chapter 5.

Alternatively, Likert and semantic differential scales may be used to judge the whole performance, or different aspects of it. A Likert scale (Figure 4.1) is one in which a person is asked to indicate which of a range of named categories, arranged in increasing order of intensity of a trait (for example, liking for something or approval), best represents their point of view.

How adequate was this performance? Place a mark (X) in the category which best describes it.

very inadequate	inadequate	adequate	more than adequate	outstanding
[0	1	2	3	4]

Figure 4.1: Likert scale

The numbering of the categories in square brackets at the bottom of Figure 4.1 does not usually appear on the rater response sheet, but responses are coded using such numerical equivalents for subsequent analysis. Commonly, Likert scales are used (Henning, 1987) 'to elicit extent of agreement with some statement of opinion or attitude' (p. 23), with typical categories being 'strongly agree', 'agree', 'undecided', 'disagree', and 'strongly disagree'. It is important to note, though, that this type of data should only be subjected to a Rasch analysis if the developer of the questionnaire compiled it to investigate a latent variable (i.e. the construct that we are trying to measure) that underlies all the items. This is in contrast to surveys that are combined to gather information from people without attempting to test an underlying theoretical construct. We will focus on the analysis of questionnaire (Likert scale) data on pages 79–89 of this chapter.

Semantic differential scales (see Figure 4.2 for two examples) similarly offer raters a range of response categories. For example, in judging a performance on successive criteria, each criterion is defined in terms of a pair of antonymous anchor terms (words which define the extremes of the attribute being assessed).

```
Complexity of sentence structure

simple _ _ _ _ _ _ _ _ _ _ _ _ _ _ _ _ complex
```

```
Sophistication of vocabulary

simple 1  2  3  4  5  6  7  8  9  10  sophisticated
```

Figure 4.2: Semantic differential scale

In general, item types in which responses may be scored with a range of marks are called *polytomous* items and these can be analysed using either the rating scale or the partial credit models. With the greater number of score points, several new threats to test fairness are introduced. In Chapter 5, we examine how we can identify such threats.

Differences between the simple Rasch model and the rating scale and partial credit models

In this section we will examine how the simple Rasch model (which we encountered in detail in Chapter 3) differs from the RSM and the PCM. This section will also introduce the main difference between the RSM and the PCM. Note that we only introduce the main difference here; we examine this in more detail on pages 78–79.

All of the basic concepts of a Rasch analysis that were discussed in Chapter 3 are applicable to the RSM and the PCM, with one major difference. These two models can be used to analyse items that attract a partial credit scoring system (i.e. polytomous items). Both the RSM and the PCM investigate the rating scale structure of these types of items. So instead of merely providing a set of measures, fit statistics, and standard errors for each item and person, the program also analyses the precise way in which the rating scale is being used. We will investigate this in detail later in this chapter.

The main difference between the RSM and the PCM is that, while an analysis using the RSM models one common rating scale for all items in the test (and therefore assumes that all items have the same rating scale structure), in a partial credit analysis, each item has its own rating scale structure. The RSM, in other words, is making a simplifying assumption; it deliberately ignores any differences in the way the rating scale might be interpreted by those using it across different items or criteria. Simplifying assumptions are routine in all walks of life, including research. A map of a metro or underground transportation system chooses to ignore, for example, differences in distances between stations in the interests of getting a clear overall picture of the system. What is lost by this assumption? What difference does it make if we adopt it? Would we get a different picture of the system if we refrained from this assumption? We will show what exactly that means in practice when we examine the output from such analyses.

Analysing polytomous data

Let us start by examining in detail the output from a partial credit analysis. The data set we will use originates from an L2 listening test. There are 22 items in the data set. Each item is scored on a partial credit scale, but the number of steps in each item differs. Some items have only three steps (0 - 1 - 2), while others have up to five steps (0 - 1 - 2 - 3 - 4). Table 4.1 presents an extract of the data from a few randomly selected students. The item numbers from 1 to 22 can be seen across the top in bold; candidates are indicated as letters A–G in the left-hand column.

While the whole data set includes 667 test takers, eyeballing the extract of data based on only seven test takers in Table 4.1 shows us that some items seem to result in more variation than others. For example, Item 4, which is out of a possible score of 2, has been answered correctly by all seven students in this table. On the other hand, Item 17, which has a possible total score of 4, has resulted in a much more varied score profile.

Forming conclusions based on eyeballing this data set is more difficult than it was with the data set we encountered in Chapter 3 (due to the number of test takers), and sorting the data as we did in Chapter 3 creates only a slightly clearer picture. Such an ordered data set is particularly difficult to interpret if items attract different total scores and there are large numbers of test takers, which is the case with our listening test. This is where a Rasch analysis can help us to identify patterns in the data. Because we have items with different total scores (for example, some items out of two, others out of three or four), we cannot use the RSM to analyse this data set. We need to draw on the PCM, which can model different scales for different items. The

	1	2	3	4	5	6	7	8	9	10	11	12	13	14	15	16	17	18	19	20	21	22
A	2	1	1	2	3	1	2	1	1	1	3	0	1	3	1	0	2	4	1	2	0	1
B	3	2	2	2	3	2	2	2	2	1	3	0	1	3	0	3	4	2	2	1	2	1
C	3	2	2	2	3	2	2	1	1	1	4	2	1	4	0	3	4	3	4	3	2	2
D	3	2	2	2	2	1	2	2	2	1	3	2	1	4	1	3	1	3	0	2	2	0
E	3	2	2	2	2	2	2	1	2	1	2	1	3	4	1	3	3	3	1	1	1	2
F	3	2	1	2	2	2	1	1	2	2	3	0	2	3	1	2	2	3	0	1	2	0
G	3	2	0	2	1	1	2	1	1	1	3	1	1	1	0	2	4	1	1	2	1	1

Table 4.1: Extract of data matrix: L2 listening test

exact differences between the models will be described later in the chapter. In the first instance, we describe an analysis using the PCM.

Conducting an analysis using the partial credit model or the rating scale model using Winsteps

A detailed account of how a data set can be read into Winsteps and then analysed using the partial credit model or the rating scale model can be found in the files offered on the companion website of this book (www.oup.com/elt/teacher/fjla). The website provides the data files used in this chapter, as well as detailed instructions accompanied by screenshots on how to read in and analyse the data and how to access the output files. We suggest readers attempt the analyses of the data sets provided on the website, and that they also attempt to analyse their own data in the same manner. We have provided some exercises at the end of the chapter to guide these activities. We will now turn to the analysis of the L2 listening data set using the partial credit model.

Understanding the results of a partial credit analysis

This section describes some of the key pieces of output from a Rasch analysis involving data with partial credit items. Most of the results are similar to those we saw in the description of a simple Rasch analysis in Chapter 3, but there are a number of key differences, which we will discuss in more detail. At the same time, this section serves to revise some of the key concepts introduced in Chapter 3. The following aspects of a Rasch analysis involving partial credit items will be discussed:

- item/person map (Wright map)
- person ability and fit
- item difficulty and fit
- rating scale analysis

Item/person map (Wright map)

The item/person map or Wright map produced as the output of a rating scale analysis or partial credit analysis differs depending on the program used. Figure 4.3 presents the Winsteps Wright map for our listening data with the full data set of 667 test takers. The map looks no different from the Wright maps we encountered in Chapter 3 when our data set comprised dichotomous data. In the case of this map, each # denotes six test takers and each full stop one to five test takers. The map is interpreted in the same way.

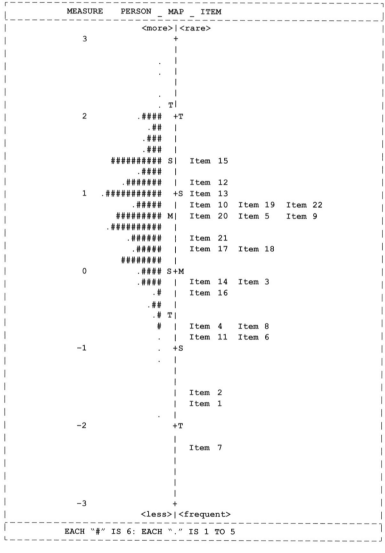

Figure 4.3: Wright map: partial credit data (Winsteps)

We can see from the Wright map that the items are slightly too easy for our sample of test takers in that there are a number of students at the high-ability end not matched by items. Similarly, there are a number of easier items (Items 1, 2, and 7) that are not matched to any, or that are matched to only very few, students. Depending on the purpose of our test, this may weaken the inferences we can draw about test takers at the higher-ability levels. At the same time, however, many items are well matched to the bulk of our test takers.

Figure 4.4, which is the Wright map produced by a different type of Rasch analysis software, the Quest program (Adams & Khoo, 1993), provides a more detailed view of our analysis. This is where we notice some differences

```
-----------------------------------------------------------------
| Item Estimates (Thresholds)                                   |
| all on all (N = 667 L = 22 Probability Level=0.50)            |
-----------------------------------------------------------------
|                                  |   15.2                     |
|   3.0                            |                            |
|                                  |   13.4                     |
|                              X   |   19.4                     |
|                                  |                            |
|                          X       |                            |
|                          X       |    5.3    10.2             |
|                          X       |                            |
|   2.0                 XXXX       |   20.4                     |
|                 XXXXXXXXXX       |    8.2    12.3   17.4  18.4 |
|                    XXXXXX        |                            |
|                    XXXXXX        |    9.2    13.3   22.2      |
|           XXXXXXXXXXXXXXXXXX     |   12.2    14.4   19.3      |
|             XXXXXXXXXXXXXXX      |   11.4                     |
|               XXXXXXXXX          |   20.3    21.2             |
|   1.0  XXXXXXXXXXXXXXXXXXXX      |    5.2    13.2   16.3      |
|        XXXXXXXXXXXXXXXXXXXXXX    |                            |
|           XXXXXXXXXXXXXXXXX      |    3.2    18.3             |
|              XXXXXXXXXX          |   17.3                     |
|            XXXXXXXXXXXXX         |   20.2                     |
|          XXXXXXXXXXXXXXXXXXX     |    6.2    12.1   14.3  19.2 |
|   0.0       XXXXXXXXXXXXXX       |    4.2    22.1             |
|               XXXXXXXX           |    9.1    17.2             |
|                XXXXXX            |   18.2                     |
|                   XXX            |    2.2    15.1   21.1      |
|                  XXXX            |    1.3    11.3   14.2  16.2 |
|                  XXXX            |   10.1                     |
|                   XX             |   20.1                     |
|  -1.0                            |    3.1    18.1             |
|                                  |    5.1     7.2             |
|                                  |   17.1    19.1             |
|                                  |    4.1    16.1             |
|                                  |    1.2    11.2             |
|                                  |   13.1    14.1             |
|                         X        |    6.1                     |
|  -2.0                            |                            |
|                                  |                            |
|                                  |   11.1                     |
|                                  |                            |
|                                  |    2.1                     |
|                                  |    1.1                     |
|  -3.0                            |                            |
|                                  |                            |
|                                  |    7.1     8.1             |
-----------------------------------------------------------------
|   Each X represents    3 students                             |
=================================================================
```

Figure 4.4: Wright map: partial credit data (Quest)

from an analysis with dichotomous data. While the Winsteps map plots the average item difficulty for each item, the Quest map charts several threshold estimates for each item.

Consider Item 15, for example. In the Winsteps map, this item has an average difficulty of approximately 1.5 logits. In the Quest map, this item appears twice, once at approximately −0.5 logits (noted as 15.1) in the logit map and then again at approximately 3.2 logits (noted as 15.2). Item 15 has three possible score points (0 - 1 - 2). What do these two item thresholds noted in the Quest map represent? The first point, 15.1, represents the point where a test taker located at the same logit value (approximately −0.5 logits) has an equal likelihood of scoring 0 or 1 on that item. Similarly, the threshold 15.2 is the point where a student at the ability measure of approximately 3.2 logits has an equal likelihood of scoring 1 or 2 on the item. We will examine in more detail how these two points are calculated on pages 74–75.

Let us recap some of the points we examined in the Wright map in Chapter 3 (see Figure 3.1). Both the Wright map in Chapter 3 and the Quest map in Figure 4.4 show us that overall, the test is not perfectly matched to the ability of our students. We have a group of items that are too easy for the majority of the students. At the same time, we have a group of students at the top of the ability spectrum who are not matched by any items. This is particularly apparent in the Winsteps map (Figure 4.3), which shows only the average item difficulty estimates. Looking at that map, we could argue that it would be better to have more items that are matched in average difficulty to the students of higher ability. But when the thresholds in the Quest map are examined, it shows that some of the individual steps of the items match the test takers at higher-ability levels.

We can further observe from the two maps that while the students are well spread and distributed, there is a small number of students (the maps are not specific here, but it looks like three students) who are significantly weaker than the larger group of students. These students are located at approximately −1.8 logits. There are several areas on the maps where many students are located but these are not matched by many or any items. For example, in the Winsteps map there are no items located at and just above the zero logit point. This is slightly less of an issue when the score points are taken into consideration, as is the case in the Quest map; however, similar areas with no or few items can be seen here as well.

Person ability

Person ability and fit in a partial credit or rating scale analysis are interpreted in the same way as was described in Chapter 3. Table 4.2 shows an extract from the Winsteps results of the person analysis. The table shows 10 test takers only, and is organized in entry order, i.e. the student who was first on our input spreadsheet is mentioned first in the table.

|ENTRY |NUMBER	TOTAL SCORE	TOTAL COUNT	MEASURE	MODEL| S.E.	INFIT |MNSQ ZSTD|	OUTFIT |MNSQ ZSTD|	PT-MEASURE |CORR. EXP.|	EXACT MATCH |OBS% EXP%|	PERSON|
	1	33	22	.28	.28|1.24	.8|1.13	.5| .38	.56| 54.5 50.8|	1	
	2	43	22	1.12	.30|1.04	.2| .91	-.2| .67	.49| 50.0 55.0|	2	
	3	51	22	1.93	.35| .99	.1| .78	-.3| .51	.39| 68.2 62.7|	3	
	4	41	22	.94	.29|1.23	.8|1.05	.3| .57	.51| 50.0 54.8|	4	
	5	44	22	1.21	.30| .93	-.1| .77	-.6| .53	.48| 68.2 55.9|	5	
	6	37	22	.61	.29| .96	.0|1.13	.5| .42	.54| 50.0 54.1|	6	
	7	32	22	.20	.28| .85	-.4| .65	-1.2| .69	.57| 63.6 50.8|	7	
	8	55	22	2.51	.42|1.14	.4|1.02	.2| .39	.32| 63.6 73.6|	8	
	9	46	22	1.40	.31| .72	-.9| .61	-1.1| .64	.46| 59.1 55.2|	9	
	10	40	22	.86	.29| .87	-.3|1.18	.6| .37	.52| 45.5 54.0|	10	

Table 4.2: Person statistics (extract)

The 'Total count' column shows the number of items each test taker responded to. The 'Total score' column shows each candidate's raw score. This is higher than the total number of items because all items were scored as partial credit items. The 'Measure' column shows the average ability of each test taker. This figure relates to their position on the logit scale. Test takers with higher values have shown more ability in this listening test, while test takers with low or negative measures have less ability. The standard error (as indicated in the 'Model S.E.' column) shows us the size of the error that is involved in the estimates of the candidate measure. Let us examine Candidate 8, who has an ability measure of 2.51, more closely. Looking back at the Wright map in Figure 4.4, we can see that Candidate 8 is one of our most proficient test takers. We cannot tell which X in the map relates to this test taker, but we can roughly estimate his/her position based on the measure value. The standard error associated with Candidate 8 is much larger than that of other test takers. The reason for this relates back to the topic of item coverage that we commented on when discussing the Wright map. There are far fewer items that are well matched with this candidate's ability than there are for a candidate like Candidate 1, for example, who has an ability measure of .28 and is therefore more in the middle in terms of ability in our larger cohort. There are therefore far more items that are targeted at the ability of Candidate 1 than Candidate 8, which provides our software with more data. Therefore, the software can be less certain about the ability estimate of Candidate 8 and for this reason the standard error is higher. Therefore, the measurement and the resulting inferences we make based on our assessment may be unfair to Candidate 8.

Person fit

As was the case with the fit statistics for dichotomous items discussed in Chapter 3, a Rasch analysis also produces four columns of fit statistics for each item: infit mean square, infit ZStd, outfit mean square, and outfit ZStd. To recap, the major difference between infit and outfit mean-square statistics is the fact that outfit statistics are more susceptible to outliers, while infit statistics only represent the most typical responses in the data set. Both infit and outfit mean-square statistics have an expected value of 1, with values higher than 1 indicating misfit and values lower than 1 indicating overfit. Although the interpretation of the polytomous statistics closely mirrors that of an analysis of a data set with dichotomous items, less has been written about the interpretation of fit statistics for polytomous fit statistics. Smith (1996) provides a detailed analysis of different possible student response patterns and how the infit and outfit mean-square statistics, as well as the point-biserial correlation, can be interpreted in relation to these response patterns. An adapted extract of Smith's table can be seen in Table 4.3. This table can be useful for language testers in the process of reviewing their tests and trying to understand the fit statistics of certain students.

Wright (1991) also provides some indication of why high- or low-ability test takers may be identified as misfitting. Able test takers might have been careless in providing or rushing their answers so that they have produced some unexpected wrong answers. Low-ability test takers, on the other hand, may have resorted to guessing or may have displayed some 'special knowledge' which led them to answering items unexpectedly correctly. If a low-ability test taker is identified as overfitting, they may have been working through the test materials too slowly, with the result that they didn't complete the test or they may have been too cautious and only answered very easy items.

While some of these patterns are not necessarily the types of response patterns we hope to see, they form a very useful starting point for the evaluation of our listening data set. For example, if we find a pattern of very high infit and outfit mean-square values for one of our test takers, it is worth checking whether the data was entered incorrectly by accident. If our data set involves a rating scale where test takers or respondents or judges choose the different categories (such as a semantic differential scale or a Likert scale), the infit and outfit mean-square statistics can give us an indication of how test takers or

Type	Response string easy .... hard	Infit MnSq	Outfit MnSq	Correlation
Modelled	33333132210000001011	.98	.99	.78
Overfitting	32222222221111111110	.21	.26	.89
Only using central categories	22222222221111111111	.24	.34	.87
Noisy outliers	32222222201111111130	.94	1.22	1.22
Random responses	03202002101113311002	2.99	3.59	−.01
Reversal of expected patterns	00111111112222222233	4.00	5.58	−.92

Table 4.3: Polytomous fit patterns (adapted extract from Smith, 1996, p. 516)

judges applied the scale. A reversal of the expected patterns can, for example, indicate that the respondent did not read the instructions carefully and applied the scale differently from others. All of these cases pose a threat to the validity of our results and therefore to test fairness. If this is the case, the researchers can decide to exclude such data from further analysis.

Item difficulty

Item difficulty for polytomous items can be interpreted in the same way as for dichotomous items. It is possible to differentiate between the average item difficulty of an item and the step difficulty of the different rating scale points. Table 4.4 provides the summary of the item statistics generated by Winsteps. The average item difficulty is indicated in the 'Measure' column in logits. Items with high positive logits are the most difficult, and items with high negative values are the easiest. Thus, Item 15 is the most difficult item in our data set and Item 7 is the easiest. These measures, also used in the Winsteps Wright map, are the average difficulty measures for each item. We will see how these are generated later in the chapter. The standard errors ('Model S.E.' column) are relatively low for our items. These provide us with an estimate of the precision of our model, that is, how confident we can be of our measure estimates. Bond and Fox (2007) show that three factors influence the size of the standard errors. Imprecision will increase (1) if the items are off-target to the population of test takers, (2) if the number of response categories increases, and (3) when the sample is small.

ENTRY NUMBER	TOTAL SCORE	TOTAL COUNT	MEASURE	MODEL S.E.	INFIT MNSQ	INFIT ZSTD	OUTFIT MNSQ	OUTFIT ZSTD	PTMEASUR-AL CORR.	PTMEASUR-AL EXP.	EXACT MATCH OBS%	EXACT MATCH EXP%	ITEM
1	1837	667	-1.65	.08	.98	-.2	1.00	.0	.33	.34	78.9	77.9	Item 1
2	1169	667	-1.59	.09	1.00	.0	.99	.0	.30	.30	76.5	76.8	Item 2
3	945	667	-.15	.06	.97	-.5	.96	-.8	.44	.41	54.9	54.6	Item 3
4	1081	667	-.68	.07	.96	-.6	.94	-.7	.41	.37	67.3	66.1	Item 4
5	963	667	.78	.05	.96	-.8	.95	-1.0	.50	.47	53.1	48.6	Item 5
6	1049	667	-.81	.07	.98	-.3	.98	-.3	.38	.36	64.8	63.5	Item 6
7	1237	667	-2.26	.11	.92	-.9	.76	-2.2	.37	.25	85.6	85.9	Item 7
8	835	667	-.78	.09	.97	-.6	.98	-.3	.35	.30	73.0	72.5	Item 8
9	692	667	.71	.06	1.04	1.1	1.05	1.1	.40	.44	47.8	47.4	Item 9
10	656	667	.84	.07	.98	-.4	.98	-.4	.39	.37	63.4	64.0	Item 10
11	2115	667	-.81	.05	1.04	.8	1.06	1.0	.41	.46	50.8	50.8	Item 11
12	752	667	1.16	.04	.95	-.9	.97	-.5	.55	.53	41.8	39.6	Item 12
13	1091	667	.97	.05	1.03	.5	1.05	.8	.50	.51	45.0	45.5	Item 13
14	1881	667	-.13	.04	1.00	.0	1.03	.6	.53	.54	41.5	40.4	Item 14
15	558	667	1.40	.08	.99	-.1	.99	-.1	.36	.34	68.7	68.0	Item 15
16	1495	666	-.33	.05	.87	-2.5	.84	-2.8	.57	.46	53.5	50.3	Item 16
17	1685	667	.27	.04	1.10	1.8	1.09	1.6	.52	.56	37.2	38.9	Item 17
18	1659	667	.35	.04	1.16	3.0	1.20	3.6	.47	.56	35.4	38.1	Item 18
19	1316	667	.80	.04	1.08	1.6	1.09	1.8	.46	.52	40.0	42.7	Item 19
20	1383	667	.67	.04	.91	-1.9	.91	-1.9	.63	.58	34.3	35.9	Item 20
21	782	667	.43	.06	1.04	.9	1.05	1.1	.41	.44	46.0	46.8	Item 21
22	655	667	.82	.06	.99	-.1	.99	-.1	.44	.44	47.1	46.8	Item 22
MEAN	1174.4	667.0	.00	.06	1.00	.0	.99	.0			54.8	54.6	
P.SD	437.8	.2	.98	.02	.06	1.2	.09	1.4			14.8	14.4	

Table 4.4: Item summary table from Winsteps: listening data

We are also provided with a more detailed analysis of each polytomous item. Table 4.5 shows an extract from a Winsteps output table which provides details of the mean ability measures of students at each score value. This table shows how many test takers achieved which score value on the partial credit scale of each item (see 'Data count' and '%' columns). We can also see at which average ability level the test takers were who received the different score points (this mirrors the output of the multiple-choice item analysis in Chapter 3). This information is invaluable for the test designer as it aids decisions about possible revisions of the scale structure of each item. For example, if very few or no test takers are scored at one of the score points, the rating scale may be collapsed.

ENTRY NUMBER	DATA CODE	SCORE VALUE	DATA COUNT	%	AVERAGE ABILITY	S.E. MEAN	OUTF MNSQ	ITEM
1	0	0	2	0	-1.09	.72	.5	Item 1
	1	1	22	3	-.04	.14	.9	
	2	2	114	17	.49	.07	1.1	
	3	3	529	79	.89	.03	1.0	
2	0	0	9	1	-.33	.25	.8	Item 2
	1	1	147	22	.47	.06	1.0	
	2	2	511	77	.89	.03	1.0	
3	0	0	79	12	.11	.08	.9	Item 3
	1	1	231	35	.62	.04	1.0	
	2	2	357	54	1.04	.03	1.0	
4	0	0	42	6	-.02	.11	.9	Item 4
	1	1	169	25	.49	.05	1.0	
	2	2	456	68	.96	.03	1.0	
5	0	0	75	11	.30	.08	1.1	Item 5
	1	1	302	45	.52	.04	.9	
	2	2	209	31	1.09	.04	.8	
	3	3	81	12	1.39	.06	1.0	

Table 4.5: Item category frequency table (extract)

Item fit

As was the case with the dichotomously scored data set in Chapter 3, Winsteps also produces fit statistics for each item. Table 4.6 shows our items ordered according to fit. Just as we saw in Chapter 3, Winsteps produces four different fit statistics, a mean-square statistic and a ZStd for each infit and outfit. To recap, the outfit statistics are more sensitive to outliers, while infit statistics ignore extreme outlying observations. Also in Chapter 3, we discussed how to identify items with good fit, misfitting items, and overfitting items, and the implications of these items for our measurement and possible revision procedures. All these principles apply equally to polytomous items such as the ones in our listening test.

ENTRY NUMBER	TOTAL SCORE	TOTAL COUNT	MEASURE	MODEL S.E.	INFIT MNSQ	INFIT ZSTD	OUTFIT MNSQ	OUTFIT ZSTD	ITEM
18	1659	667	.35	.04	1.16	3.0	1.20	3.6	Item 18
17	1685	667	.27	.04	1.10	1.8	1.09	1.6	Item 17
19	1316	667	.80	.04	1.08	1.6	1.09	1.8	Item 19
11	2115	667	-.81	.05	1.04	.8	1.06	1.0	Item 11
9	692	667	.71	.06	1.04	1.1	1.05	1.1	Item 9
13	1091	667	.97	.05	1.03	.5	1.05	.8	Item 13
21	782	667	.43	.06	1.04	.9	1.05	1.1	Item 21
14	1881	667	-.13	.04	1.00	.0	1.03	.6	Item 14
1	1837	667	-1.65	.08	.98	-.2	1.00	.0	Item 1
2	1169	667	-1.59	.09	1.00	.0	.99	.0	Item 2
15	558	667	1.40	.08	.99	-.1	.99	-.1	Item 15
22	655	667	.82	.06	.99	-.1	.99	-.1	Item 22
6	1049	667	-.81	.07	.98	-.3	.98	-.3	Item 6
8	835	667	-.78	.09	.97	-.6	.98	-.3	Item 8
10	656	667	.84	.07	.98	-.4	.98	-.4	Item 10
3	945	667	-.15	.06	.97	-.5	.96	-.8	Item 3
12	752	667	1.16	.04	.95	-.9	.97	-.5	Item 12
4	1081	667	-.68	.07	.96	-.6	.94	-.7	Item 4
5	963	667	.78	.05	.96	-.8	.95	-1.0	Item 5
7	1237	667	-2.26	.11	.92	-.9	.76	-2.2	Item 7
20	1383	667	.67	.04	.91	-1.9	.91	-1.9	Item 20
16	1495	666	-.33	.05	.87	-2.5	.84	-2.8	Item 16
MEAN	1174.4	667.0	.00	.06	1.00	.0	.99	.0	
P.SD	437.8	.2	.98	.02	.06	1.2	.09	1.4	

Table 4.6: Item characteristics table—in fit order (extract)

Let us look more closely at our results. According to the criteria we established in Chapter 3, none of our items are misfitting or overfitting. It is important to note at this point, however, that item fit is to some degree dependent on sample size. Smith et al. (2008) modelled this phenomenon on a large data set from a patient health questionnaire and were able to show that the mean-square statistics were less susceptible to sample size than the ZStd statistics, and that published recommended ranges for these mean-square statistics were suitable for identifying misfit.

If misfitting items are identified in a data set, a Rasch analysis using the partial credit model provides us with additional data about each item—an analysis of the rating scale properties of our items. This is described in more detail below. As mentioned earlier, it is important to remember that the difference between the rating scale model and the partial credit model lies in the fact that the rating scale model assumes the step structure[3] of all items to be identical and therefore only models one set of statistics across all items. The step structure of a scale or each item can be compared to a set of stairs. The rating scale model assumes that all steps within a set of stairs (one for each item) are of equal height. The partial credit model is different as it assumes the step structures to be potentially different for different items; it is possible that some steps in one set of stairs are much higher or much lower than those of the other sets of stairs. While we would like each step to have the same height, the partial credit model reveals differences which are of interest to us.

Rating scale analysis

As part of a partial credit model analysis, Rasch measurement programs like Winsteps also produce statistical output for each item. This is worth reviewing for the purpose of understanding rating scale functioning, and is a useful tool in identifying potential threats to the quality of our measurement and therefore to fairness to test takers. Table 4.7 presents the output for Item 6, an item with three categories, o - 1 - 2. The 'Observed count' and '%' columns show how many of our test takers fell into each of these categories. The average measure provides us with the average test taker ability at each score level.

The infit and outfit mean-square statistics are the average infit or outfit values associated with the responses of each category. The infit values have an expected value of 1.0; much higher values are problematic as they show misfit. Both infit and outfit mean-square values of over 1.5 are problematic. The outfit mean-square value is, as always, sensitive to highly unexpected responses. The Andrich threshold can be found in the last column in Table 4.7. The way in which this is generated will be discussed later in the chapter. This value is also sometimes called *Rasch-Andrich thresholds, step difficulty, step calibration, tau,* or *delta parameter (delta).* The Rasch-Andrich thresholds are expected to increase with category value. They can sometimes be disordered, which indicates that a certain category is rarely observed. This may indicate a problem with the rating scale.

While Table 4.7 provides useful information when the rating scale of each item is examined, there are a number of further very useful graphs which form part of the regular output of most Rasch analysis programs. In this section we will examine the following charts and terms:

- category probability curves, including:
    - o Rasch-Andrich thresholds (deltas)
    - o average item difficulty for partial credit items
- cumulative probability curve, including:
    - o Rasch-Thurstone thresholds
- item characteristic curves (ICCs)

| CATEGORY | | OBSERVED | OBSVD | SAMPLE | INFIT | OUTFIT | | ANDRICH |
LABEL	SCORE	COUNT	%	AVRGE EXPECT	MNSQ	MNSQ		THRESHOLD
0	0	28	4	.00	.07	.97	1.01		NONE
1	1	229	34	.52	.53	.98	.95		−.99
2	2	410	61	.98	.97	1.00	1.00		.99

Table 4.7: Rating scale statistics: Item 6 (extract)

Category probability curves

Figure 4.5 shows the category probability curve for Item 9 in our data set from the listening test. This item has three response categories, which are labelled 'o', '1', and '2'. The three curves on the graph show the probability of the three different responses to the item in relation to the ability of the students. The y-axis represents the probability of a response category, that is, the chance of someone receiving a certain score level expressed as a proportion of 1; the x-axis shows the ability of test takers in terms of logits.

The probability of a 'o' score on Item 9 steadily decreases as the ability of test takers increases. Therefore, for someone with a very low listening ability, a score of '2' is very unlikely on this item. Similarly, for someone with high listening ability, the probability of scoring 'o' is also very unlikely. The probability of a response of '1' first increases as we move from low ability to high ability on the horizontal logit scale and then decreases again as the likelihood of scoring a '2' increases. For every level of ability, the probabilities of the three response categories in Figure 4.5 add up to one.

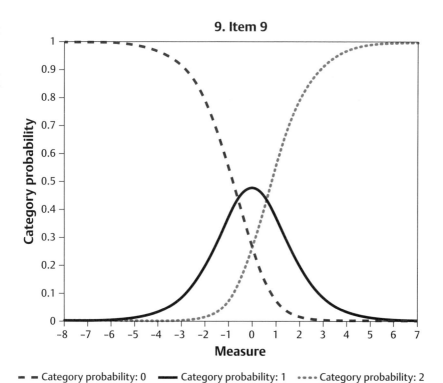

Figure 4.5: Category probability curve: Item 9

We can learn a number of important things from this curve. First of all, the location of the curve on the logit scale shows us how difficult an item is overall. The individual curves for each score point also give us an indication of how likely it is that test takers score a certain score point. Figure 4.6 shows the item characteristics curve of Item 16. It can be seen that the curve for the score of '1' is most likely only for a very narrow range of abilities, whereas the score curve for '2' is much more likely (i.e. a much wider ability range is likely to score '2').

The situation in Figure 4.6 can be even more pronounced, so that a curve for a certain score point is never most probable. This is the case for score point '2' in Item 12 in Figure 4.7, which does not have an individual peak in the graph. There has been much debate in the Rasch literature over this phenomenon, also referred to as 'disordered thresholds' (see for example, Adams, Wu, & Wilson, 2012) and whether this is an issue of how well the data fits the model. Adams et al. (2012) examine several scenarios where disordered thresholds can occur, and provide possible solutions.

These curves provide us with important information about the functioning of the rating scale of each item. By simply reviewing the graphs, we can get

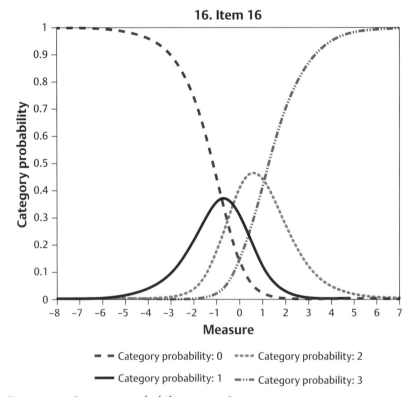

Figure 4.6: Category probability curve: Item 16

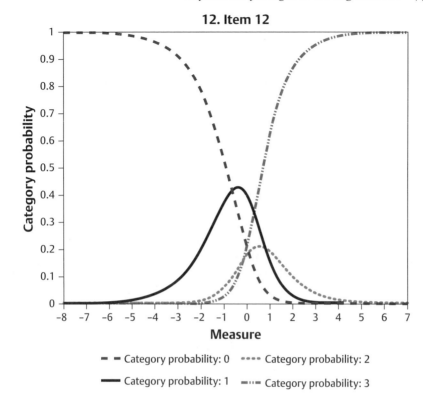

12. Item 12

— — Category probability: 0   •••• Category probability: 2

—— Category probability: 1   —··— Category probability: 3

Figure 4.7: Category probability curve: Item 12

an indication of the difficulty of an item, how likely each score category is for groups of students of a certain ability, how likely each score category is overall, and whether any of the score points are never most likely. If this is the case, the test designer might want to review the scoring system of the item by, for example, collapsing two adjacent categories or revising the scoring criteria.

It is important to remember, however, that the parameter estimates of this estimation are only stable if there are at least 10 observations at each score point. For this reason, it is important to establish that these minimum numbers have been reached before making any decisions in relation to revising the item in question.

Rasch-Andrich thresholds and average item difficulty

Figure 4.8, which shows the probability curve of Item 6, can help us understand how programs like Winsteps and Quest generate the Wright maps relating to a partial credit analysis.

We noted above that these two programs provide us with slightly different Wright maps when we undertake a partial credit analysis. While Winsteps only maps the average difficulty of each item onto the map, Quest provides us with information about the location of each step. So where do these two locations on the logit scale come from? We have inserted two vertical black lines and a shorter vertical grey line into Figure 4.8. The grey line indicates the point on the logit scale where the lowest and the highest score points in our item (i.e. scores of 'o' and '2' in Item 6) intersect. This is the *average item difficulty* of the item and the location of the item on the Winsteps Wright map. The two vertical black lines in Figure 4.8 indicate the locations on the logit scale where the adjacent score categories intersect. For example, at about logit –1.80, the response categories 'o' and '1' cross. This is the point where it is equally likely that someone of this ability would score either of these score points. This point is sometimes called the *delta parameter*, or the *Rasch-Andrich threshold*. The second vertical black line can be found where the scale categories of '1' and '2' intersect. This indicates the delta parameter where these two scores are of equal probability. These delta parameters are what is shown on the Wright map in the Quest output.

The distances between the delta parameters can provide us with an indication of the relative distances between the steps on the rating scale of each item. Consider Item 20 (Figure 4.9), for example. The lines indicating the locations

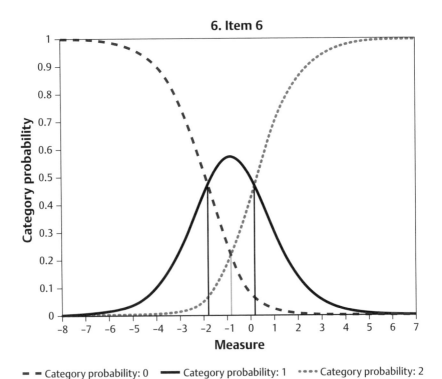

Figure 4.8: Category probability curve: Item 6 with Rasch-Andrich thresholds

20. Item 20

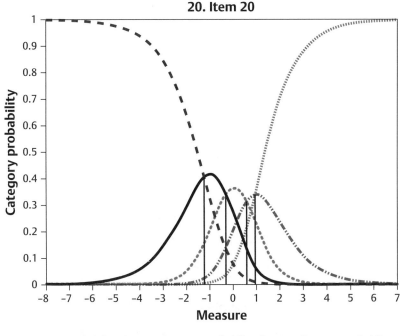

- – Category probability: 0 ••• Category probability: 2 """"" Category probability: 4
— Category probability: 1 —••— Category probability: 3

Figure 4.9: Category probability curve: Item 20

of the deltas on the logit scale show that the distance between the delta between score points '2' and '3', as well as the delta between score points '3' and '4', are much closer together than the other deltas. Therefore, the range of abilities where score point '3' is most probable is much narrower than for the other score points. One could therefore argue that a student has to increase their abilities on the latent variable by much more to move from score '1' to score '2' than when moving from score '3' to score '4'. This information has implications for our understanding of the scale as well as for rater training. It draws our attention to the fact that scales are not necessarily linear with equal intervals. This characteristic is in stark contrast to reporting scales, such as the CEFR, which are depicted as equal interval scales (which of course is not true).

Cumulative probability curves

The probability curves for each item can also be presented in a different way—as cumulative probability curves. Figure 4.10 is the cumulative probability curve for Item 19. The y-axis again represents the probability of a test taker receiving a certain score and the x-axis shows the logit scale depicting the candidate ability measures. As the name of the curves indicates, the graph shows the cumulative probability of a certain score point rather than the probability of individual scores.

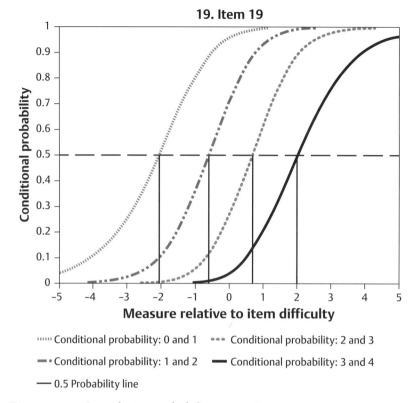

Figure 4.10: Cumulative probability curve: Item 19

The vertical black lines in Figure 4.10 are the *Rasch-Thurstone thresholds*. The first vertical black line on the left is the Rasch-Thurstone threshold, where the probability is 50% of a test taker of that ability level scoring 1 or higher. The next Rasch-Thurstone threshold is the point where the probability of scoring 2 or higher is 50%, and so on. Large testing organizations often make use of these probability curves to communicate results to stakeholders. To do this, they usually make a decision regarding the point at which a pass/fail cut-off is located on such graphs. Note, however, that this graph only displays one item, and that pass/fail decisions are usually based on whole tests.

Item characteristic curves (ICCs)

A further type of graph generated by Rasch software programs are item characteristic curves or ICCs.

Figure 4.11 shows the model and empirical item characteristic curves for Item 20. The thick grey line in the middle represents the model ICC and the line connected by small x marks represents the empirical ICC. The thin grey lines represent the 1.96 model standard errors above and below the model ICC and therefore form the two-sided 95% confidence interval around the model ICC. So how do we interpret these ICCs? The y-axis in this case represents the score on Item 20, while the x-axis represents the average ability

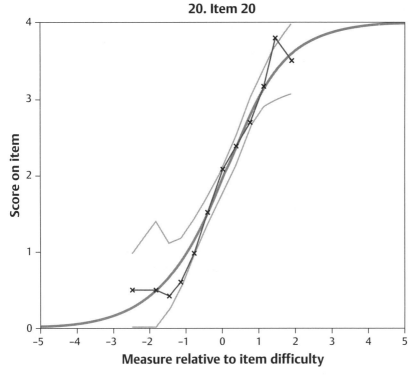

Figure 4.11: Item characteristic curve: Item 20

measure of our test takers. The closer to the left of our logit scale the graph is situated, the easier the item is for test takers.

The graph also provides us with information about the discrimination of the item: the steeper the curve, the more discriminating the item is between high- and low-ability test takers. The confidence intervals can provide us with information about misfit, as ideally we would like our empirical line to be within the confidence interval. For example, for Item 20 in Figure 4.11, test takers at about 1.2 logits are scoring higher on the item than would be expected. If an item displays this type of misfit across a larger group of students at a certain ability level (for example, high performers), then this could be a reason to review the item with the intention of making that item fairer for those test takers. It may be possible that this item is functioning differently for different groups of students and, as a result, not measuring what we intended.

Summary of rating scale analysis

After reviewing all the statistics available for rating scale analysis, it is important to summarize which of these are key for researchers and practitioners. Linacre (1999, 2002b, 2004) makes the following recommendations:

1 There should be more than 10 observations per category. If this condition is not fulfilled, it is possible that the findings are unstable.

2 Average measures should advance approximately by the same value at each score point.
3 Average measures should not be disordered.
4 The frequency of data points in each category should result in a smooth distribution, i.e. the distribution should not be jagged.
5 Average measures should be near their expected values.
6 Mean-square values should be less than 2.
7 Rasch-Andrich thresholds (step difficulty, step calibration) should increase at each score level by 1.4 or more, but no more than 5 logits.

These guidelines are useful for researchers investigating scale structure. We also suggest eyeballing the graphs presented earlier in this chapter for any obvious problems, such as disordered thresholds, and revising any items or scales that do not seem to be functioning well.

A closer look at the differences between the partial credit model and the rating scale model: when do we use which?

As mentioned earlier in this chapter, when we have a data set with items that attract more values than simply right or wrong answers, we have the option of choosing either the Andrich rating scale model (RSM) or the partial credit model (PCM) for our Rasch analysis. Sometimes, the researcher can choose which model to use; at other times, only one model will be suitable for the analysis. This section sets out to clarify these differences.

The major difference between the two models is that when we use the Andrich rating scale model, we assume the same scale structure for all items in the data set, and therefore that the item characteristic curves we discussed in the previous section are the same for all items in the data set. The only difference between the graphs will be their location on the logit scale (i.e. the difficulty of each item will vary). This is useful for certain situations, for example when we are using Likert scale items where the response structure for each item is intended to be the same. When we apply the partial credit model, the category probability curve for each item is different. Each item is therefore allowed to define its own category probability structure. The Andrich rating scale model can, however, only be used when all items in the analysis have the same number of response categories. Because this was not the case for our listening trial data set, we had no choice but to use the partial credit model for this analysis.

When using the PCM, our data should fit each item slightly better than for the RSM, but we lose some of the generality of the rating scale categories. Each partial credit structure is also estimated with less data, which means that the thresholds are less stable. Therefore, it is generally accepted that we need more data for stable rating scale structure threshold parameter estimates when using the PCM. For this reason, the rule that we need 10 observations per category is important to keep in mind. The RSM is therefore often used if not enough data is available to use the PCM. An analysis with the RSM is more robust to accidents in the data and should therefore be the first model chosen if possible. It is always advisable when conducting Rasch analyses to choose the most parsimonious model first. We recommend that, if possible, a researcher use the RSM first and then compare the item parameters with a partial credit analysis of the same data set. Often, the differences between the results of the two analyses are negligible; further, it is important to keep in mind that because the RSM is simpler, it simplifies communication with stakeholders.

The rating scale model: using Rasch to analyse questionnaire data

A further data type that can be analysed with the Rasch model is Likert scale questionnaire data. Likert scale items (Likert, 1932) are often used to elicit attitudes data. In language assessment, this type of scale is sometimes used in self-assessment questionnaires, in peer feedback, or in directed self-place-ment. Although this is a common data type used in the area of applied linguistics, it is rarely analysed using the Rasch model. As mentioned earlier in this chapter, it only makes sense to analyse questionnaire data using a Rasch model if the questions are designed to measure one underlying con-struct. In this section we will explore how questionnaire data can be analysed using the Rasch model exemplified by a data set from PISA (Programme for International Student Assessment). PISA is a worldwide study by the Organization for Economic Cooperation and Development (OECD) of 15-year-old students' performance in mathematics, science, and reading. It was first performed in 2000 and has since been repeated every three years. Nearly half a million students from 65 nations participated in 2009.

The data set we will be examining in this section is based on an 11-item reading attitudes questionnaire administered alongside PISA and is based on the responses of 14,251 Australian students in the 2009 administration of PISA.[4] The questionnaire questions can be found in Figure 4.12. It can be seen that these questions are all based around the concept of students' attitudes to reading, that is, they are all designed to measure the same underlying construct.

Q24 How much do you agree or disagree with these statements about reading?

a) I read only if I have to.
b) Reading is one of my favourite hobbies.
c) I like talking about books with other people.
d) I find it hard to finish books.
e) I feel happy if I receive a book as a present.
f) For me, reading is a waste of time.
g) I enjoy going to a bookstore or a library.
h) I read only to get information that I need.
i) I cannot sit still and read for more than a few minutes.
j) I like to express my opinions about books I have read.
k) I like to exchange books with my friends.

Figure 4.12: Questionnaire items

Students were asked to select one of the following response categories for each item:

strongly disagree (1)   disagree (2)   agree (3)   strongly agree (4)

Current approaches to questionnaire analysis

Questionnaire research is common in the area of second language research, but the techniques used for analysis are mostly based on linear inferential statistical techniques (such as factor analysis, correlational analyses, etc.) or purely based on description of the data (see, for example, Brown, 2001; Dörnyei, 2003). As an example, for Item b in the reading questionnaire from PISA, a researcher might state that the students, on average, disagree with this item as can be seen in the graph in Figure 4.13.

Often, scores across all items in such a questionnaire are averaged and an overall reading attitude (or anxiety or motivation) score is calculated. This score might then be used for further analysis (for example, for correlation with other variables, such as test scores). In other cases, sub-sections of questionnaire questions are averaged and then correlated with each other, or used as input for more sophisticated techniques such as exploratory or confirmatory factor analyses.

The data analysis approaches outlined above, however, all assume that the data is interval in nature and that scores can merely be added to one another for other analyses, for example to perform factor analyses. It also assumes that the units (agree, strongly agree, etc.) on the Likert scale are at equal distances from each other. Finally, all items are given equal strength in the questionnaire. Bond and Fox (2007) demonstrate clearly how this practice is

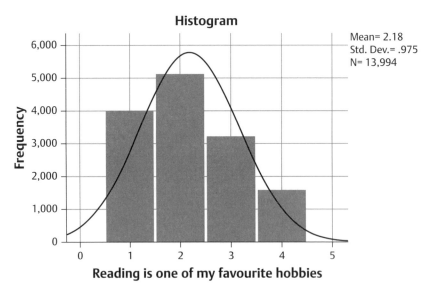

Figure 4.13: Histogram: Item b (Reading is one of my favourite hobbies)

inappropriate and also highly dependent on what numerical codes are assigned to the different categories on the Likert scale (for example, 0, 1, 2, 3, 4 or 1, 2, 3, 4, 5). They argue that traditional analyses assume that the questionnaire items constitute an ordered block of answers, just as the answer options are arranged on the sheet when answered. That is, they assume that the distances between the score points are equal for all items and that the items are all equally likely to be endorsed or not to be endorsed. But it is quite unlikely that this will be shown when the data is analysed.

Let us examine our data more closely. It is clear from reading the different questionnaire items in Figure 4.12, that some of these are worded negatively and others positively. For example, Item a (*I only read if I have to*) and Item b (*Reading is one of my favourite hobbies*) are worded in such a way that they have opposite meanings. To analyse these items, we need to reverse the Likert scale of one of these items to be able to make meaningful comparisons.[5] Items that are not reversed would be measuring a different underlying construct, or latent variable, and may show up as misfitting in the analysis.

Reviewing the content of the different items, one could assume that some of these are items that indicate higher levels of reading attitude. For example, we can assume that it is easier for students to endorse an item such as Item e (*I feel happy if I receive a book as a present*) than Item k (*I like to exchange books with my friends*). However, if we use classical analysis techniques such as the ones described above, all items are given equal weighting in the questionnaire.

Questionnaire analysis using Rasch

We can now make the connection to the description of Rasch analyses earlier in this chapter. An analysis of this type of Likert scale data can give us an indication of how well each item fits the data set as a whole, and is therefore able to contribute to the overall latent variable of 'attitudes towards reading'. By scrutinizing the Wright map and the item statistics, we will see which items are more difficult to endorse for students, and which are easier to endorse. It is important to note that a good Likert scale questionnaire requires items to be at different levels of the construct we are trying to measure, a condition that is ignored in an analysis using more traditional descriptive inferential statistics such as the ones often employed in applied linguistics. It is therefore important to choose a statistical technique that does not treat all items as being at the same level on the trait in question.

It is also important to remember the rule we encountered on page 73 relating to sample size and the number of responses required for each response category. Just as we said for the partial credit model data above, to ensure precision in our measurement we need sufficient observations in each cell of our data matrix, that is, sufficient responses to each option on our Likert scale. The rule of thumb of 10 observations per category (Linacre, 1999, 2002b, 2004) is also relevant to this type of data. While it is possible to analyse data with fewer observations, the estimates generated by the Rasch program will be less exact.

Questionnaire reliability and Wright map

Figure 4.14 presents the Wright map based on the analysis of our data using the rating scale model. We can analyse this data set using the rating scale model, because all items have the same structure (i.e. the same Likert scale options) and the same number of response categories. The rating scale model will assume the same structure for all items in the data set.

Before the analysis, we reversed the response categories for the following items, as these had been worded negatively:

a) I read only if I have to.
d) I find it hard to finish books.
f) For me, reading is a waste of time.
h) I read only to get information that I need.
i) I cannot sit still and read for more than a few minutes.

We start our examination of the data with a quick look at the questionnaire reliability (Table 4.8). This is important in order to have a sense of how well and reliably the questionnaire is measuring the construct we are interested in. In this case, the Cronbach's alpha is high (.94). For an explanation on how to interpret the Rasch reliability indices and Cronbach's alpha, see pages 51–53 in Chapter 3.

Figure 4.14 presents the Wright map for the 11 items in the PISA reading attitudes questionnaire. It can be seen that, just as we expected, some are easier to endorse for the students than others. The reversed items for *waste of time* and *cannot sit still* were the easiest to agree to while *exchange books*, *favourite hobby*, and *talk about books* were the hardest to approve. It can also be seen from the Rasch map that the 11 questionnaire items, at least when indicated by their average item measures, do not fully account for the reading attitudes of our student population. There are few or no items matching the attitudes of students at the higher and lower levels of the Rasch map. It seems therefore, that to more fully measure the reading attitudes of this population, a longer questionnaire might have provided us with more information, in particular about the test takers at the more extreme ends. However, this may have not been practical in the context of the PISA test.

	TOTAL SCORE	COUNT	MEASURE	MODEL S.E.	INFIT MNSQ	INFIT ZSTD	OUTFIT MNSQ	OUTFIT ZSTD
MEAN	27.5	10.9	.01	.55				
P.SD	8.0	.5	2.10	.22				
S.SD	8.0	.5	2.10	.22				
MAX.	44.0	11.0	6.32	2.10				
MIN.	1.0	1.0	-6.14	.46				

REAL RMSE	.65	TRUE SD	1.99	SEPARATION	3.05	Studen RELIABILITY	.90
MODEL RMSE	.59	TRUE SD	2.01	SEPARATION	3.38	Studen RELIABILITY	.92
S.E. OF Student MEAN = .02							

Student RAW SCORE-TO-MEASURE CORRELATION = .97
CRONBACH ALPHA (KR-20) Student RAW SCORE "TEST" RELIABILITY = .94

Table 4.8: Questionnaire reliability indices

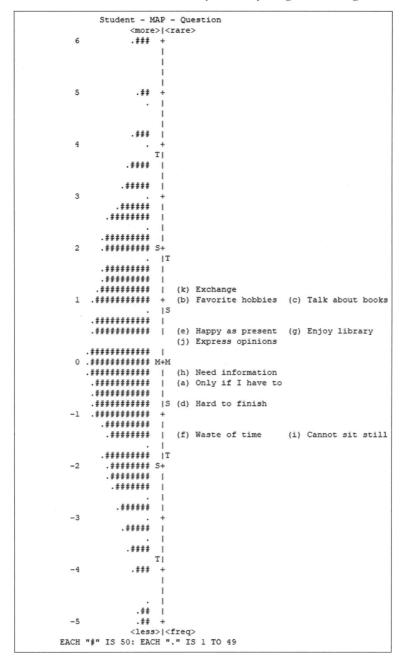

```
                Student - MAP - Question
                    <more>|<rare>
        6            .###  +
                           |
                           |
                           |
                           |
        5            .##   +
                      .    |
                           |
                           |
                           |
                     .###  |
        4             .    +
                         T|
                    .####  |
                           |
                   .#####  |
        3             .    +
                  .######  |
                 .#######  |
                      .    |
                .########  |
        2       .######### S+
                      .    |T
               .########   |
               .########   |
              .#########   |  (k) Exchange
        1   .###########   +  (b) Favorite hobbies   (c) Talk about books
                     .     |S
             .###########   |
             .###########   |  (e) Happy as present   (g) Enjoy library
                              (j) Express opinions
            .############   |
        0  .############## M+M
            .###########   |  (h) Need information
            .###########   |  (a) Only if I have to
            .###########   |
            .###########   |S (d) Hard to finish
       -1   .###########   +
             .#########    |
              .########    |  (f) Waste of time      (i) Cannot sit still
                    .      |
              .########    |T
       -2     .######## S+
              .#######    |
               .#######    |
                    .      |
                .######    |
       -3          .       +
                 .#####    |
                   .       |
                 .####     |
                         T|
       -4        .###     +
                           |
                           |
                           |
                  .        |
                 .##       |
       -5        .##       +
                  <less>|<freq>
        EACH "#" IS 50: EACH "." IS 1 TO 49
```

Figure 4.14: Wright map of questionnaire responses (Winsteps)

We can also see from the Rasch map that there are differing distances between the questionnaire items as they advance from easiest to agree with to hardest to endorse (from the bottom of the Wright map to the top). For example, the distance from 'I like to express my opinions about books I have read' to 'I enjoy going to a bookstore or library' is much smaller than the distance from

'I enjoy going to a bookstore or library' to 'I like talking about books with other people'. Details like these are difficult to identify if we only rely on techniques from classical test theory or simple descriptive statistics.

Figure 4.15 shows the Wright map as presented by the program Quest. As we discussed earlier in this chapter, rather than merely providing us with the average item difficulty indices, as is the practice in the Winsteps program, Quest shows the Rasch-Andrich thresholds for each item. There are three thresholds: threshold 1 indicates an equal chance of a respondent at that level choosing either 'strongly disagree' or 'disagree'; threshold 2 indicates an equal chance that a respondent at the same level on the logit scale will choose either 'disagree' or 'agree'; and threshold 3 indicates an equal likelihood of a respondent selecting 'agree', or 'strongly agree'.

From this map we are able to predict the most likely responses provided by participants who are located at different positions on the logit scale. For example, a person located at logit 1.0 is likely to choose 'agree' to Question 10 (express opinions). This is because threshold 2, which is the 50% chance that they are likely to endorse either 'disagree' or 'agree', is some way lower on the logit scale.

The Quest item/person map also shows us that the questionnaire items provide fairly good coverage in comparison to our respondents, with only the respondents at the very top and bottom of the scale not covered by items.

Item analysis

As was the case with both the analysis of dichotomous data in Chapter 3 and the data set of the listening test with polytomous items we analysed earlier in this chapter, an analysis using the rating scale model also produces a table of item statistics (Table 4.9). In this case, we have chosen to have this table displayed in measure order, from the hardest-to-endorse to the easiest-to-endorse item.

The 'Total count' column indicates how many participants responded to this item. The 'Measure' column provides us with the average location of each item on the logit scale. This location is where the highest and lowest response categories in our Likert scale are equally probable and is the point that Winsteps uses for the locations of the items on the Wright map. In the case of our data set, the standard error (S.E. column) is very low. This is due to the large number of participants in the PISA questionnaire sample we are using. The low S.E. indicates that we can be fairly confident of the accuracy of the item locations on the Wright map.

We can again see columns with fit statistics in this table and these are interpreted in the same manner as we discussed in Chapter 3 (see page 40). According to the criteria we established previously, one item in our questionnaire (Item 4, 'I find it hard to finish books') is borderline to being misfitting (depending on which criteria we draw on). Further investigation of this item may be necessary. On the whole, however, the analysis of our data shows that the items in the reading questionnaire seem to be good at accounting for the construct it was designed for.

More details of the response categories for each item can be found in the item category frequency table, an extract from which is shown in Table 4.10. Here we can see how many students chose each response category and the

```
 ---------------------------------------------------------------------
| Item Estimates (Thresholds)                        31/ 8/2016 12:15 |
| all on all  (N = 14251 L = 11 Probability Level=0.50)               |
 ---------------------------------------------------------------------
|    5.0                              |                                |
|                         XXX         |                                |
|                                     |                                |
|                                     |                                |
|    4.0                              |                                |
|                       XXXXX         |                                |
|                                     |                                |
|                                     |                                |
|                     XXXXXXX         |     11.3                       |
|                                     |      2.3                       |
|    3.0              XXXXXXXX         |      3.3                       |
|                                     |                                |
|                   XXXXXXXXXX        |      7.3    10.3               |
|                                     |      5.3                       |
|               XXXXXXXXXXXXX         |                                |
|    2.0        XXXXXXXXXXXXX         |      8.3                       |
|                                     |      1.3                       |
|              XXXXXXXXXXXXXX         |                                |
|              XXXXXXXXXXXXXX         |      4.3                       |
|              XXXXXXXXXXXXXX         |                                |
|                                     |                                |
|    1.0        XXXXXXXXXXXXXXXX      |      6.3    9.3    11.2        |
|              XXXXXXXXXXXXXXXX       |                                |
|              XXXXXXXXXXXXXXXX       |      2.2    3.2                |
|              XXXXXXXXXXXXXXXX       |                                |
|            XXXXXXXXXXXXXXXXXX       |      7.2    10.2               |
|    0.0       XXXXXXXXXXXXXXXXX      |      5.2                       |
|              XXXXXXXXXXXXXXXXXX     |                                |
|                                     |                                |
|              XXXXXXXXXXXXXXXXX      |      8.2                       |
|              XXXXXXXXXXXXXXXX       |      1.2                       |
|              XXXXXXXXXXXXXXXX       |                                |
|   -1.0       XXXXXXXXXXXXXXXXX      |      4.2    11.1               |
|             XXXXXXXXXXXXXXXX        |      2.1    3.1                |
|              XXXXXXXXXXXXX          |      6.2                       |
|              XXXXXXXXXXXXX          |      9.2                       |
|               XXXXXXXXXXX           |      5.1    7.1    10.1        |
|   -2.0                              |                                |
|             XXXXXXXXXXXXX           |                                |
|             XXXXXXXXXXXXX           |      8.1                       |
|                                     |      1.1                       |
|              XXXXXXXXXX             |                                |
|               XXXXXXXX              |      4.1                       |
|   -3.0                              |                                |
|               XXXXXXXX              |                                |
|                                     |      6.1    9.1               |
|                                     |                                |
|                 XXXXX               |                                |
|   -4.0                              |                                |
|                                     |                                |
|                                     |                                |
|                 XXXX                |                                |
|                                     |                                |
|   -5.0                              |                                |
 ---------------------------------------------------------------------
|  Each X represents    33 students                                   |
 =====================================================================
```

Figure 4.15: Wright map of questionnaire responses (Quest)

ENTRY NUMBER	TOTAL SCORE	TOTAL COUNT	MEASURE	MODEL S.E.	INFIT MNSQ	INFIT ZSTD	OUTFIT MNSQ	OUTFIT ZSTD	PTBISERL-EX CORR.	PTBISERL-EX EXP.	EXACT MATCH OBS%	EXACT MATCH EXP%	Question
11	28896	13998	1.26	.01	1.10	7.9	1.07	4.3	.68	.71	61.9	60.7	(k) Exchange
2	30454	13994	.94	.01	.73	-9.9	.71	-9.9	.81	.71	68.5	59.5	(b) Favorite hobbies
3	30504	13987	.93	.01	.84	-9.9	.84	-9.9	.75	.71	66.9	59.5	(c) Talk about books
7	32967	13984	.44	.01	.92	-6.9	.90	-8.1	.76	.72	62.9	58.5	(g) Enjoy library
10	32985	13991	.43	.01	1.06	5.0	1.11	8.6	.67	.72	62.2	58.5	(j) Express opinions
5	33543	13958	.31	.01	.94	-5.3	.96	-3.1	.72	.72	63.5	58.5	(e) Happy as present
8	36515	13999	-.26	.01	.94	-5.2	1.04	3.1	.70	.72	64.7	58.6	(h) Need information
1	37342	14004	-.42	.01	.85	-9.9	.85	-9.9	.77	.71	67.3	58.9	(a) Only if I have to
4	39331	13993	-.83	.01	1.49	9.9	1.50	9.9	.57	.71	54.6	60.0	(d) Hard to finish
6	41689	13974	-1.34	.01	.92	-6.5	.84	-9.9	.77	.70	68.4	61.8	(f) Waste of time
9	42247	13990	-1.46	.01	1.25	9.9	1.24	9.9	.65	.69	62.3	62.5	(i) Cannot sit still
MEAN	35133.9	13988	.00	.01	1.00	-1.9	1.01	-1.4			63.9	59.7	
P.SD	4390.7	12.3	.89	.00	.20	7.9	.21	8.2			3.8	1.3	

Table 4.9: Item statistics: questionnaire data

ENTRY NUMBER	DATA CODE	SCORE VALUE	DATA COUNT	DATA %	ABILITY MEAN	P.SD	S.E. MEAN	INFT MNSQ	OUTF MNSQ	PBSX CORR.	Question	
11	1	1	4465	32	-1.82	1.65	.02	1.3	1.2	-.57	(k) Exchange	1 Strongly disagree
	2	2	5148	37	-.03	1.21	.02	1.0	.9	.00		2 Disagree
	3	3	3405	24	1.53	1.24	.02	1.0	.9	.42		3 Agree
	4	4	980	7	3.27	1.87	.06	1.3	1.5	.34		4 Strongly agree
	MISSING ***		253	2#	-.21	2.14	.29			.00		
2	1	1	4015	29	-2.17	1.37	.02	.8	.8	-.66	(b) Favorite hobbies	1 Strongly disagree
	2	2	5119	37	-.22	.95	.01	.6	.6	-.07		2 Disagree
	3	3	3239	23	1.44	.92	.02	.6	.5	.42		3 Agree
	4	4	1621	12	3.26	1.48	.04	.9	1.0	.49		4 Strongly agree
	MISSING ***		257	2#	-.59	1.97	.26			-.01		

Table 4.10: Extract from Item category frequency table

precise mean student measures at each score level. Just as we discussed earlier in the chapter, we would like the mean measures of the test takers to advance with each category of the Likert scale because we expect higher categories to be chosen by students with higher levels of enjoying reading. This means we expect students who like reading more to be more likely to select 'agree' or 'strongly agree' than students who like reading less. Occasionally when we administer questionnaires this is not the case, which means that we have a case of disordered thresholds, as we discussed on page 72. If that is the case, we need to investigate further why respondents are more likely to endorse some steps on the Likert scale than others.

As we saw earlier with the listening test data that we analysed using the partial credit model, an analysis of questionnaire data also yields output about the rating scale used. In this case, because we chose the rating scale model, we only receive this information in relation to all our 11 items at once (rather than different information for each item). This is because the rating scale assumes that the step structure or scale structure of all items is identical. Table 4.11 presents us with the rating scale properties for the PISA questionnaire. Here, we can apply the same criteria put forward by Linacre (1999, 2002b, 2004) that were discussed on page 77–8. For example, we can examine whether we have sufficient observations (no fewer than 10) in each category ('Observed count' column), and whether the average measures advance monotonically. In the case of this data set, all the criteria set out are fulfilled. With smaller or less carefully developed and trialled data sets, this may not always be the case. If any problems are found, researchers need to evaluate whether the items can be revised, or whether they should be deleted from the data set altogether. The table also provides us with fit statistics for each Likert scale answer category, as well as the Rasch-Andrich thresholds we encountered earlier.

Finally, as we saw with the partial credit data presented earlier in this chapter, Winsteps also produces a category probability curve (see Figure 4.16). Only one curve is produced for all our eleven items and we can examine this to ascertain whether each response category has a distinct peak. As we discussed on page 71, this curve shows us which response category participants are most likely to choose at different locations on our logit scale (and therefore at different locations on our construct). The probability at each location adds up to 1. For example, in Figure 4.16, a candidate at reading attitude level −1, is most likely to choose a '2' and a candidate at level 1 is most likely to

```
-------------------------------------------------------------------
|CATEGORY    OBSERVED|OBSVD SAMPLE|INFIT OUTFIT|| ANDRICH  |CATEGORY|
|LABEL SCORE COUNT  %|AVRGE EXPECT|  MNSQ MNSQ||THRESHOLD| MEASURE |
|--------------------+------------+-------------++---------+--------|
|  1    1   28660  19| -2.50 -2.53|  1.11  1.18||  NONE   |( -3.37)| 1 Strongly disagree
|  2    2   44805  29|  -.94  -.87|   .85   .82||  -2.18  |  -1.23 | 2 Disagree
|  3    3   53425  35|   .83   .77|   .86   .88||   -.24  |   1.13 | 3 Agree
|  4    4   26982  18|  2.57  2.62|  1.21  1.22||   2.42  |(  3.57)| 4 Strongly agree
|--------------------+------------+-------------++---------+--------|
|MISSING     711   0|  -.58      |           ||         |        |
-------------------------------------------------------------------
```

Table 4.11: Rating scale properties

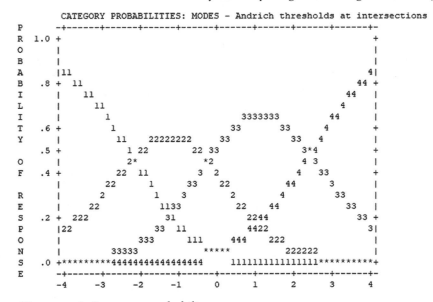

Figure 4.16: Response probability curve

choose a '3'. At just below zero, this balance between 2 and 3 slowly shifts and there is a point where both 2 and 3 are likely.

Summary of questionnaire analysis using Rasch

We have seen in this section that Rasch analysis offers an alternative data analysis method for questionnaire data designed to elicit a specific underlying construct. This has several advantages over traditional analyses: we are able to see where the items are located on our construct in question, how well they are matched to our population of respondents, the distances between items on the logit scale (indicating how much more is required by respondents to endorse an item), how well our Likert scale functions, and whether any of the questionnaire questions are not measuring the same underlying construct as the others. Most importantly, we have a much better way of knowing where our questionnaire respondents are located on our construct. The person measure can then be used for further analyses such as factor analyses, correlation, and so on. Such analyses are crucial if we want to get a fuller understanding of the functioning of a questionnaire. This is particularly important for questionnaires that are used for decision-making, such as directed self-placement questionnaires, for example, or self-assessment questionnaires.

In a directed self-placement questionnaire, a series of questions, once modelled in Rasch, can be used to make more precise decisions about the placement of a student, resulting in more accurate placement decisions and hence a fairer instrument for the candidate. While placement decisions are often low-stakes, misplacement can result in lower student satisfaction and may increase the administrative load of both teachers and other staff members.

Summary

In this chapter we introduced Rasch models that are suitable for analysing data with items with more score points than simply right or wrong, namely the rating scale model and the partial credit model. We examined the differences between these two models and discussed criteria for selecting which of the two models we should use for our analysis. Later, in Chapters 6 and 7, we will show how some of these analyses can be applied to identify differential item functioning (DIF) to explore whether any test items are unfairly advantaging or disadvantaging subgroups of test takers (for example, females or males, or subgroups from different L1 backgrounds). We will also show how researchers have used the techniques exemplified in Chapters 3 and 4 to examine the quality of their testing instruments to ensure fair decisions about test takers.

In the final section of the chapter we showed the usefulness of Rasch analysis for analysing questionnaire data. We explained that this type of analysis is only suitable for questionnaire data that is designed to examine an underlying construct (in our case 'attitudes to reading'). Although not usually used to analyse questionnaire data in language assessment or applied linguistics more broadly, Rasch analysis can provide us with answers, to questions that more traditional analyses may fail to answer, and as a result it may lead to fairer decisions about students (for example, following self-assessment or directed self-placement).

In Chapter 5 we will examine data that includes more than two facets, i.e. that is not only focused on candidate ability and item difficulty. Such data can be analysed using many-facets Rasch measurement.

Activities on the website

The data sets used in this chapter are provided on the companion website (www.oup.com/elt/teacher/fjla). Interested readers are encouraged to download the files and complete the activities.

Notes

1 For a historical perspective of the development of the different Rasch models, see Chapter 8.
2 This term has several senses: (1) the overall sense expressed here, (2) data from a rating scale as distinct from a Likert or semantic differential scale, and (3) data analysed using Andrich's rating scale model as compared with Masters' partial credit model.
3 The step structure refers to the distance between different points on the rating scale. When we use the Andrich rating scale model, this assumes that all items have the same number of steps and the same distances between the steps. The partial credit model does not assume this.
4 The data from the PISA project is available for download from the following website: http://www.oecd.org/pisa.
5 Note that the practice of merely switching around (or changing the polarity of) Likert scale items is not without its problems, but for the sake of this analysis, we have taken this simple approach.

5

Introducing raters and ratings: the many-facets Rasch model

Introduction

The assessment of writing and speaking performances often involves human judges, termed 'raters' in the language testing world. This is appropriate because, despite development in automated assessment systems on computers, humans can make much more complex decisions about a spoken or written performance. We all know, however, that human judges do not necessarily agree: think of the differences among judges in popular song or dance competitions on television, or in sports at the Olympic Games, where complex performances (such as gymnastics or diving) need to be judged as a whole in all their complexity. Participants encountering a strict judge would be disadvantaged in comparison to another participant encountering a lenient judge. For this reason, most testing agencies, as well as smaller, localized tests, put at least some measures in place to account for these differences, including double marking, rater training, and rater moderation.

In this chapter we will examine the issue of rater variability more closely. We will start out by describing types of rater effects that are a source of construct-irrelevance, that is, the scores that reflect not only candidate ability but arbitrary and irrelevant rater differences. These pose a threat to the validity of the score interpretations we make, and thus constitute a risk to test fairness. We will explore how difficult it is to identify these effects using more traditional measures of rater quality. The chapter then introduces another, more complex Rasch model, the many-facets Rasch model (Linacre, 1989), which can help us with both identifying rater variation and calculating a fairer score for candidate performances (rather than relying on raw scores only). The chapter concludes with a summary of rater effects and the statistics that can be used to identify these.

Understanding rater variability

Traditionally, best practice in language assessment ensures that the following measures are taken during a performance assessment:

1 Raters have been trained carefully and have demonstrated the required level of rating accuracy before being accredited as raters.
2 Raters regularly take part in ongoing rater moderation sessions.
3 Rating criteria have been carefully developed and trialled, and are reflective of candidates' discourse. The delineations between performance levels are clear and easy to apply.
4 Samples of performances at different score levels are available to raters.
5 Performances are routinely rated by more than one rater.

Despite all these measures, it is common for rater differences to persist. McNamara (1996) provides the example of two candidates (Michael and Paula) completing a speaking task as part of a test of English for Academic Purposes. Michael's performance is rated by a strict rater and receives a score of 5 on the nine-point scale. Paula is rated by a lenient rater and receives a score of 6. Paula and Michael also had a choice of topic. Michael's topic was relatively difficult and Paula's was quite easy. The scenario (from McNamara, 1996, p. 118) is summarized in Table 5.1. We can see from the table that although Michael's raw score was lower, he was the candidate with the higher ability, while Paula received a higher score, but actually had the lower ability. Thus we can see that raw scores can mask the true nature of the situation. The table also illustrates the interplay of several facets (candidate ability, topic difficulty, and rater leniency/harshness) that came into effect here.

Candidate	Rater	Topic	Rating	Ability
Michael	harsh	tough	5	(higher)
Paula	lenient	easy	6	(lower)

Table 5.1: How raw scores can disguise differences in ability in performance assessment settings (adapted from McNamara, 1996, p. 118)

It has long been acknowledged that differences between raters exist, and that numerous factors in the assessment situation can contribute to this. This is because—in contrast to fixed-response-type assessments, where the assessment score is directly arrived at from the instrument (as was the case, for example, for our dichotomously scored assessment in Chapter 3)—scores on performance assessments are directly mediated by a number of aspects, or *facets*, in the assessment context. We have already encountered two such facets—the rater and the task—but there are many others that we could think of as well. McNamara (1996) showed the complex interaction between performance, task, rater, and assessment score graphically. We have updated McNamara's figure to also include the interlocutor (for example, the rater or a paired test taker) as a possible facet, as presented in Figure 5.1. The interlocutor (who could be the rater as represented by the long arrow) is also relevant to interactive speaking assessments or writing assessments that include an element of interaction, such as in email interaction or interactive chat.

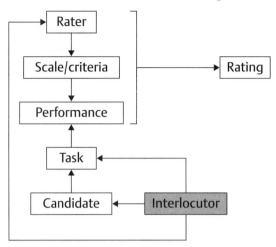

Figure 5.1: Factors influencing the score in a performance assessment (adapted from McNamara, 1996, p. 86)

Other authors (Fulcher 2003; Knoch, 2009; Skehan, 1998) have expanded this figure over the years to include further aspects that impact candidates' scores. In Figure 5.2, for example, we have reproduced Knoch's (2009) expanded model of writing performance, which is based on Fulcher's (2003)

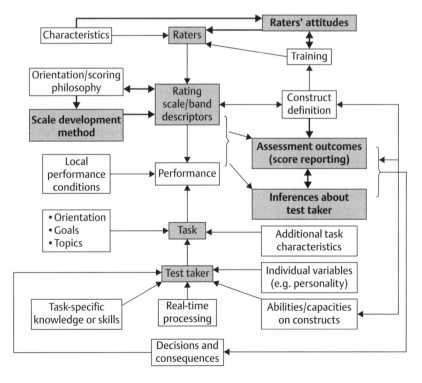

Figure 5.2: Knoch's (2009) expanded model of writing performance (p. 227)

model. It can be seen that there are many additional factors that can impact a score on a performance assessment when compared with McNamara's expanded model depicted above. There are, for example, three variables that directly influence raters, namely their characteristics, their attitudes, and their training. The rating scale in use is influenced by the scoring philosophy of the test, the scale development method, and the construct definition. The performance is influenced by the local performance conditions. The task is influenced by its orientation, goals, and topics as well as other task characteristics. Test takers bring with them task-specific knowledge or skills as well as individual variables and specific abilities on constructs. Based on the performance, which is determined through the use of the rating scale, assessment outcomes are determined and inferences about test takers are made.

Eckes (2011), in his framework of rater-mediated assessment, referred to the factors in grey in the middle column (i.e. task, test taker, rater, and rating scale and criteria/band descriptors) as proximal factors that have an immediate impact on the scores, and the other factors (for example, rater characteristics, task characteristics, test taker individual variables), which are on the outside of the figure, as distal factors (as their impact is less direct and they are therefore slightly more difficult to isolate). It is also important to note that many of these factors can interact. For example, a writing task requiring test takers to describe a narrative based on a series of pictures of a soccer match might be easy for some test takers with background knowledge of soccer, but very difficult for others lacking this knowledge. Raters might interact in a certain way with specific categories on the rating scale (for example, rating more harshly when rating grammatical accuracy and more leniently when grading content). Any of the aspects mentioned so far are facets of the assessment situation, and any of them can cause variation among raters.

Let us examine in more detail some of the ways that raters can differ from each other (see Eckes, 2011; Knoch, 2009; McNamara, 1996; Myford & Wolfe, 2003, 2004). A number of rater effects have been described in the literature, and each of these pose a direct threat to fairness for the candidates if they are not controlled. For the purpose of this chapter we will focus on six of these effects, which are described in more detail below.

1 Raters can differ from each other in their overall leniency and harshness. This may be because they differ in their sense of what constitutes an average performance, and apply the higher- and lower-scale steps accordingly.

2 When rating using an analytic rating scale, some raters may also display a *halo effect*, which means they fail to recognize distinct traits in a performance and apply more holistic views across the different rating scale criteria, resulting in very 'flat' rating profiles. For example, when using a rating scale with five categories, each with five levels, a rater might award scores of 4, 4, 4, 4, 4.

3 Others display a *central tendency effect*, which means they avoid using the outer rating scale levels, focusing most of their ratings on the inside levels in the majority of cases, despite encountering both excellent and poor performances. For a rating scale such as the one described in (2) above, a rater displaying a central tendency effect might overuse the middle range of the rating scale, but generally avoid using 1s and 5s.

4 Raters may also be rating *inconsistently* when compared to the group of raters, that is, without a clear pattern of leniency and harshness. This has been termed 'randomness' by Myford and Wolfe (2003); it is defined as a rater's tendency to apply one or more rating scale categories in a way that is inconsistent with the way in which others apply the same scale, but without a clear pattern such as leniency or severity, as described above.

5 Raters may also display leniency or harshness not overall, but to a specific aspect of the rating situations, such as a specific group of candidates or certain rating scale criteria. For example, a rater may always rate candidates with an Indian accent higher than other raters, or may always rate particularly harshly when scoring the organization criterion on an analytic rating scale for writing. In the first example, there is an interaction between the rater and a type of candidate, while in the second there is an interaction between the rater and a particular criterion. This has also been called a *bias effect*.

6 Raters may be interpreting the scale steps of the rating scale slightly differently. McNamara (1996), for example, shows that while rating scales are presented as having steps that are equal distances apart, that is, they represent equal degrees of difference in ability, raters may not interpret them in that way. Figure 5.3 shows how the scale is presented to raters as a set of equal steps, so that there are regular increments in ability as we move up the scale (a)—and how two raters may interpret the scale steps differently (b and c)—awarding the next higher score after only a small increase in ability (1 to 2 or 3 to 4 in (c), 5 to 6 in (b), or after an unusually large increase (3 to 4 in (b)).

Figure 5.3: Rating scale layout (a) and different rater interpretations of scale steps (b and c) based on McNamara (1996, p. 124)

Identifying variation in ratings—the traditional approach

Traditional approaches to identifying rater differences have mostly focused on pairs of raters, and have generally drawn on either indices of consensus or consistency, or both (see, for example, Stemler, 2004; Stemler & Tsai, 2008).

Consensus refers to the extent to which raters provide the exact same ratings of a particular performance. *Consistency*, on the other hand, examines whether they arrive at the same relative ranking of the performances. Unfortunately, these two groups of indices have been inconsistently used in the literature and their meaning is often misunderstood. Let us examine how this plays out in practice. In Table 5.2, we present the ratings of two raters on ten performances. The raters used a five-point scale when rating these samples.

It can be seen that Rater 2 is almost always rating one score point lower than Rater 1, but relatively consistently so. In terms of consensus, these two raters would score low (as they only agreed once, i.e. in 10% of the samples). In terms of consistency, however, they would be found to be highly consistent as they are ranking the performances in almost exactly the same way. If we were only interested in ranking candidates, this would not be a problem; but if we have a score above which a person passes, and below which the person fails (a so-called *cut score*), then this could have serious consequences for candidates: some would be passed by one judge but not by the other. We can therefore see that neither of these two types of indices by themselves provides us with the full picture of the rating patterns of our two raters. Neither of them can provide us with information about the full range of rater effects described above.

These more traditional indices are also often restricted to describing rating patterns of pairs of raters, and therefore do not reflect well the reality of large-scale assessments, where raters may not always be neatly paired up to rate a group of performances. In Table 5.3 we simulate how raters might be assigned in a high-stakes setting using a small data set. It can be seen that using

Performance sample	Rater 1	Rater 2
1	5	4
2	4	3
3	1	1
4	4	3
5	3	2
6	5	4
7	5	4
8	2	1
9	4	3
10	3	2

Table 5.2: Sample ratings of two raters

Rater	1	2	3	4	5	6	7	8
Test takers 1–10	X	X						
Test takers 11–20		X	X					
Test takers 21–30			X	X				
Test takers 31–40				X	X			
Test takers 41–50					X	X		
Test takers 51–60						X	X	
Test takers 61–70							X	X
Test takers 71–80	X							X

Table 5.3: Sample rating design matrix

reliability indices focusing on pairs of raters is not particularly helpful in gaining a picture of the overall reliability of the rater group.

Moreover, if tests are using an analytic rating scale, it is even more difficult to identify rater effects, and testing organizations often conduct their analyses only on averaged, overall raw scores. Furthermore, thinking back to McNamara's (1996) example of Michael and Paula (see Table 5.1) and the influence of other facets beyond the rater and the influence on the resulting score, indices of consistency and consensus do not help us gain a better understanding of whether the raw score was influenced by an easier task or whether there were any interactions between facets of the rating situation. Finally, raw scores do not provide us with a clear picture of how raters apply the step structure of the rating scale in use.

Using many-facets Rasch to model rater effects

Rasch measurement provides us with a way to overcome the issues with traditional measures used to calculate inter-rater reliability. The Rasch models we encountered in Chapters 3 and 4 are not sufficient to analyse this data, as they include only two facets of the rating situation: person and item. Because of this limitation, Linacre (1989) developed the many-facets Rasch model, which allows us to add additional facets into the analysis. We have already discussed, in the example of Paula and Michael, the fact that the rater and the task might have an influence on the assessment outcome.

These aspects of the assessment (i.e. raters and tasks) can be seen as facets of the assessment situation. Many-facets Rasch measurement (also referred to as multi-facet(ed) Rasch measurement) is able to model these facets so we can evaluate their impact on the scores. We have chosen to analyse our data set (described further below) using a computer program called FACETS

(Linacre, 2015). As was the case with the analyses in the previous chapters, we have included detailed instructions on how to use FACETS on the companion website (www.oup.com/elt/teacher/fjla). There, you will find the data files used in this chapter, the input files, and detailed instructions accompanied by screenshots on how to prepare a data file and how to run the analysis in the FACETS program. Interested readers may want to conduct the analyses in this chapter at home or analyse their own data sets using the same procedures. We have included some activities to facilitate practice.

The data set we will draw on in this chapter was collected as part of a research project that set out to trial a new rating scale for a writing assessment for academic purposes. The raters were introduced to the new rating scale in a rater training session; following that, all ten trained raters rated the writing samples of 100 students using an analytic rating scale with five criteria (content, organization, academic style, grammar, and vocabulary and spelling) on a nine-point scale (from 1 to 9). All raters rated all 100 writing scripts, providing us with a fully crossed design. (We will discuss issues of sample size, missing data connectivity, and rating designs in Chapter 7.) The analysis included three facets (candidate, raters, and rating scale criteria).[1] This provides the FACETS program with a number of different pieces of information. We have data from all ten raters about each candidate's performance. We also have information about how different raters apply the same five criteria. An extract of the data matrix can be seen in Table 5.4. The first column shows the candidate number, the second column the rater number, and the other five columns show the raw scores provided by the raters.

	Rater	Content	Organization	Academic style	Grammar	Vocabulary and spelling
Candidate 1	1	4	5	3	5	4
Candidate 1	2	6	5	5	5	4
Candidate 1	3	5	5	4	4	4
.....	.....					
Candidate 1	10	6	4	5	5	5
.....						
Candidate 100	1	7	8	7	7	7
.....	.....					
Candidate 100	10	8	8	7	8	7

Table 5.4: Data matrix: writing assessment for academic purposes (extract)

The FACETS program (or any other many-facets Rasch measurement program) evaluates each cell within the data matrix in light of the information from the other cells. It identifies patterns in the data, and provides summaries both of these patterns and of how predictable they are. For example, let us focus on the first score line in Table 5.4. The line shows the scores received by Candidate 1 when rated by Rater 1. The first cell in the 'Content' column shows the score for content, for which the candidate received a score of 4. FACETS evaluates how predictable this score is in light of the other scores in the data set. It is able to calculate whether Rater 1 is generally harsh or lenient in comparison with the other raters, or whether this rater is harsh or lenient when scoring content. The program can also evaluate whether it is generally harder or easier for candidates to receive high scores on Content. This is achieved by evaluating all the other information in the data set. FACETS assumes that each data point in the data set is predictable from the other information available. A summary is then provided of the extent to which—for each candidate, rater, and criterion—a predictable pattern of responses is found. Where a sufficiently consistent pattern is found, we can then generalize. For example, we can show that the patterns of scores for a particular rater on a particular criterion is higher than that of the other raters—thus letting us identify differences in rater severity. These differences in severity (for raters) or ability (for test takers) are again expressed in terms of measures expressed on the logit scale, which we have already encountered in previous chapters.

For the purposes of the first part of this chapter, we are going to specify in FACETS that we would like to run this analysis using the rating scale model, which assumes that all our rating scale criteria (i.e. content, organization, etc.) have the same underlying rating scale structure. Following this introduction to many-facets Rasch measurement using the rating scale model, we will discuss other possible models we can run in FACETS.

Interpreting the results of a many-facets Rasch analysis

In this section we will examine the different aspects of the output from a many-facets Rasch analysis using the rating scale model. More specifically, we will examine the following:

- the Wright map
- the candidate measurement report
- the rater measurement report
- the criterion (trait) measurement report
- the rating scale category functioning.

Wright map

Figure 5.4 presents the Wright map for the data set described in the previous section. It looks very similar to the maps we encountered in Chapters 3 and 4, but with two differences. We now have two extra columns in the map that we did not see previously, one entitled 'Rater' and the other 'Scale'. The column on the left ('Measr'—measure) shows the equal interval logit scale we first encountered on pages 32–34. The second column (Candidate) shows our test takers (with each candidate being represented by a star). We can see that these are spread over about five logits. This facet is positively oriented, with candidates with higher ability at the higher end of our logit scale, while weaker candidates are depicted lower down (in the negative logits).

The next column ('Rater') shows our ten raters identified by their rater number. Rater 2 (the rater depicted highest up in the figure) is the harshest rater and Rater 9 is the most lenient. We can see that our raters differ in severity quite substantially. The most lenient and the most severe raters are nearly two logits apart, which could make a difference of nearly two raw score points, and represents more than a third of the spread of the test takers. This shows that our group of raters are far from homogeneous, and if we were basing our decisions on raw scores only, this would have significant impact on the outcomes for the test takers, and constitute a threat to test fairness.

The column entitled 'Criterion' depicts the five rating scale criteria in terms of their relative difficulty, with harder criteria located higher up on the scale. We can see that content is located higher than the other criteria on our logit scale. This means that it is harder for students to get a certain score on content than it is on the other criteria. Academic style and grammar are similar in terms of difficulty.

The final column on our map shows our five-category rating scale, depicted as one overall scale (rather than showing our individual criteria).[2] The highest and lowest observed scale levels are shown in brackets. When comparing the locations of the candidates on the logit scale with the rating scale in the right-hand column, we can see what score candidates would be likely to receive at specific logit levels. For example, candidates at a logit value of 2 would be likely to score a 7 on the rating scale. The horizontal lines in this column are category thresholds or Rasch-half-point thresholds. They depict the point at which a candidate at that same logit level would score a half score point. A candidate at about 2.5 logits would be likely to receive a score of 7.5.

Note also that the average rater severity and the difficulty of the criteria are set at zero and that the candidates are set to float around that. A negative score for a candidate thus means that this candidate is facing a rater of average severity and on a criterion of average difficulty would have a less than 50% chance of achieving a given score from that rater on that criterion—the score indicated on the scale at zero logits, that is, a score of 6.

```
+------------------------------------------------------------------------+
|Measr|+Candidate |-Rater    |-Criterion                           |Scale|
|-----+-----------+----------+-------------------------------------+-----|
|  4 +            +          +                                     + (9) |
|     |           |          |                                     |     |
|     | *         |          |                                     |     |
|     |           |          |                                     |     |
|     |           |          |                                     |     |
|     | *         |          |                                     |     |
|     | *         |          |                                     |     |
|     |           |          |                                     |  8  |
|  3 + **         +          +                                     +     |
|     |           |          |                                     |     |
|     | *         |          |                                     |     |
|     | ***       |          |                                     |     |
|     | ******    |          |                                     |     |
|     | ***       |          |                                     | --- |
|     | ***       |          |                                     |     |
|     | ***       |          |                                     |     |
|  2 + *          +          +                                     +     |
|     | ****      |          |                                     |     |
|     | *****     |          |                                     |     |
|     | **        |          |                                     |  7  |
|     | ***       |          |                                     |     |
|     | ***       |          |                                     |     |
|     | **        |          |                                     |     |
|     | ******    |          |                                     |     |
|  1 + ****       +          +                                     +     |
|     | *****     | 2        |                                     | --- |
|     | ***       |          |                                     |     |
|     | ********* |          |                                     |     |
|     | ******    |          |                                     |     |
|     | **        |          | Content                             |     |
|     | *         | 3        |                                     |     |
|     | **        | 10       |                                     |  6  |
*  0 * **         * 1  4  6  * Academic Style   Grammar            *     *
|     | ****      | 7        | Organisaton                         |     |
|     | **        | 5  8     | Vocabulary                          |     |
|     | ****      |          |                                     |     |
|     |           |          |                                     |     |
|     |           |          |                                     | --- |
|     |           | 9        |                                     |     |
|     | ****      |          |                                     |     |
| -1 +            +          +                                     +     |
|     | *         |          |                                     |     |
|     | *         |          |                                     |  5  |
|     |           |          |                                     |     |
|     |           |          |                                     |     |
|     |           |          |                                     |     |
|     |           |          |                                     |     |
| -2 +            +          +                                     + (3) |
|-----+-----------+----------+-------------------------------------+-----|
|Measr| * = 1     |-Rater    |-Criterion                           |Scale|
+------------------------------------------------------------------------+
```

Figure 5.4: Wright map: writing assessment for academic purposes

Candidate measurement report

Candidate ability

Table 5.5 presents an extract from the candidate measurement report for the data set. The output is similar to that encountered in the previous two chapters. Let us examine each column in detail. The first column ('Total score') needs to be read in combination with the second column ('Total count'). Each candidate was rated by ten raters on five criteria. This results in the total count of 50 observations for each student. The total score is the sum of all the scores the candidate received. So Candidate 1, for example, received a total score of 263. If we divide this by 50, we can see that the average rating across the five criteria and the ten raters was 5.26. This is confirmed in the third column ('Observed average'). The fourth column ('Fair average') is a column we have not encountered previously as this is specific to many-facets Rasch measurement. These fair averages are computed using information of relative rater severity and show what score a test taker would have received if the test taker had been rated by 'average' raters in the group.

The fair averages in our data set are not remarkably different from the observed average. This is because we used a fully crossed design, which means that each candidate was rated by all ten raters. This design takes care of rater differences automatically in some ways as the observed average is based on all ten raters; however, it is not a practical rating design and not one that any testing centre or language school could afford. This data was collected purely for research purposes. In the case of data sets with fewer raters, the fair average could result in larger differences between the observed scores and the fair average. In Table 5.6, for example, taken from another data set in which

```
+---------------------------------------------------------
| Total   Total   Obsvd  Fair(M)|         Model  |
| Score   Count  Average Average|Measure  S.E.   |
|------------------------------------+-----------+
|   263     50     5.26   5.25  |  -.92    .17  |
|   265     50     5.30   5.29  |  -.86    .17  |
|   328     50     6.56   6.56  |   .95    .17  |
|   302     50     6.04   6.04  |   .19    .17  |
|   381     50     7.62   7.63  |  2.55    .18  |
|                               |               |
|   292     50     5.84   5.84  |  -.09    .17  |
|   319     50     6.38   6.38  |   .68    .17  |
|   353     50     7.06   7.06  |  1.69    .17  |
|   318     50     6.36   6.36  |   .65    .17  |
|   339     50     6.78   6.78  |  1.27    .17  |
|   341     50     6.82   6.82  |  1.33    .17  |
|   321     50     6.42   6.42  |   .74    .17  |
|   329     50     6.58   6.58  |   .97    .17  |
|------------------------------------+-----------+
|   333.7   50.0    6.67   6.68  |  1.14    .17  |
|    36.7    .0      .73    .74  |  1.09    .01  |
|    36.9    .0      .74    .74  |  1.10    .01  |
+---------------------------------------------------------
```

Table 5.5: Candidate measurement report (extract)

```
+-----------------------------------------------------+
| Total    Total    Obsvd  Fair(M) |             |
| Score    Count   Average Average|  Nu Rater    |
|-------------------------------------+-----------|
|   203      48      4.23    4.06 |    1  1      |
|   183      39      4.69    4.20 |   21 21      |
|   361      75      4.81    4.26 |   18 18      |
|   475     102      4.66    4.26 |    5  5      |
|   100      21      4.76    4.61 |   23 23      |
|   319      66      4.83    4.61 |    9  9      |
|   250      57      4.39    4.64 |   15 15      |
|   212      39      5.44    4.68 |   31 31      |
|-------------------------------------+-----------|
```

Table 5.6: Sample data set illustrating differences between observed and fair averages

each performance was only rated by two raters, it can be seen that the differences between observed and fair averages are larger. The reported scores to students, if rounded, may be quite different. Even more importantly, if a cut score is used on the test, the differences between the two averages may mean a candidate moves above or below a pass/fail line if the fairer score, the fair average is used. It is important to understand here that FACETS uses the whole group of raters as a reference group to calculate the fair averages; that is, the fair average assumes an average rater in the group of raters.

The final two columns in Table 5.5 present the 'Measure' column and the 'Standard error' column. As we saw in the previous chapters, the measure provides us with a test taker's position on the logit scale. This is essentially the program's estimation of each candidate's ability in our writing assessment. The standard error gives us an indication of the precision of the measure. High standard errors signal that the program does not have sufficient information about the location of a test taker on the logit scale. This is again not a problem in the case of our data set. The standard errors in Table 5.5 indicate that we can be relatively sure of the locations, although some error does exist. However, as mentioned earlier, not all data sets have this much information included; that is, it is rare that all candidates are rated by all raters. Table 5.7 shows a data set where the standard errors are significantly higher and more varied than those in our main data set in this chapter. This means we can have less confidence about the precision of the candidates' location on the logit scale and therefore their ability, and the claims we can make about these candidates have to be more cautious. In many language testing situations, we deal with smaller data sets, so higher standard errors are not uncommon. It is, however, important for researchers to understand what these indicate.

Candidate fit

Candidate fit indices give an indication of the predictability of the pattern of scores awarded by a rater in relation to the wider data set. They therefore give us information about the consistency of raters. As we saw in previous

Total Score	Total Count	Obsvd Average	Fair(M) Average	Measure	Model S.E.	Nu Rater
203	48	4.23	4.06	3.90	.31	1 1
183	39	4.69	4.20	3.05	.35	21 21
361	75	4.81	4.26	2.78	.27	18 18
475	102	4.66	4.26	2.78	.23	5 5
100	21	4.76	4.61	1.41	.47	23 23
319	66	4.83	4.61	1.40	.28	9 9
250	57	4.39	4.64	1.28	.30	15 15
212	39	5.44	4.68	1.10	.46	31 31
330	69	4.78	4.73	.90	.27	10 10
647	135	4.79	4.77	.70	.20	3 3
304	63	4.83	4.77	.70	.28	16 16
497	105	4.73	4.79	.62	.22	13 13
392	81	4.84	4.81	.52	.25	2 2

Table 5.7: Extract from candidate measurement report

chapters, we again have four columns of fit statistics. We discussed issues relating to fit in detail on pages 40–51, so we will only recap the main concepts in this chapter in relation to Table 5.8.

The first two columns present the infit statistics and the second two columns the outfit statistics. The outfit statistics are influenced by outliers, while the infit statistics are not influenced by such unusual observations. The mean-square statistics have an expected mean of 1 and range from zero to infinity. As discussed in Chapter 3, a number of authors have described different acceptability levels for mean-square statistics. Let us, for our purpose, use the range proposed by McNamara (1996), who stated that the range of acceptability extends from 0.7 to 1.3. Candidates with higher mean-square statistics than 1.3 are misfitting; values below 0.7 indicate overfit. So what does this mean for our analysis? While overfit is not a threat to our measurement, as it does not introduce 'noise' into our measurement as described in Chapters 3 and 4, misfit is. This can provide us with two types of information: information about individual test takers and information about the whole test. Let us focus on Candidate 95, for example. The program is indicating that this test taker is slightly misfitting, with an infit mean-square value of 1.32. This shows us that, for some reason, this candidate is not well measured; this person's scores do not fit well with the program's expectations, which are drawn from the entire data matrix, including how the same raters rated other candidates in relation to this candidate. If we were making high-stakes decisions based on this test, we could not be fully confident that we had measured this candidate well, and that the inferences we were to make based on this candidate's score were well supported. We have identified a potential source of unfairness in the assessment process for this candidate. This can be addressed by ensuring that candidates that are misfitting are re-rated. These additional scores

```
------------------------------------------------------------+
| Infit       Outfit     |Estim.| Corr. |                   |
| MnSq ZStd   MnSq ZStd  |Discrm| PtBis | Num Candidate      |
+------------------------+------+-------+-------------------|
| 1.07   .4   1.07   .4  | .89  | .28  |   1  1             |
|  .82  -.9    .82  -.9  | 1.13 | .10  |   2  2             |
|  .74 -1.3    .74 -1.3  | 1.27 | .12  |   3  3             |
|  .66 -1.9    .65 -1.9  | 1.38 | .42  |   4  4             |
|  .72 -1.5    .72 -1.6  | 1.33 | .35  |   5  5             |
|                                                            |
|  .93  -.3    .93  -.3  | 1.07 | .35  |  93 93             |
|  .91  -.3    .91  -.4  | 1.10 | .14  |  94 94             |
| 1.32  1.5   1.31  1.4  |  .70 | .34  |  95 95             |
| 1.09   .5   1.09   .4  |  .89 | .21  |  96 96             |
|  .77 -1.1    .76 -1.2  | 1.25 | .36  |  97 97             |
|  .85  -.7    .85  -.7  | 1.14 | .48  |  98 98             |
|  .77 -1.2    .77 -1.1  | 1.22 | .25  |  99 99             |
|  .76 -1.2    .75 -1.3  | 1.25 | .31  | 100 100            |
+------------------------+------+-------+-------------------|
| 1.01  -.1   1.00  -.1  |      |      | .24  | Mean (Count: 100)  |
|  .34  1.7    .34  1.7  |      |      | .13  | S.D. (Population)  |
|  .34  1.7    .34  1.7  |      |      | .13  | S.D. (Sample)      |
------------------------------------------------------------+
```

Table 5.8: Fit statistics from candidate measurement report

can be added to the analysis to see whether the misfit is resolved. If not, it is worth scrutinizing the raw scores to see whether a particular rater may be causing the misfit. In that case, we suggest deleting the scores from that rater for this particular candidate.

If we examine the level of candidate misfit at the whole-test level, we can get some indication of how well our test works. If there is significant candidate misfit (i.e. if more than 2–5% of all candidates are identified as misfitting, depending on the stakes of the test), test developers need to re-examine whether the test is functioning well for the population for which it was designed. Revisions to the test or the scoring criteria may be necessary; alternatively, we may need to add a second task that can contribute more information about each candidate and resolve substantial misfit. In the case of our data set, the level of misfit was high: 15 of the 100 candidates were identified as misfitting. It is possible that this happened because it was the first time the raters had used the rating scale in this study and they were therefore not intimately familiar with it. The high level of misfit would have to be monitored if the rating instrument were adopted in a high-stakes context. The ZStd has a mean of 0 and can be either positive or negative. It indicates whether the misfit is significant, whereas the mean-square value tells us about the size of the misfit. ZStd values beyond the range of −2 and +2 indicate significant deviations from the expectations of the Rasch model. ZStd is sensitive to sample size, so that in big samples, even a small misfit value will become significant, and it may therefore make sense to change the upper and lower bounds of acceptability of this value for large test contexts. The infit mean square and ZStd rules we have provided here do not always align, as can be seen in the example of Candidate 95, who shows a slightly misfitting infit mean-square value, but a ZStd value of 1.5. We recommend that researchers evaluate these values in tandem. In this way, as the infit mean-square value is only just over 1.3, we can assume that this candidate's measurement is not of too much concern.

Candidate summary statistics

Directly below the candidate measurement report, we can discover some useful summary statistics about our population of test takers. We have reproduced this section of the candidate measurement report in Table 5.9.

The fixed chi-square test tests the hypothesis that all candidates are at the same level of performance (Myford & Wolfe, 2003). We can see a chi-square value, the degrees of freedom (99 in our case, as we have a sample of 100 candidates) and a p-value. A significant result indicates that at least two elements (i.e. two candidates) are significantly different, which is the case in our test. It is unlikely that we would find a case where this statistic was not significant for candidates, as this would indicate that our test was not functioning at all in separating our students into distinct levels of ability. More revealing, therefore, is the candidate separation index (indicated as 'Strata' in our table), which is calculated using the candidate separation ratio (indicated as 'Separation' in Table 5.9)—a measure of the spread of the candidate performance in relation to their precision (Fisher, 1992). The candidate separation index indicates the number of measurably different levels (or strata) of candidate performance in our sample. In our data we can see that there are 8.67 statistically distinct groups of students in our sample. The reliability of the candidate separation index ('Reliability' in Table 5.9) is interpreted in a similar way to Cronbach's alpha or KR20, and provides us with an indication of the reliability with which the candidates in the sample are separated. If the aim is to differentiate among candidate performance, as is often the case in language assessments, then we would aim for high candidate reliability indices.

```
Model, Populn: RMSE .17  Adj (True) S.D. 1.08  Separation 6.22  Strata 8.63  Reliability .97
Model, Sample: RMSE .17  Adj (True) S.D. 1.08  Separation 6.25  Strata 8.67  Reliability .98
Model, Fixed (all same) chi-square:  3827.1  d.f.: 99  significance (probability): .00
Model, Random (normal) chi-square:   96.6  d.f.: 98  significance (probability): .52
```

Table 5.9: Summary statistics from candidate measurement report

Rater measurement report

Earlier in this chapter we discussed the problem of identifying a number of rater effects identified in the literature using the more traditional rater reliability measures of consensus and consistency. The rater measurement report (Table 5.10) provides us with some evidence of the performance of the raters in our sample.

Total Score	Total Count	Obsvd Average	Fair(M) Average	Measure	Model S.E.	Infit MnSq	Infit ZStd	Outfit MnSq	Outfit ZStd	Estim. Discrm	Correlation PtMea	Correlation PtExp	Exact Agree. Obs %	Exact Agree. Exp %	Nu Rater
3326	500	6.65	6.67	.04	.05	1.10	1.5	1.09	1.4	.89	.70	.68	36.9	33.3	1 1
3030	500	6.06	6.07	.91	.05	1.35	5.1	1.35	5.1	.63	.60	.68	28.7	28.5	2 2
3247	500	6.49	6.51	.27	.05	1.16	2.5	1.18	2.7	.83	.80	.68	35.1	32.8	3 3
3343	500	6.69	6.70	-.01	.05	1.03	.4	1.02	.4	.99	.70	.68	39.4	33.4	4 4
3429	500	6.86	6.88	-.27	.05	.82	-2.9	.83	-2.9	1.18	.74	.67	37.7	33.0	5 5
3322	500	6.64	6.66	.05	.05	.97	-.3	.97	-.4	1.02	.62	.68	37.4	33.3	6 6
3360	500	6.72	6.74	-.06	.05	.77	-3.9	.78	-3.8	1.23	.64	.68	42.0	33.4	7 7
3436	500	6.87	6.89	-.29	.05	1.16	2.4	1.15	2.3	.84	.61	.67	38.8	33.0	8 8
3583	500	7.17	7.19	-.74	.06	1.03	.4	1.02	.4	.99	.74	.67	36.1	30.6	9 9
3297	500	6.59	6.61	.12	.05	.61	-7.4	.61	-7.3	1.42	.64	.68	41.9	33.2	10 10
3337.3	500.0	6.67	6.69	.00	.05	1.00	-.2	1.00	-.2		.68				Mean (Count: 10)
135.5	.0	.27	.27	.40	.00	.21	3.5	.20	3.5		.06				S.D. (Population)
142.8	.0	.29	.29	.43	.00	.22	3.7	.22	3.6		.07				S.D. (Sample)

Model, Populn: RMSE .05 Adj (True) S.D. .40 Separation 7.32 Strata 10.09 Reliability (not inter-rater) .98
Model, Sample: RMSE .05 Adj (True) S.D. .42 Separation 7.72 Strata 10.63 Reliability (not inter-rater) .98
Model, Fixed (all same) chi-square: 542.8 d.f.: 9 significance (probability): .00
Model, Random (normal) chi-square: 8.9 d.f.: 8 significance (probability): .35
Inter-Rater agreement opportunities: 22500 Exact agreements: 8416 = 37.4% Expected: 7302.3 = 32.5%

Table 5.10: Rater measurement report

Rater severity

The rater measurement report is structured in the same way as the candidate measurement report shown in Table 5.5 (see page 102). Let us focus on the key components only.

Table 5.11 presents an extract of the first few columns of the rater measurement report. It is worth checking the first two columns ('Total score' and 'Total count') to ensure we have made no data-entry errors. The 'Total count' column in particular gives us an indication of how much data each rater contributed. This may differ wildly for exams where raters can choose how many candidates they mark and may have a direct impact on the standard error for those raters and the associated precision of the locations of the measures (the estimate of the relative severity of that rater). As usual, the 'Measure' column provides us with the exact location of each rater on the logit scale, and therefore indicates how lenient and severe they are in relation to the group. The mean logit for the group of raters is centred at zero. We can see that the rater severity differs by about 1.65 logits, with Rater 2 being the most severe and Rater 9 the most lenient. A quick check of the 'Standard error' column shows us that, because of the large number of observations in our sample, the estimation of the rater measures is relatively precise (i.e. it has a low S.E.).[3] Examining the rater measures can give us an indication of the relative severity or leniency of the raters. We can see from the Wright map in Figure 5.4 that Rater 2's severity would result in a 0.5 score difference overall for candidates when compared to an average rater. This might not result in much of a difference for some candidates in some situations, while it could have a relatively significant impact for candidates around the cut-score in tests with high stakes. The differences in severity of the raters in our sample is fairly typical of most tests. It is important, however, to monitor raters at the extreme ends of the rater group and see whether well-targeted feedback on their rating (see

```
+-------------------------------------------------------------------------+
| Total    Total    Obsvd    Fair(M)|    -     Model |                     |
| Score    Count   Average  Average|Measure   S.E.  | Nu Rater            |
|-----------------------------------+----------------+---------------------|
|  3326     500      6.65     6.67  |   .04     .05  |  1  1               |
|  3030     500      6.06     6.07  |   .91     .05  |  2  2               |
|  3247     500      6.49     6.51  |   .27     .05  |  3  3               |
|  3343     500      6.69     6.70  |  -.01     .05  |  4  4               |
|  3429     500      6.86     6.88  |  -.27     .05  |  5  5               |
|  3322     500      6.64     6.66  |   .05     .05  |  6  6               |
|  3360     500      6.72     6.74  |  -.06     .05  |  7  7               |
|  3436     500      6.87     6.89  |  -.29     .05  |  8  8               |
|  3583     500      7.17     7.19  |  -.74     .06  |  9  9               |
|  3297     500      6.59     6.61  |   .12     .05  | 10 10               |
|-----------------------------------+----------------+---------------------|
|  3337.3   500.0    6.67     6.69  |   .00     .05  | Mean (Count: 10)    |
|   135.5      .0     .27      .27  |   .40     .00  | S.D. (Population)   |
|   142.8      .0     .29      .29  |   .43     .00  | S.D. (Sample)       |
+-------------------------------------------------------------------------+
```

Table 5.11: Rater measurement report (extract)

for example, Elder, Knoch, Barkhuizen, & von Randow, 2005; Knoch, 2011) is not able to move them closer to the mean of the group in terms of severity. At the same time, it is important to remember that rater severity is not a significant issue if candidate fair averages are used to report scores and to make subsequent score interpretations, since fair averages account for such differences. But this involves having the performances scored by two raters, and the multi-faceted analysis run before the candidates receive their scores so that they can receive a fair score. This may not be practical or affordable in many situations, but the analyses reported here show the potential cost in terms of fairness to candidates of not adopting these procedures.

Rater fit

Rater severity can be estimated by examining the 'Measure' column in the rater measurement report. Most other rater effects can be identified by scrutinizing the rater fit statistics. The rater measurement report again includes four columns of fit statistics, two with infit statistics and two with outfit statistics. The outfit statistics are sensitive to outliers and the infit statistics are based on the most typical data only. Fit statistics provide us with an indication of the consistency of each rater within the group of raters. We discussed acceptable ranges for fit statistics on page 44 in relation to item fit in tests with dichotomously scored tests. As a reminder, some authors have suggested 0.7 as the lower limit and 1.3 as the upper limit (for example, Bond & Fox, 2015; McNamara, 1996), while others, like Linacre (2002a), have suggested a lower limit of 0.5 and an upper limit of 1.5. These same ranges apply to rater fit statistics equally, and should be chosen depending on the stakes of the test. High mean-square values (for example, those above 1.3, depending on the range chosen) such as those identified for Rater 2 indicate that a rater is misfitting. This means that the rater is at times rating more harshly than expected and at other times more leniently than expected in an unpredictable way. Inconsistent raters pose a threat to test validity and hence to test fairness because the ratings cannot be adjusted in the fair average due to the randomness of their responses. Retraining can often also prove difficult, as there are no clear guidelines for what inconsistent raters can do to change their rating behaviour. Raters could re-familiarize themselves with pre-rated samples, try to rate more slowly, and possibly be paired with a senior rater for a period of time, regularly discussing scripts during the assessment period in order to have access to formative feedback.

Raters can also be found to be overfitting, as indicated by relatively low mean-square values (for example, below 0.7). This means that the rater is rating with less variation than is predicted by the Rasch model. This may mean that the rater is displaying one of two rating effects: a *halo effect* or a *central tendency effect*. A rater displaying a halo effect usually assigns very similar ratings across analytic scoring criteria. For example, a candidate might be rated as a 5, 5, 5, 5, 5. This is an unusually flat profile, in particular for L2 learners, who often have areas of strengths and weaknesses across our criteria. Raters rating in such a way may form a holistic impression of a candidate and then assign this score level across all criteria. A central tendency effect is identified if a rater avoids the extreme categories of a rating scale and favours the inner categories. It again reflects a less-than-desirable variability in the ratings: the rater is not distinguishing among the candidates in the way that is shown to be possible by the performance of the other raters. This lack of variability may sometimes simply reflect the reality of the sample of test takers, but it is not typical of a more varied sample of test takers. Overfitting raters pose less of a threat than misfitting raters to our measurement, but it is still helpful to make raters aware of such rating patterns as they may not notice such tendencies in their own ratings. It is possible that inconsistent raters, following feedback, may resort to displaying a central tendency effect if they are being over-cautious.

Rater summary statistics

Below the rater measurement report we can locate the rater summary statistics. These are interpreted in a similar manner to the candidate summary statistics, but they have slightly different meanings and implications for our measurement. We have reproduced the rater summary statistics in Table 5.12 for convenience.

```
Model, Populn: RMSE .05  Adj (True) S.D. .40  Separation 7.32  Strata 10.09  Reliability (not inter-rater) .98
Model, Sample: RMSE .05  Adj (True) S.D. .42  Separation 7.72  Strata 10.63  Reliability (not inter-rater) .98
Model, Fixed (all same) chi-square:  542.8  d.f.: 9  significance (probability): .00
Model, Random (normal) chi-square:  8.9  d.f.: 8  significance (probability): .35
Inter-Rater agreement opportunities: 22500  Exact agreements: 8416 = 37.4%  Expected:  7302.3 = 32.5%
```

Table 5.12: Rater summary statistics

We will start again by examining the fixed chi-square statistic. The fixed chi square for the raters 'tests the hypothesis that all raters exercised the same level of severity when evaluating candidates, after accounting for measurement error' (Myford & Wolfe, 2003, p. 409). A significant chi-square value, as we have in the case of our data set, indicates that at least two raters rated significantly differently from each other. Again, it is highly unlikely that we would ever find a situation where this statistic was not important in a real data set; it is a simple and oft-repeated finding that raters vary, that the variability is significant, and that it is likely to have important implications for the fairness of the assessment if it is not addressed. Possibly more useful than the fixed chi-square statistic are the rater-separation ratio (indicated as 'Separation' in the table) and the rater-separation index ('Strata'). The rater-separation ratio of 7.32 in our data set indicates that the differences between the rater severities are over seven times greater than the error with which the severities are measured (Myford & Wolfe, 2004). The rater-separation index of 10.09 indicates the number of distinct levels of rater severity our ten raters fall into. Our data shows that there are about 10 distinct levels of rater severity, one for each rater, indicating that our raters are not rating statistically alike in terms of severity. Finally, the reliability of the rater-separation index is interpreted in the opposite way to traditional rater reliability indices. In this case, if our raters rated in the same manner, i.e. not displaying differences in terms of lenience and harshness, the reliability index would be zero. However, this index (.98) also confirms that our raters are not a homogeneous group and that they are in fact highly distinct. The rater separation statistics can provide us with some information about how the raters are rating as a group and whether there are raters who are likely to be lenient and harsh within the group of raters.

Criterion (trait) measurement report

The criterion (or trait) measurement report in Table 5.13 presents the same kind of information we are used to from the reports on the other facets, namely information on the relative difficulty of the criteria and the fit of each.

```
+-------------------------------------------------------------------------------------------------------+
| Total   Total   Obsvd  Fair(M)|   -    Model | Infit      Outfit    |Estim.| Corr. |                 |
| Score   Count   Average Average|Measure S.E. | MnSq ZStd  MnSq ZStd |Discrm| PtBis | N Criterion     |
|-------------------------------------------------------------------------------------------------------|
| 6752    1000    6.75   6.77  |  -.11   .04 | .99  -.1   1.00   .0  | 1.00 |  .38  | 1 Organisaton    |
| 6399    1000    6.40   6.41  |   .41   .04 | 1.49  9.0  1.49  9.0  |  .48 |  .35  | 2 Content        |
| 6693    1000    6.69   6.71  |  -.03   .04 | .91  -2.0  .91  -2.0  | 1.10 |  .52  | 3 Academic style |
| 6695    1000    6.70   6.71  |  -.03   .04 | .81  -4.6  .81  -4.5  | 1.21 |  .56  | 4 Grammar        |
| 6834    1000    6.83   6.85  |  -.24   .04 | .79  -5.1  .79  -5.1  | 1.24 |  .55  | 5 Vocabulary     |
|-------------------------------------------------------------------------------------------------------|
| 6674.6  1000.0  6.67   6.69  |   .00   .04 | 1.00  -.6  1.00  -.6  |      |  .47  | Mean  (Count: 5) |
| 147.0     .0     .15    .15  |   .22   .00 | .26  5.1   .26  5.1   |      |  .09  | S.D. (Population)|
| 164.4     .0     .16    .17  |   .24   .00 | .29  5.7   .29  5.7   |      |  .10  | S.D. (Sample)    |
+-------------------------------------------------------------------------------------------------------+

Model, Populn: RMSE .04  Adj (True) S.D. .22  Separation 5.57  Strata 7.76  Reliability .97
Model, Sample: RMSE .04  Adj (True) S.D. .24  Separation 6.24  Strata 8.66  Reliability .97
Model, Fixed (all same) chi-square:  161.1  d.f.: 4  significance (probability):  .00
Model, Random (normal) chi-square:   3.9  d.f.: 3  significance (probability):  .27
```

Table 5.13: Criterion measurement report

Criterion difficulty

The criterion measurement report confirms what we could already see in the Wright map (Figure 5.4, on page 101); that is, most of our rating scale criteria (apart from 'Content') are located close together. It is, therefore, slightly harder for students to achieve a certain score on content than it is on the other criteria. However, with a logit value of .41, content is not unusually difficult. In fact, as Myford and Wolfe (2004) have pointed out, if we would like to define a construct of increasing difficulty, it is useful to have a number of traits spread out along the logit scale, all working together to measure the construct. This is the case for the criteria in this data set.

Criterion fit

The fit indices indicate that not only is 'content' slightly more difficult than other criteria, but it is also misfitting with an infit mean-square value of 1.49. This shows that the content criterion is possibly measuring a slightly different ability than the other criteria. Considering that 'content' is focused on the *ideas* that students produce in their writing, rather than the language, this makes sense.

It is important to note at this point that, in the case of the criteria, fit is more than just a technical matter. It goes right to the heart of empirical validation of the constructs we measure, and can provide us with important information that helps us understand in more detail what performance assessments are measuring. This issue will be explored further in Chapter 6.

Criterion separation statistics

Table 5.14 presents the criterion separation statistics from the bottom of the criterion measurement report, reproduced here for convenience. We can see from this information that our traits are not all equal in difficulty. This is shown by the significant chi square and the separation ratio (indicated as 'Separation' in the table) and the separation index ('Strata'), which both show that there are a number of distinct levels of difficulty among the criteria. Finally, as Myford and Wolfe (2003) point out, for the reliability of the criterion separation index, we would like high separation reliability (just as was the case for the candidate separation reliability). This shows that our test includes a number of traits/criteria that are calibrated along the construct we are aiming to measure.

```
Model, Populn: RMSE .04  Adj (True) S.D. .22  Separation 5.57  Strata 7.76  Reliability .97
Model, Sample: RMSE .04  Adj (True) S.D. .24  Separation 6.24  Strata 8.66  Reliability .97
Model, Fixed (all same) chi-square:  161.1  d.f.: 4  significance (probability): .00
Model,  Random (normal) chi-square:    3.9  d.f.: 3  significance (probability): .27
```

Table 5.14: Criterion separation statistics

So how can we interpret this information about the criteria? It is acceptable to have criteria with different levels of difficulty; however, criteria that are misfitting are interpreted by the raters differently than the other, fitting, criteria. This means that the construct is interpreted differently and may have implications for score reporting. It is also worthwhile examining whether any of the criteria are more discriminating than others. This can be done by running an analysis of each criterion individually and extracting the range of candidate measures. A higher range of candidate measures indicates a higher discrimination. It is important to examine this discrimination, as it may be that raters are far better at discriminating performance on some criteria than on others. This practice is likely to be fairer to candidates who are very able on the criteria that are less discriminating.

Rating scale category functioning

The output of a Rasch analysis also provides us with very useful information relating to the functioning of the rating scale. We can see how the rating scale categories are spread in the Wright map shown in Figure 5.4 (see page 101). Beyond this, FACETS also presents a separate table with category summary statistics; this is shown in Table 5.15.

Linacre (1999, 2002b, 2004) reports how these statistics are interpreted and what qualities are desired in a rating scale for optimal functioning. These

| DATA | | | | QUALITY CONTROL | | RASCH-ANDRICH | | EXPECTATION | | MOST | | RASCH- | Cat |
| | Category Counts | | | Cum. | Avge | Exp. | OUTFIT | Thresholds | | Measure at | | PROBABLE | THURSTONE | PEAK |
Score	Total	Used	%	%	Meas	Meas	MnSq	Measure	S.E.	Category	-0.5	from	Thresholds	Prob
3	4	4	0%	0%	-.52	-1.20	1.4			(-5.64)		low	low	100%
4	141	141	3%	3%	-.55*	-.69	1.2	-4.52	.50	-3.23	-4.67	-4.52	-4.58	65%
5	596	596	12%	15%	-.02	-.08	1.1	-1.83	.09	-1.28	-2.12	-1.83	-1.99	46%
6	1406	1406	28%	43%	.56	.62	.9	-.59	.05	.14	-.56	-.59	-.57	47%
7	1693	1693	34%	77%	1.37	1.38	1.0	.81	.04	1.60	.85	.81	.83	50%
8	910	910	18%	95%	2.17	2.13	.9	2.38	.04	3.16	2.36	2.38	2.35	49%
9	250	250	5%	100%	2.82	2.78	1.0	3.76	.07	(5.00)	4.18	3.76	3.94	100%
										(Mean)	(Modal)	(Median)		

Table 5.15: Rating scale statistics

guidelines are identical to those we discussed in Chapter 4 in relation to scale properties for partial credit data analysed using the rating scale or partial credit model. The guidelines are repeated here for convenience:

1 There should be more than ten observations per category. If this condition is not fulfilled, the findings may be unstable.
2 Average measures should advance approximately by the same value at each score point.
3 Average measures should not be disordered.
4 The frequency of data points in each category should result in a smooth distribution; that is, the distribution should not be jagged.
5 Average measures should be near their expected values.
6 Mean-square values should be less than 2.
7 Rasch-Andrich thresholds (step difficulty; step calibration) should increase at each score level by 1.4 or more, but by fewer than 5 logits.

For FACETS to return reliable results, each scale category (band level) needs to include at least ten observations (Guideline 1). We can check whether this guideline holds by scrutinizing the second column in Table 5.15. This is not the case for our Level 3 band, where there were only four observations across the five analytic sub-scales. If the test taker population were representative, then revisions might be required to the scale. It seems that Level 3 is being used so infrequently by raters that it may be redundant. Linacre (1999, 2002b, 2004) further argues that the observations in column 2 should be more or less normally distributed—not displaying more than one peak, for example (Guideline 4). In the case of our data, this condition is more or less achieved. There is a clear peak at band level 7 although the observations are not completely normally distributed. The next guidelines proposed by Linacre state that the average measure shown in column 6 should advance monotonically and should not be disordered (Guidelines 2 and 3). This is not the case for our scale, where the average measure of test takers rated at Level 3 is slightly higher than Level 4. At the same time, if we were to collapse the three observations at Level 3 into the Level 4 data, this problem would be solved. Guideline 5 states that the average measures should be near their expected values. This is again a particular issue at the lower end of our scale, where the expected measure for Level 3 is much lower than that which we observed. Guideline 6 states that the mean-square values should be less than 2. When we scrutinize column 8, we can see that this condition is observed in our data. Finally, Guideline 7 posits that the Rasch-Andrich thresholds should advance monotonically by between 1.4 and 5 logits. This again is not the case in our data set, where a number of thresholds do not advance by as many as 1.4 logits. Overall, our scale seems to be performing adequately, although some changes may be necessary to ensure that raters are using the rating scale appropriately. We may want to consider collapsing Levels 3 and 4, as the results from the analysis show that score Level 3 has been underused and the average candidate measures at Level 4 are slightly lower than Level 3. It is important, however, that after such changes to a scale, the instrument is monitored to ensure the change has the desired effect of increasing fairness in the rating process.

Beyond the category statistics table (Table 5.15), FACETS also produces scale category probability curves, which provide information about the rating scale. Figure 5.5 presents the probability curve for our data set. Probability curves are a visual representation of the rating scale statistics. The horizontal axis represents the candidate proficiency scale (in logits) and the vertical axis shows the probability of a certain score being awarded. When examining this curve, as we discussed in Chapter 4 (see page 71), we should ensure that there is a separate peak for each scale level and that the curves appear as an evenly spaced series of hills. In our data set we can see that the Level 4 peak is much higher, and that the peaks for Levels 5 and 6 are much flatter in comparison. If there are categories that never become most probable (i.e. do not display a separate peak), then that may indicate that the raters are having problems applying that band level and are not interpreting the scale as envisaged by the developer. The points where each of the scale categories intersect are the

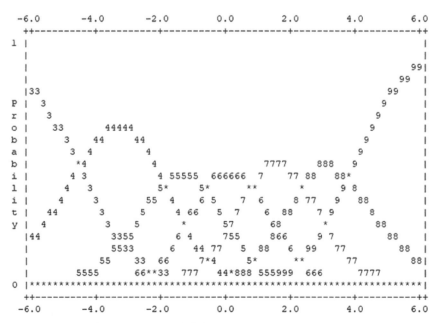

Figure 5.5: Scale category probability curve

rating scale category thresholds (or Rasch-Andrich thresholds) and represent the points at which there is a 50% probability of a test taker of that ability being rated at either level.

The statistics in Table 5.15 and the probability curves in Figure 5.5 are useful in providing us with an overall sense of how the rating scale is functioning; however, it is important to remember that this only presents us with a summary of our overall scale and does not give us an indication of how our individual analytic scale categories have been used by raters. As a reminder, the raters were required to rate the writing scripts on five criteria (organization, content, academic style, grammar, and vocabulary and spelling), each employing a nine-point scale. We can, however, get a sense from the table that the ten raters in the research project made no or very limited use of the lowest three band levels (Levels 1 to 3), which essentially changed the scale into a six-band instrument.

As mentioned earlier, FACETS only provided us with statistics for the overall rating scale rather than for all our analytic criteria separately. This is because we specified the Andrich rating scale model for this initial analysis. FACETS is, however, able to provide more detailed information about our rating scale criteria (and all other facets in our analysis) if we make changes to the model specifications. What this means, and what additional output we can get from such an analysis to help us identify rater variability (and therefore threats to test fairness for the test takers), will be covered below.

Understanding basic many-facets Rasch analysis models

The output we explored in detail above was generated using the many-facets Rasch version of the Andrich rating scale model. This would have provided us with sufficient information about our rating scale if a holistic scale had been used. Unfortunately, however, it does not give us any detailed information about the analytic scale in our data set.

As mentioned above, it is possible, however, to specify hybrid many-facets Rasch models in FACETS. These models are called hybrid models because they differentially apply the rating scale and the partial credit model (Eckes, 2011; McNamara, 1996; Myford & Wolfe, 2003). These hybrid models can be used to answer a variety of different questions in relation to our data set. Remember that we conducted an analysis with three facets: (1) candidates (test takers), (2) raters, and (3) rating scale criteria. We can change our model specifications quite easily to ask FACETS to generate more detailed statistics for particular facets or to explore interaction between facets. The exact model specifications for each of these models can be found on the companion website (www.oup.com/elt/teacher/fjla), and a summary of the models will be presented later in this chapter (see Table 5.19 on page 125).

Using the many-facets Rasch hybrid model to explore the functioning of analytic rating scales

The first hybrid model we would like to introduce is similar to the rating scale model we explored in detail on pages 97–99. However, this one also provides more information about our analytic rating scales, rather than assuming that they all share the same scale structure. We can do this by asking FACETS to apply a partial credit model to our criterion facet. Let us look at two aspects of the output: the Wright map and the rating scale statistics.

Wright map

Figure 5.6 presents the Wright map of such an analysis. We can see that now, rather than just having an overall scale represented in the Wright map, we have a column for each rating scale criterion. The criteria are represented in

```
+--------------------------------------------------------------------------------+
|Measr|+Candidate|-Rater    |-Criterion             | S.1 | S.2 | S.3 | S.4 | S.5 |
|-----+----------+----------+-----------------------+-----+-----+-----+-----+-----|
|  4 +          +          +                       + (9) + (9) + (9) + (9) + (9) |
|     |          |          |                       |     |     |  ---|     |     |
|     |          |          |                       |     |     |     |     |     |
|     |          |          |                       |     |     |     |     |     |
|     |          |          |                       |     |     |     |     |     |
|     |          |          |                       |     |  ---|     |     |     |
|     | *        |          |                       |     |     |     |     |  ---|
|  3 +          +          +                       +     +     +     + --- +     |
|     |          |          |                       |  8  |     |  8  |     |     |
|     |          |          |                       |     |     |     |     |     |
|     | *        |          |                       |     |     |     |     |     |
|     | *        |          |                       |     |     |     |     |     |
|     | **       |          |                       |     |     |     |     |     |
|     |          |          |                       |     |  8  |     |  8  |  8  |
|  2 + *        +          +                       + --- +     + --- +     +     |
|     | ******   |          |                       |     |     |     |     |     |
|     | *****    |          |                       |     |     |     |     |     |
|     | ****     |          |                       |     |  ---|     |     |  ---|
|     | *        |          |                       |     |     |     |     |     |
|     | ***      |          |                       |     |     |  7  | --- |     |
|     | *****    |          |                       |  7  |     |     |     |     |
|  1 + ****     +          +                       +     +     +     +     +     |
|     | ***      | 2        |                       |     |     |     |     |     |
|     | ****     |          |                       |     |  7  |     |  7  |     |
|     | ***      |          | Content               |     |  ---|     |     |  7  |
|     | **       |          |                       |     |     |     |     |     |
|     | ******   | 3        |                       |     |     |     |     |     |
|     | *******  | 10       | Grammar               | --- |     |     |     |     |
*  0 * *****    * 1   4   6   7 * Vocabulary & spelling *   --- *     * --- *     *
|     | ******** |          | Organisation          |     |     |  6  |     |  ---|
|     | *******  | 5    8   | Academic Style        |     |     |     |     |     |
|     | ***      |          |                       |     |     |     |     |     |
|     | *        | 9        |                       |     |  6  | --- |  6  |     |
|     | *****    |          |                       |     |     |     |     |  6  |
| -1 + **       +          +                       + 6   +     +     +     +     |
|     | ****     |          |                       |     |     |     | --- |     |
|     |          |          |                       |     |  ---|  5  |     |  ---|
|     |          |          |                       |     |     |     |     |     |
|     | ****     |          |                       |     |     |     |     |     |
| -2 + **       +          +                       + --- +     + --- + 5   +     |
|     |          |          |                       |     |     |     |     |  5  |
|     |          |          |                       |     |  5  |     |     |     |
|     |          |          |                       |     |     |     |     |     |
|     |          |          |                       |     |     |  4  |     |     |
| -3 +          +          +                       + (4) + (4) + (3) + (4) + (4) |
|-----+----------+----------+-----------------------+-----+-----+-----+-----+-----|
|Measr| * = 1    |-Rater    |-Criterion             | S.1 | S.2 | S.3 | S.4 | S.5 |
+--------------------------------------------------------------------------------+
```

Figure 5.6: Wright map: hybrid model with separate scale criteria

the order they were entered into the analysis: (1) organization, (2) content, (3) academic style, (4) grammar, and (5) vocabulary and spelling.

We can see in Figure 5.6 that each rating scale seems to have a different step structure, a fact we could not see from our previous analysis, precisely because the model we had specified (the rating scale model) made the simplifying assumption that the step structure was the same for each criterion. We can now see what score on each of the scales a candidate at a given ability level is likely to be awarded. For example, a candidate located at logit –1 is likely to be awarded a score of 6 across all criteria apart from academic style, where the candidate is likely to be awarded a score of 5. This information is important when score reporting is considered, particularly in certain testing contexts. If detailed feedback is valued in a particular test (for example, in a diagnostic assessment context), then providing sub-scores is fairer to candidates than an overall composite score, as this may mask strengths and weaknesses of test takers. The use of the hybrid model for this is preferable to merely reporting raw scores.

Scale step statistics

In this hybrid model, FACETS provides us with separate tables with rating scale statistics for each criterion. In Table 5.16, we have depicted the table for the rating scale statistics for the criterion 'Content'. We chose content because this was identified as misfitting in our overall analysis shown on page 111.

```
+------------------------------------------------------------------------------------------------+
|        DATA            |        QUALITY CONTROL |RASCH-ANDRICH|  EXPECTATION  |  MOST  |  RASCH- | Cat|
|     Category Counts        Cum.| Avge  Exp. OUTFIT| Thresholds |  Measure at  |PROBABLE| THURSTONE|PEAK|
|Score Total      Used    %    % | Meas  Meas  MnSq |Measure S.E.|Category  -0.5 |  from  |Thresholds|Prob|
|------------------------------------+-------------------+-----------------+---------+----------+----|
|  4      45        45   5%   5%| -1.09 -1.83  1.8 |            | ( -4.08)      |  low   |   low    |100%|
|  5     174       174  17%  22%|  -.91 -1.16  1.6 | -2.85      | -2.23  -3.26| -2.85  |  -3.04   | 49%|
|  6     333       333  33%  55%|  -.46  -.44  1.4 | -1.45  .09 |  -.68  -1.43| -1.45  |  -1.43   | 50%|
|  7     263       263  26%  82%|   .22   .31  1.5 |  .17   .08 |   .69   .03|  .17   |   .07    | 43%|
|  8     155       155  16%  97%|   .75  1.00  1.4 | 1.19   .10 |  2.20  1.39| 1.19   |  1.30    | 53%|
|  9      30        30   3% 100%|  1.30  1.59  1.2 | 2.95   .20 |( 4.14)  3.28| 2.95   |  3.08    |100%|
+--------------------------------------------------------- (Mean) --------- (Modal) -- (Median) ------+
```

Table 5.16: Rating scale criteria statistics: content

We can see that the average measures for several band levels are not near the expected measures and that not all the Rasch-Andrich thresholds advance by more than 1.4. This could provide an indication as to why this criterion was misfitting in the overall analysis. It is clear that at least some raters are oriented to this criterion in a way that is different from their orientation to the other criteria. Put another way, candidates who are considered to be able in relation to content—perhaps because their content is interesting, engaging, complex, or clear—are not necessarily as able in terms of the other criteria, and vice versa.

Using the many-facets Rasch hybrid model to explore how each rater employed the rating scale as a whole

Let us suppose we are interested in exploring whether the ten raters in our sample applied the rating scale in the same way. We may want to do this to examine whether the raters in our data set are displaying the sixth rater effect described earlier in this chapter (i.e. raters are interpreting the scale steps of the rating scale slightly differently). We can examine this with a different hybrid model by asking FACETS to analyse the raters with a partial credit model and the rating scale with the rating scale model. In this case, we will get information about how each of the ten raters applied the rating scale as a whole.

Wright map

Figure 5.7 presents the Wright map for such an analysis. We can see from the Wright map that FACETS has modelled each rater separately in order of entry. This shows us how each rater interpreted the scale structure as a whole. We can see that the scale steps are in different locations for each rater, indicating that the raters implemented the rating scale differently. This type of analysis is likely to be too time-consuming to be routinely used in most testing programs. However, it can be used to analyse persistent rater inconsistencies and to diagnose specific problems raters may encounter when using a rating scale. The Wright map visually presents the threat to fairness here: test takers at different ability levels would be likely to receive very different scores if they encountered two different raters.

Scale step statistics

In this analysis, FACETS also produces a separate set of rating scale statistics and probability curves for each rater, illustrating how they apply the scale as a whole. The rating scale statistics for these two raters, Raters 7 and 8, are shown in Table 5.17 (see page 120), and the probability curves in Figure 5.8 (see page 121).

We can see in the probability curves in Figure 5.8 that for Rater 7, there are even peaks for each score level. Table 5.17 also shows that the observations are well distributed across the scale categories for this rater. For Rater 8, however, there are issues at the lower end of the scale. Band levels 4 and 5 are not used much and Level 5 is never the most probable in the probability curve in Figure 5.8. The statistics indicate that Raters 7 and 8, at least, apply the scale steps differently. Rater 8, in particular, may require further monitoring and possible retraining to be able to produce scores that are fairer to test candidates.

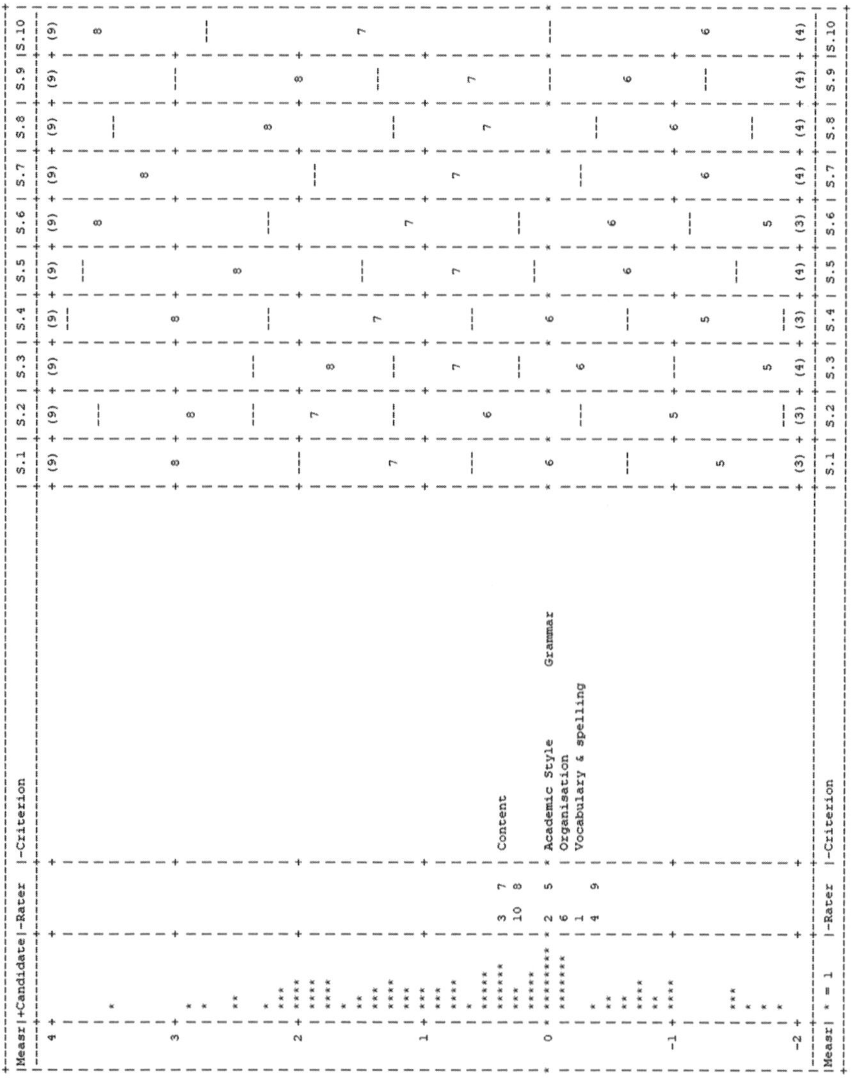

Figure 5.7: Wright map: hybrid model modelling each rater separately: rating scale as a whole

Rater 7 (top)

	DATA				QUALITY CONTROL			RASCH-ANDRICH		EXPECTATION	MOST PROBABLE	RASCH-THURSTONE	Cat
Score	Total	Used	%	Cum. %	Avge Meas	Exp. Meas	OUTFIT MnSq	Thresholds Measure	S.E.	Measure at -0.5 Category	from low Thresholds	from low Thresholds	PEAK Prob
4	3	3	1%	1%	-1.01	-1.69	1.4			(-5.17)	low	low	100%
5	39	39	8%	8%	-.99	-1.13	1.2	-3.99	.59	-3.12	-3.99	-4.13	55%
6	155	155	31%	39%	-.46	-.40	.9	-2.16	.18	-1.21	-2.16	-2.15	55%
7	205	205	41%	80%	.39	.43	1.0	-.27	.11	.72	-.27	-.27	56%
8	94	94	19%	99%	1.36	1.27	.9	1.64	.13	3.23	1.64	1.71	70%
9	4	4	1%	100%	2.17	1.97	.9	4.79	.51	(5.90)	4.79	4.82	100%
										(Mean)	(Modal)	(Median)	

Rater 8 (bottom)

	DATA				QUALITY CONTROL			RASCH-ANDRICH		EXPECTATION	MOST PROBABLE	RASCH-THURSTONE	Cat
Score	Total	Used	%	Cum. %	Avge Meas	Exp. Meas	OUTFIT MnSq	Thresholds Measure	S.E.	Measure at -0.5 Category	from low Thresholds	from low Thresholds	PEAK Prob
4	15	15	3%	3%	-.80	-1.49	2.1			(-3.53)	low	low	100%
5	33	33	7%	10%	-.84*	-.97	1.2	-2.03	.29	-2.16	-2.03	-2.53	32%
6	126	126	25%	35%	-.29	-.33	1.2	-1.99	.18	-.99	-1.99	-1.69	48%
7	177	177	35%	70%	.31	.40	1.1	-.31	.12	.45	-.31	-.32	49%
8	125	125	25%	95%	1.12	1.19	1.1	1.14	.12	2.24	1.14	1.21	57%
9	24	24	5%	100%	2.08	1.88	.9	3.20	.23	(4.37)	3.20	3.29	100%
										(Mean)	(Modal)	(Median)	

Table 5.17: Rating scale statistics for Rater 7 (top) and Rater 8 (bottom)

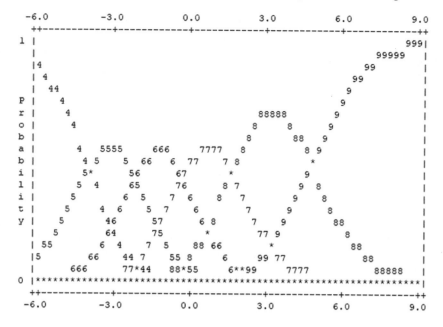

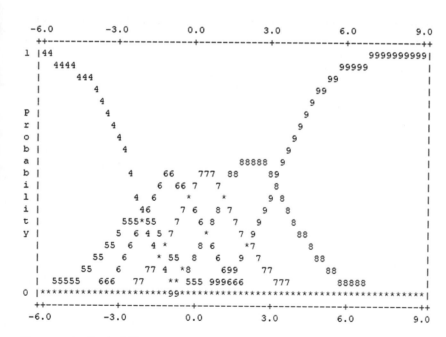

Figure 5.8: Probability curves: Rater 7 (top) and Rater 8 (bottom)

Using the many-facets Rasch hybrid model to explore how each rater employed each individual rating scale

In the first hybrid model we explored how the raters as a whole applied each individual rating scale, and in the second model we explored how each individual rater applied the rating scale as a whole. We can also take this one step further and explore in FACETS how each individual rater applied each individual rating scale. In this case, FACETS produces rating scale category statistics for each rater, for each scale, and a probability curve for each rater applying each individual scale. To arrive at reliable results, this type of analysis requires more data points. Such an analysis is unlikely to be used in routine testing contexts, but could potentially be useful for research projects examining particular aspects of rater functioning. Readers will find the data file for Chapter 5 with the results of such an analysis on the companion website (www.oup.com/elt/teacher/fjla). By simply following the instructions on how to change the model statement, this analysis can be conducted by interested readers.

Bias analysis: modelling interactions in a many-facets Rasch analysis

The three hybrid models presented above are all designed to facilitate understanding of the main facets (in particular raters and rating scales) in more detail. It is also possible to examine interactions between facets with a many-facets Rasch analysis. When examining Figure 5.2 in this chapter, we discussed how it is conceivable for there to be interactions between different aspects in our performance assessment situation. For example, it is possible that individual raters display a bias when rating female candidates (i.e. they consistently rate female candidates more highly than male candidates, or vice versa). It is also imaginable that raters display a bias when applying particular rating scale criteria (for example, they consistently rate more leniently when rating content or consistently more harshly when rating grammar). We can uncover such interactions by conducting a *bias analysis*. For the purpose of illustration, we will explore whether any raters display a bias when applying one or more of the five rating scale criteria.

In this case the bias analysis uses the overall severity of each rater (across all criteria) and the overall difficulty of each criterion. These have already been estimated as the basis for determining whether this overall pattern holds for particular raters with particular criteria. It then predicts the likely score a rater would give when applying a certain criterion if this were applied in the same way that the rater applied the other criteria. If the predicted and the actual scores are sufficiently different, and such differences happen consistently when the rater is applying this criterion, bias is detected.

Table 5.18 presents the bias/interaction report for the two facets we are interested in: rater and rating scale criterion. The table has been arranged in

Observd Score	Expctd Score	Observd Count	Obs-Exp Average	+Bias Size	Model S.E.	t	d.f.	Prob.	Infit MnSq	Outfit MnSq	Rater Sq	Rater Nu	Rater Ra	-measr	Criterion N	Criterion	-measr
677	637.46	100	.40	.59	.12	4.78	99	.0000	1.2	1.2	11	1	1	.04	2	Content	.41
696	673.81	100	.22	.33	.12	2.71	99	.0079	.3	.3	27	7	7	-.06	3	Academic style	-.03
697	676.33	100	.21	.31	.12	2.53	99	.0131	.7	.7	4	4	4	-.01	1	Organisaton	-.11
709	689.00	100	.20	.31	.12	2.46	99	.0157	.8	.8	28	8	8	-.29	3	Academic style	-.03
660	640.91	100	.19	.28	.12	2.31	99	.0228	1.7	1.7	14	4	4	-.01	2	Content	.41
707	689.20	100	.18	.27	.12	2.19	99	.0310	.9	.9	38	8	8	-.29	4	Grammar	-.03
705	687.80	100	.17	.26	.12	2.11	99	.0371	.6	.6	35	5	5	-.27	4	Grammar	-.03
668	651.42	100	.17	.25	.12	2.01	99	.0469	1.2	1.2	33	3	3	.27	4	Grammar	-.03
653	636.65	100	.16	.24	.12	1.98	99	.0505	1.4	1.4	16	6	6	.05	2	Content	.41
680	665.54	100	.14	.22	.12	1.76	99	.0812	1.1	1.1	43	3	3	.27	5	Vocabulary & spelling	-.24
731	718.56	100	.12	.20	.13	1.56	99	.1229	.9	.9	39	9	9	-.74	4	Grammar	-.03
589	578.13	100	.11	.16	.12	1.32	99	.1893	1.7	1.7	12	2	2	.91	2	Content	.41
677	667.17	100	.10	.15	.12	1.20	99	.2336	.7	.7	10	10	10	.12	1	Organisaton	-.11
622	613.84	100	.08	.12	.12	.99	99	.3258	1.3	1.3	2	2	2	.91	1	Organisaton	-.11
709	701.53	100	.07	.11	.12	.92	99	.3578	.6	.6	45	5	5	-.27	5	Vocabulary & spelling	-.24

Table 5.18: Bias analysis (extract)

order of bias, with the higher level of bias presented first. Let us examine the first line of the table. We can see an interaction between Rater 1 and the criterion 'Content'. The observed score for this rater on this criterion is 677 and the expected score is 637.46; the difference between the observed and expected score is shown in the 'Obs – Exp Average' column (where '–' is minus). The bias size is indicated in log odds units; this shows us on the logit scale how much of a difference the bias represents. The interaction is significant as indicated by a significant p-value ('Prob' column below .05). This means that Rater 1 is rating significantly more leniently than expected when rating content. There are several other statistically significant interactions in the table as well.

So what can we do with information from a bias analysis? Uncovering and understanding biases is the first step in addressing such unfairness to certain groups of test takers. Earlier in this chapter we mentioned that insights we gain from a many-facets Rasch analysis of rating data can be used to provide feedback to raters. As well as the information from the overall analysis we showed on pages 106–111 (in particular, information about overall leniency and harshness in relation to the wider group of raters and consistency), we can also give raters feedback on any biases they display. This has been done in several studies as part of rater training (for example, Elder et al., 2005; Knoch, 2011; Wigglesworth, 1993) with varying success, and may be a worthwhile tool for high-stakes large-scale tests to enhance rater reliability on an ongoing basis and raise consciousness among raters of specific rating patterns they may not be aware of.

Summary of many-facets Rasch hybrid and interaction models

We have seen that there are a number of many-facets Rasch hybrid models and interaction models available for carrying out further analyses of rating behaviour and scale functioning that we cannot see using the many-facets Rasch rating scale model. Detailed descriptions of how to conduct the analyses using these models in FACETS are provided on the companion website (www.oup.com/elt/teacher/fjla). Here, though, we would like to provide a summary of the models, including the basic model statement used in the FACETS specification file. Table 5.19 summarizes the five models we have examined in this chapter.

In this chapter we have limited our discussion of the many-facets Rasch models to fairly basic models with only three facets (candidate, rater, and criterion). Any of the models described in Table 5.19 can, of course, be further expanded by including additional facets. One obvious example may be the facet 'task', but other possible facets (testing time, rater background, rater group, candidate background, etc.) could also be included if they are useful for providing us with information about our performance assessment that can be used to ensure the fairness and validity of the scores and score interpretations we make.

Model	Model statement in control file	Basic features	Section in this chapter
Many-facets Rasch rating scale model	?,?,? (candidate, rater, criterion)	All rating scale criteria modelled to have the same scale structure.	pp. 97–114
Many-facets Rasch hybrid model to explore the functioning of analytic rating scales	?,?,# (candidate, rater, criterion)	Analytic rating criteria are modelled to each have their own scale structure.	pp. 115–116
Many-facets Rasch hybrid model to explore how each rater employed the rating scale as a whole	?,#,? (candidate, rater, criterion)	Models how each rater used the rating scale (but all analytic rating scales modelled to have the same scale structure).	pp. 117–119
Many-facets Rasch hybrid model to explore how each rater employed each individual rating scale	?,#,# (candidate, rater, criterion)	Models how each rater used each analytic rating scale.	p. 119
Interaction model (bias analysis)	?,?B,?B (candidate, rater, criterion)	Examines whether any of the raters exhibit any individual biases against any of the rating criteria.	pp. 119–120

Table 5.19: Many-facets Rasch models for investigating rating behaviour in FACETS

In Chapter 6 we will show how analyses using many-facets Rasch measurement with three or more facets have been used to explore issues of fairness in testing contexts. For example, studies have investigated rater performance over time to explore whether rater quality is stable over time (and to what extent experience is a factor). Other studies have examined raters from varying backgrounds and levels of experience to establish whether this aspect has an impact on rater quality. Finally, studies have also examined the test method as a facet, to see whether, for example, taking an exam on-screen or on paper makes a difference for test takers. See Chapter 6 for some sample studies of this kind.

Summary

At the start of this chapter (see pages 94–95), we discussed the various rater effects that have been described in the literature. These included the following:

1 overall leniency and harshness of raters
2 halo effect
3 central tendency effect
4 rater inconsistency
5 rater scale interpretation effect
6 bias effect (leniency or harshness towards specific aspects of rating situation, such as specific score criteria, specific task, specific test-taker group)

We also showed how it is difficult to identify these effects based on traditional analyses, such as indices of consensus and consistency. Throughout this chapter we have seen how useful many-facets Rasch measurement is in identifying these effects.

As well as identifying rater effects, it is also important to ensure that the rating scale used is functioning as intended. We have seen in this chapter that the many-facets Rasch model provides us with a powerful tool for exploring how the raters as a group apply a scale, including each rating scale criterion and how each rater applies each rating scale. These types of analyses are worthwhile during the development of a scale, as well as in high-stakes testing once a scale is operational. They also have a role in research. In Chapter 6 we will describe some of the types of research questions that can be explored with this kind of analysis. Table 5.20 summarizes which many-facets Rasch model to use when examining rater variability and rating scale functioning, and which specific statistics we can draw on to identify each of these rater effects.

Not only does Rasch measurement help us to easily recognize patterns in our data, such as rater effects or scale functioning, but it also provides us with a simple way of dealing with these effects by generating a 'fair score' for candidates that takes any systematic effects into account. In the following chapter we will examine how Rasch analysis has been used in the literature to address issues of fairness.

Activities on the website

The data file used in this chapter is provided on the companion website (www.oup.com/elt/teacher/fjla), with some activities for readers who are interested in exploring issues relating to rater-mediated assessment further.

Rater effect	Model	Statistics
rater overall leniency or harshness in relation to a group of raters	many-facets Rasch rating scale model	'Measure' column in rater measurement report and Wright map
halo effect	many-facets Rasch rating scale model	rater fit statistics in rater measurement report plus examination of raw data
central tendency effect	many-facets Rasch rating scale model	rater fit statistics in rater measurement report; category counts in rating scale statistics table; examination of raw data
rater inconsistency	many-facets Rasch rating scale model	rater fit statistics in rater measurement report
rater scale interpretation effect	hybrid models (see Table 5.19)	Wright map rating scale statistics
bias effect	many-facets Rasch model with interaction analysis	bias analysis statistics

Table 5.20: Summary of rater effects and the appropriate Rasch models and statistics for detecting the effects

Notes

1 There are many other possible aspects of performance assessment we could explore with such an analysis. For example, in the assessment of speaking, we could examine the L1 background of the candidate or the gender of the rater as possible interaction effects. Alternatively, it may be interesting to examine whether experienced raters show different rating patterns as compared with new raters. The physical setting of the assessment could also be a factor; for example, a particular group of candidates may have been assessed on a particularly noisy day or the audio input for a writing assessment may have been difficult to hear. Finally, in some speaking assessments, candidates interact either with other candidates or a trained interlocutor rather than the rater, and it is possible that the person they interact with has an impact on the scores.

2 FACETS is able to map all rating scale criteria onto this map in the same way that it maps the overall 'Scale' column in this figure. We will look at this in more detail later in this chapter when examining various many-facets Rasch hybrid models.

3 A large standard error (SE) in the rater measurement report indicates that we cannot be confident of the exact location of the raters on the logit scale; that is, FACETS is not confident of the precision of the modelling of the raters' leniency and harshness.

6

Investigating fairness using Rasch measurement

Introduction

How, specifically, do we investigate fairness issues in assessments using the tools of Rasch analysis? In this chapter we give examples of how this has been done in some recent research studies in language assessment using Rasch analysis. To do this, we collected and analysed research papers or commentaries published in recent years in leading international journals in the field of language assessment. We consider, in particular, the kinds of fairness issues that have been investigated by Rasch analysis in such studies, and ways in which the analysis may enhance the fairness of the test instruments and procedures under analysis. Through synthesizing these studies we demonstrate the vitally important role of Rasch analysis in investigating a wide range of issues that are essential to test fairness.

Mapping the terrain

In order to get an overview of recent research using Rasch analysis in language testing research, we decided to partially replicate a study conducted by McNamara and Knoch (2012) that traced the growing acceptance of Rasch methods since 1984, when they were first introduced. We looked at the papers published between January 2010 and September 2016 in the four leading international journals in the field of language assessment: *Language Testing*, *Language Assessment Quarterly*, *Assessing Writing*, and *Papers in Language Testing and Assessment*.

We chose papers from the four journals in which, in the case of empirical papers, Rasch analysis constituted at least one of the methods that the researchers employed to address the research questions, or, in the case of research commentaries, the Rasch model was substantially discussed or constituted one of the foci. We found 57 articles that met these criteria. We then slightly revised the coding scheme from McNamara and Knoch (2012) to classify the articles. The coding scheme addressed the following six questions: (1) Which Rasch model was used? (2) What skills were measured in the test? (3) Where was the author based? (4) Was the Rasch analysis a primary focus of the study, or one of several foci? (5) Did the paper use Rasch as an analytic tool, or simply discuss it? (6) What research questions were answered by the Rasch analysis? (Questions 3 and 5 are less relevant to the focus of this chapter, but we included them for the sake of comparison with the earlier study.) We will first present an overview of the findings in relation to these six questions, before moving on to the main focus of this chapter, i.e. a discussion of the kinds of fairness issues that have been investigated in these studies, using examples selected to show how fairness was a focus of the analysis.

Table 6.1 presents an overview of the published research in the four journals during the period of January 2010 to September 2016. The major trends that emerge from this table are: (1) a preponderance of the many-facets Rasch model (MFRM) over other Rasch models; (2) much more research focusing on productive language skills (i.e. writing and speaking) than on receptive skills (for example, listening and reading); (3) the use of Rasch together with other statistical models or qualitative methods; (4) the strong representation of research from the Americas and an increasing number of research studies from Asia; (5) FACETS and Winsteps being the two Rasch software programs that have been most frequently used by language assessment researchers.

Essentially, the results of the analyses resonate with McNamara and Knoch's (2012) findings, which were based on a review of published research in the same four journals from the periods 1990 to 1999 and 2000 to 2009. Nevertheless, two differences need highlighting. First, we noticed that the number of articles using and/or discussing Rasch measurement has been increasing steadily in language assessment. For example, McNamara and

Model used	Basic (6)	RCM/PCM (5)	MFRM (39)	Other/ Unknown (6)	N = 56[a]
skills in test	speaking (16), writing (21)	reading (1), listening (6)	vocabulary (4), grammar (1)	other or more than one (8)	N = 57
author affiliation	Australia, NZ (6)	North and South America (27)	Asia (16)	UK, Europe (8)	N = 57
role of Rasch	primary (24)	one of several (33)			N = 57
function of Rasch	discuss (3)	use (52)	both (2)		N = 57
program used	FACETS (39)	Winsteps (12)	(Con)Quest (2)	others/ unknown (2)	N = 55

Note: PCM = partial credit model; RSM = rating scale model; MFRM = many-facets Rasch model; NZ = New Zealand; UK = United Kingdom
[a]The totals in these cells differ, as some authors did not specify the models they used. With regard to the program used, some empirical papers used more than one program, while some discussion papers did not use any program. In total, 57 articles were included in the sample.

Table 6.1: Published journal research using Rasch measurement, 2010–2016 (N = 57)

Knoch (2012) collected 36 articles published during the period 1990 to 1999, and 47 during the period 2000 to 2009; we collected 57 articles published between 2010 and 2016. This suggests a growing enthusiasm for embracing Rasch measurement in the field of language assessment. Second, regarding author affiliation, we noticed a substantial increase of research from the Americas (primarily North America) and Asia (in particular Japan), as opposed to the over-representation of Australian research found in McNamara & Knoch (2012), which tracked the published research from 1984 to 2009. This trend suggests that while Australia continues to be a Rasch stronghold, other countries and regions are increasingly adopting Rasch measurement in language assessment research.

What kinds of fairness issues does Rasch-based research address?

When we look in detail at the 57 studies included in this survey, it is possible to identify a number of recurring issues that Rasch measurement has been used to investigate. Unsurprisingly, rater effects in performance language assessment (for example, writing and speaking) is the topic that has been most frequently investigated in these studies. As we saw in earlier chapters, this issue is crucial to the fairness of performance language assessments, given the important role that raters play in determining the scores that test takers receive. In addition to rater effects, Rasch analysis has explored the technical quality of the instruments used in tests (for example, items, rating scales). This kind of research is germane to fairness in the sense that it addresses the fundamental question in language testing, i.e. whether the test scores truly reflect the test takers' language abilities that are targeted by the test. Two other topics—the effect of test method on test performance and the functioning of test items on different subgroups of test takers—also feature prominently in the research we have surveyed. We will now look in detail at examples of how Rasch analysis has been used to investigate these topics in the studies surveyed, and how the investigation of each topic helps to enhance test fairness.

Rater effects

Research on rater effects is of various kinds. Some research simply investigates the extent of rater variability, and consistently demonstrates that such variability is an inevitable feature of performance assessment. Having established that such variability exists, the next question is whether it can be reduced by understanding what factors (for example, the background of the raters, their training, their L1) have a systematic effect on rating quality. Research has also explored whether providing detailed feedback to raters on their rating behaviour can improve their subsequent performance. We will look in detail at selected papers to show how Rasch analysis has been used in these studies, and how this has impacted on the issue of fairness in each case.

Rater variability

The many-facets Rasch model (MFRM) has typically been used to examine rater variability in severity and consistency in contexts of standardized assessment. Rater variability has also been examined in other contexts. With the increasing use of alternative assessment procedures such as self- and peer-assessment in classroom settings, the quality of ratings by self- and peer-assessors has become an important issue, particularly if they are used for summative purposes. There is also the question of the cultural context in which peer- and self-assessment takes place, as it has been argued that cultural values (for example, modesty or competitiveness) will affect the capacity of peer- and self-assessors to provide ratings that are consistent with those of arguably more objective observers such as teachers. Esfandiari and Myford (2013) investigated the severity differences among self-assessors, peer-assessors, and teacher assessors in rating EFL essays in Iran. Employing MFRM as the primary data analysis method, the researchers found that teacher assessors were the most severe while self-assessors were the most lenient; the average severity levels of teacher assessors and peer-assessors were not significantly different. They discuss their findings, and consider how they contrast with findings from other cultural contexts such as Japan, in the light of cultural differences across contexts. The study is of particular interest to those who would like to use self- and peer-assessment in decision-making, particularly in non-Western learning contexts.

Another important context in which rating takes place is in standard setting, when expert judges are required to judge whether performances at particular levels reach a given standard. The score associated with a performance agreed by the judges to define a level is known as a 'cut point' or 'cut score'. Standard setting is obviously important to test fairness, as where the cut point is set is going to govern decisions with important consequences for test takers—to admit them (or not) to professional practice or to university education, for example. Two recent papers have shown the usefulness of Rasch measurement in standard-setting in language testing contexts, in the tradition of studies conducted since the early 1990s, when many-facets Rasch analysis had just appeared (Lumley, Lynch, & McNamara, 1994). The first, by Hsieh (2013), used many-facets Rasch analysis to examine the severity and consistency in panelists' judgements of the difficulty of test items as part of the Angoff procedure for cut score setting. The study outlines the multiple practical advantages of using Rasch tools within standard-setting. These include, in relation to the behaviour of the panelists, information provided by the analysis on the following issues: Are the judgements among panelists significantly different? How much agreement about the panelists' judgements on items is there? How is each rating different from its expected value? Which panelist ratings appear to be higher or lower than expected? What is revealed can be factored into decisions about standards. The second study, by Pill and McNamara (2016), also used MFRM in a study of standard-setting in a revised test of communication for immigrant health professionals, the

Occupational English Test (OET). The study was designed to set new standards for a revised speaking sub-test, in which additional criteria had been introduced that more adequately reflected the views of health professionals on what counted in successful communication between clinicians and patients. The standards were set using the judgements of health professionals themselves, rather than language raters. This raised the issues of the commensurability of the two types of judges, and the consistency of the judgements of the health professionals, which were addressed using MFRM. The results from analyses using MFRM were generally reassuring: health professionals were found to be consistent in assessing test takers' speaking performances, and they also showed considerable score agreement with language-trained raters in their ranking of test takers, although it was less clear whether agreement on the test construct was the basis of that agreement. This study further demonstrates the usefulness of Rasch analysis in augmenting the rigour of standard-setting, which, in turn, has implications for test fairness.

Research into variability in rater behaviour helps to uncover sources of variability, and hence has implications for rater training. Studies have investigated whether accurate and inaccurate raters engage in different processes in decision-making. Zhang (2016) examined how raters' cognitive and meta-cognitive strategies influence their rating accuracy in the context of the writing section of College English Test Band 4 in China. MFRM was used to analyse raters' ratings and to classify them into accurate and less accurate raters. Qualitative data was collected to explore their mental processing while rating. The results revealed that, compared with less accurate raters, accurate raters are better at integrating information from target essays and more self-conscious about their rating accuracy. These cognitive and meta-cognitive strategies were believed to contribute to their better rating performance. The study has implications for rater training and the revision of rating rubrics, and ultimately for fairer assessment for candidates. For example, testing agencies may attempt a screening evaluation of raters' performance as part of rater training, and then provide differentiated training schemes targeting different cognitive and meta-cognitive strategies for more and less competent raters.

Rater behaviour over time

Two recent longitudinal studies have used Rasch analysis to examine change in rater behaviour over time. The first examined the effect of experience in general; the second explored the effectiveness of targeted feedback to raters on the basis of an analysis of their recent performance.

Lim (2011) investigated the performance of novice and experienced raters, in terms of both rater severity and consistency, on the writing section of the Michigan English Language Assessment Battery (MELAB), an international English proficiency test used for various high-stakes academic and professional purposes. This study was intended to reveal the developmental patterns of the performance of novice and experienced raters. MFRM was used to investigate how novice raters' rating quality developed over time in comparison to experienced raters, and the extent to which raters could maintain their rating quality over time. The data came from a larger study that examined three specific time periods within a four-and-a-half-year span. The data comprised a total of 20,662 ratings provided by 11 raters over the three time periods, ranging from 12 to 21 months. Analyses using MFRM followed three steps. First, the complete four-and-a-half-year data set was run through FACETS to generate difficulty estimates for each writing prompt, as well as average ability estimates for groups of test takers based on their L1 background. Following this, the prompt and L1 background estimates were used as anchors in FACETS, which specified separate runs for each month covered by this study. Finally, month-on-month estimates were generated for each rater in order to observe their performance over time.

The results revealed that, at the outset, novice raters might differ significantly from the more experienced raters in terms of severity. However, they learned to adjust their severity levels relatively quickly, and gradually their severity could not be distinguished from the more experienced ones. It was also revealed that once novice raters became acceptably moderate in their ratings, they could maintain their severity levels throughout the periods of time over which they were tracked. For the more experienced raters, their severity levels remained stable throughout the periods being tracked. Rater consistency was evaluated through the infit mean-square statistics in the output of FACETS. A similar pattern was observed to that found in relation to rater severity. Novice raters were found to lack consistency at the beginning. However, their consistency kept improving, and gradually became indistinguishable from their more experienced counterparts, whose consistency remained acceptably stable throughout the time periods that were tracked.

This study has implications for language-testing agencies in rater recruitment, training, and management. For example, it suggests a relationship between rating volume and rating quality—that is, that rating experience leads to better rater performance. Thus, raters should be required to rate a certain number of performances before they can be fully certified.

In the second study, Knoch (2011) investigated the value of individualized feedback provided to raters in both writing and speaking over several administrations of a test, on a longitudinal basis. The study was conducted in the context of the Occupational English Test (OET). Using MFRM and raters' perception questionnaires, the study tracked the rating behaviour of 19 OET raters over eight administrations to investigate the effectiveness of individualized feedback.

MFRM was implemented in FACETS to generate detailed performance profiles of raters' rating behaviour, which included rater severity, bias, consistency, and the use of rating scale categories. The feedback was provided to raters after each administration. Furthermore, MFRM was also used to evaluate whether the feedback was successful or, in other words, whether raters' behaviour improved through the provision of such feedback. Measures of consistency (infit mean-square values), bias (z-scores), and severity (logits) for each rater at each administration provided by FACETS were used to develop accessible descriptions of rating behaviour for each rater.

The results were disappointing. The study revealed that the raters were rating no better when receiving the feedback than when they had not received feedback, and neither speaking nor writing raters were able to incorporate the feedback successfully. Although the raters were generally positive about the value of the feedback and its effectiveness, there was no relationship between their perceptions of the feedback and its success. Several reasons were believed to explain the limited effect of individualized feedback, such as raters' failure to internalize the feedback, or the inappropriate timing of the feedback. As argued by the author, future studies could be undertaken using methods such as retrospective interviews with raters to clarify why the feedback failed to take effect. The value of feedback to raters has been studied using Rasch techniques for over 20 years, with mixed results and still no clear answer. Clearly, the bases of rater behaviour lie deep in the attitudes and value systems of the raters; we need to keep studying rater behaviour in order to better understand it, given that we know it is the primary source of unfairness in tests of speaking and writing.

Raters' language background

There has been much discussion recently of the extent to which native-speaker norms are an appropriate target for second language proficiency. Given that most communication in English, for example, occurs among speakers of different L1 backgrounds, constituting what is now commonly called English as a lingua franca (ELF) communication, there is ongoing discussion relating to what norms are appropriate in judging this communication. More specifically, questions have been raised about whether native English speakers (NESs) and non-native English speakers (NNESs), both of whom are involved in ELF communication, are equally competent to judge its success. The idea of the end of native-speaker privilege has, however, encountered resistance (perhaps understandably) from native speakers, and also from non-native-speaker learners. It raises questions of both fairness and justice. In terms of fairness, are the test taker's chances of success affected by the native- or non-native-speaker status of the person judging them? In terms of justice, what norm or standard should we use in judging English language proficiency—the traditional native-speaker norm, or norms derived from an understanding of the nature of ELF communication?

In order to explore the fairness issue, Zhang and Elder (2011) investigated whether NES and NNES teacher raters had different evaluations and interpretations of oral English proficiency as elicited by the Chinese national College English Test – Spoken English Test (CET–SET). Research data was collected from a group of 19 NES and 20 NNES teachers, who rated CET–SET speech samples from 30 test takers, and who also wrote comments to justify the ratings they had assigned.

Two kinds of analysis were conducted: a quantitative analysis using MFRM and a qualitative study of the raters' retrospective written comments on the holistic ratings they had given. The results of the two studies were rather different. Results from Rasch analysis confirmed the intra-group consistency of both the NES and NNES raters. (In both cases, the infit mean-square values summarizing rater consistency were within the acceptable range.) In terms of relative severity, the results revealed that the holistic ratings assigned by NES and NNES groups were equal, suggesting that the two groups assigned ratings at the same severity level. In summary, the MFRM analysis revealed that overall, any differences in ratings observed between rater groups were marginal and not statistically significant. No obvious difference was observed in the consistency or severity of each rater group when judging performance. This was an encouraging finding from the point of view of fairness; test takers had little to be concerned about in terms of their scores, whether they were judged by native or non-native speakers.

A somewhat different picture emerged from the qualitative analysis of rater reflections, which revealed that the NES raters focused on a wider range of abilities in judging test takers' oral test performance than did the NNES raters, suggesting that the two groups were drawing upon different constructs of oral proficiency when assigning ratings. This has important implications for the conceptualization of ELF communication: What is the definition of the construct? What criteria should be used in judging its success? This study concluded that both NES and NNES raters are equipped to evaluate oral English proficiency in performance language assessment, and that the native/non-native dichotomy is not meaningful in that raters from different backgrounds, in spite of their different orientations, ranked candidates in the same way. Given that the two groups of raters drew upon different constructs of oral proficiency, however, the finding has important implications for the construct of ELF assessment, which ultimately involves questions of policy (and therefore of justice) as well as fairness.

A study by Yan (2014) returned to one important aspect of the ELF assessment issue, i.e. whether NNES raters rate differently from NES raters. In his evaluation of rater performance on the Oral English Proficiency Test (OEPT), Yan (2014) examined the potential role of raters' L1 in the ratings that they assigned to test-taker subgroups with different L1s. Developed at a large public North American university, the OEPT is a computer-based, semi-direct spoken English test, targeting the prospective international teaching assistants (ITAs) whose first language is not English. Data in this study consisted of 253 OEPT test takers and 11 trained OEPT raters, two of whom were native speakers of Chinese. Bias analysis was performed in MFRM to explore the potential interactions between raters and test takers with the same L1s. The results showed that L1 Chinese raters were significantly more lenient in relation to Chinese test takers and significantly more severe towards Indian test takers. L1 English raters, on the other hand, were significantly more lenient towards Indian test takers. Reassuringly, the effect sizes of rater–examinee L1 interactions were all small, with the exception of the moderate interaction effect between L1 Chinese raters and Indian test takers.

A related fairness issue arises in the context of large-scale testing programs growing in terms of the number of test takers they have, and needing to expand their rater pools by employing speakers of heterogeneous language backgrounds as raters. One aspect of the language background issue is whether native speakers of English who may have learned the L1 of the candidates they are rating in an English proficiency test perform differently from those with no such knowledge. For example, if I have studied Chinese as an L2, is this likely to make a difference to my ratings of L1 speakers of Chinese who are candidates in an English language test? Does it make me more or less sympathetic to them, or does it make no difference?

Winke, Gass, and Myford (2013) investigated whether raters' L2 background, defined as raters' familiarity with test takers' accent in this study, constituted a source of bias in rating oral performance. The data comprised 107 raters' ratings on 432 TOEFL iBT speech samples from 72 test takers (each test taker performed six tasks). The raters in this study were L2 speakers of Spanish, Chinese, or Korean, while the test takers comprised three native-speaker groups (24 each) of Spanish, Chinese, and Korean.

The study conducted an MFRM analysis of the scores using FACETS. Did subgroups of raters with differing knowledge of the languages of the candidate subgroups behave differently? The possibility of this kind of interaction can be studied with the bias analysis function in FACETS. A bias analysis was therefore conducted to investigate whether raters' L2 familiarity interacted with test takers' L1 background when raters assigned ratings to test takers. Two of the interactions were statistically significant: (1) the raters with Spanish as an L2 were significantly more lenient towards test takers who had Spanish as an L1; and (2) the raters with Chinese as an L2 were significantly more lenient towards test takers who had Chinese as an L1. However, in both cases the effect sizes were small, suggesting that the difference may not warrant attention in practice. No significant interactions were found between the raters with Korean as an L2 and test takers with Korean as an L1. The findings are reassuring in terms of fairness.

The findings from these three studies mostly concur with other research reported in our collection of papers. For example, Wei and Llosa (2015) examined whether differences existed between Indian and American raters when rating Indian test takers' responses to the Test of English as a Foreign Language Internet-Based Test (TOEFL iBT) speaking tasks. Results of MFRM analysis indicated that the two groups of raters did not differ in their use of scoring criteria; nor did they differ in terms of internal consistency and severity of the test scores. It is worth noting that a different result emerged from Marefat and Heydari (2016), who compared native English speakers' and Iranian teachers' evaluations of Iranian students' English essays in the Iranian context. MFRM analysis indicated that Iranian raters were significantly more severe than native-English-speaker raters in awarding scores to students' essays.

So why is this finding inconsistent with other research? We noticed that this research was conducted in an English as a Foreign Language (EFL) context and the language skill involved was writing, whereas other studies that were conducted involved speaking skills, and took place in contexts where English was the first language. Therefore, it seems plausible to assume that language skill (for example, speaking or writing) and the research context might play a role in affecting the research results. Future research is warranted to ascertain whether this is the case. Though the results are generally encouraging in terms of test fairness, it should be noted that the studies with a qualitative component all indicated that NES and NNES raters tended to draw upon different aspects of the L2 speaking or writing construct. In other words, while the overall ratings awarded to test takers are fair to test takers (as NES and NNES raters do not differ in consistency or severity), test fairness may be attenuated if fine-grained information about test takers' performance is requested, or if the test is used for diagnostic purposes. Additionally, there is the more problematic construct issue of what exactly is being measured in these assessments, as raters with different backgrounds seem to be oriented to different features of the performance.

Overall, these studies are examples of how aspects of the rating setting can be explored and how the threats to fairness from rater variability can be evaluated using Rasch techniques. More interestingly, and perhaps even more importantly, the analyses can help us understand what it would mean to adopt ELF communication as the relevant construct for the communicative assessment of English proficiency; this is perhaps the greatest challenge facing English language assessment at the current time (McNamara, 2014).

The quality of test instruments

Rasch measurement theory can be used to investigate the measurement properties of language test instruments, which are crucial considerations in investigating the fairness of tests. More powerfully, analysis of test performance data can also be used to explore the construct measured in the test. The Rasch model, as we have seen, can generate item and person measures that are calibrated on the same logit scale so that they can be directly compared with each other. The item and person distribution on the variable map can be used to test *a priori* hypotheses concerning the underlying variable being measured in the test and person responses to that variable. The Rasch model can also be used to examine differences between observed responses and the responses expected by the model through fit analysis. Furthermore, the dimensionality of the data can be assessed through an analysis of item residual variances. Because of these strengths, Rasch measurement theory has a unique role to play in research on the validation of test instruments in the interests of greater fairness and greater meaningfulness of test scores.

Beglar (2010) provides a representative example of this kind of research. The study investigated the validity of the Vocabulary Size Test (VST), which is designed to measure written receptive knowledge of the most frequent 14,000 words of English. The data was collected from 19 native speakers of English and 178 native speakers of Japanese at different English proficiency levels. The Rasch measurement model was selected because, as the author claimed, it provided a wealth of validity evidence to lend support (or the lack thereof) to several aspects of Messick's (1989) validation framework. Given that all test items assumed the format of four-option multiple-choice questions, the Rasch dichotomous model was used to analyse the data.

The results generated by Rasch analysis generally supported the validity of the VST. For example, the overwhelming majority of the items were found to display good fit to the Rasch model. In addition, the items displayed a high degree of unidimensionality, with the Rasch model accounting for 85.6% of the variance. Also, it was revealed that various combinations of items provided precise measurement for this sample of examinees, as indicated by high Rasch reliability estimates. Given the various strands of evidence in support of the validity of the VST, the study concluded that it provides teachers and researchers with a new, valid instrument for measuring written receptive vocabulary size.

A similar study was reported by Pae, Greenberg, and Morris (2012), who investigated the psychometric properties of the Peabody Picture Vocabulary Test (PPVT), a receptive vocabulary or verbal ability test that has been widely used in the United States for decades. The test has important consequences for test takers: the results guide intervention in cases of slow vocabulary development, and are used to identify children who are at risk for language delay. The test is increasingly used with adults in clinical and research contexts, but little research has been carried out on its use for such populations, particularly given that adults may perform differently in the test depending on their cultural background. The use of a test like this on markedly different populations of test takers in terms of age and cultural background raises important questions of fairness, as decisions that may be crucial to the well-being of those being tested are dependent on the quality and relevance of the information provided by the test. In this study, struggling African-American adult readers were administered the test. Rasch analysis was used to calibrate the difficulty of items in PPVT for this cohort, and to investigate whether the PPVT had a unidimensional internal structure, and whether the items functioned equivalently on different groups of test takers in terms of gender and overall ability. The results were generally reassuring about the suitability of the test for this population. Given that the test is administered to individuals of varying ethnic background, it might have been more revealing to have analysed the performance of struggling adult readers who are not African-American to see if differential item and test functioning is a problem for this test.

Goodwin et al. (2012) also studied the suitability of a widely used literacy test for an ethnic minority population, in this case the Extract the Base Test (EBT), an English derivational morphology test for third- to fifth-grade children in the United States. In this study, the performances of children from English-speaking and Spanish-speaking backgrounds were included in the data set. Rasch analysis was used to examine the test reliability and item difficulty. In addition, it was used to test whether the functioning of the items fit the Rasch model; subgroup analyses were also carried out. However, the study design precluded the use of differential item functioning analysis, which would normally have been the method of choice. The results of this study supported the reliability and validity of using the EBT for educational assessment and for making instructional decisions for the children from ethnic minority backgrounds, thus confirming the fairness of the test for this population.

With the growing realization of the need for assessment research to support the work of classroom teachers, Rasch analysis has been used to develop instruments for classroom assessment. Hirai and Koizumi (2013) developed a Story Retelling Speaking Test (SRST) to be used in classrooms as a test of speaking ability in English as a foreign language. For the purposes of evaluation, the researchers developed three possible rating scales for teachers to use. One is the empirically derived, binary-choice, boundary-definition scale, also known as the EBB scale. The researchers developed two such scales, one with four criteria (communicative efficiency, content, grammar and vocabulary, and pronunciation) (EBB1), and the other a modified version of EBB1 with three criteria (communicative efficiency, grammar and vocabulary, and pronunciation) (EBB2). The EBB2 was a modified version of EBB1 because the latter was found to be problematic in previous research. In addition, a more conventional multiple-trait (MT) scale was developed from the EBB2 scale, but using a conventional analytic scoring format. The study compared the three scales in order to determine which was best suited to the SRST.

In this study, MFRM analysis was implemented to investigate the discrimination of the three rating scales. Further, it was used to examine the three scales in terms of rater separation, reliability, and variability on the scales and rating scale properties. Results showed that overall the EBB2 scale functioned the best. It discriminated between good and poor performances reliably. In comparison with the other two scales, the EBB2 was also better at achieving agreement among raters. Furthermore, it showed the best distribution of scores across the available categories. The MT scale, in contrast, turned out to be the least discriminating among the three scales, and rater consistency was found to be problematic when applying this scale.

Overall, the authors concluded that EBB2 was the best of the three scales in terms of its measurement properties, and hence its fairness to test takers. The authors also concluded that scale format affects rater consistency: compared with the MT scale, both of the EBB scales yielded more consistent ratings. However, a follow-up questionnaire survey revealed that raters found the MT scale easy to use in practice. This is because the MT scale is akin to the conventional analytic scale, which enabled raters to see the full range of the scale at once; this is not true for the EBB scales. The study is an excellent example of how Rasch analysis can reveal issues of balancing reliability, validity, and practicality in classroom assessment contexts.

Test method and test performance

Understanding the factors that affect test takers' performance on language tests has long been of interest to language assessment researchers (for example, Bachman, 1990; Bachman & Palmer, 1996). Research along these lines can help test developers and users understand more clearly the constructs that are being assessed, as well as the meaning and interpretability of test scores. Among the plethora of variables that are believed to affect test performance, test method factors are particularly pertinent to test fairness, primarily because of the potential interactions between test methods and test-taker characteristics. Some test takers might have better performance on items presented in one format than on items presented in another, even though the items are used to assess the same language ability. It is thus necessary to understand the potential test method effect on test performance.

A number of recent studies have used Rasch analysis to investigate whether test method affects test performance. Filipi (2012), for example, investigated whether questions written in the target language in a listening comprehension test are likely to be more difficult than the same items presented in the test takers' first language. The target test in this study is the Assessment of Language Competence (ALC) certificate test, an annual international testing program developed by the Australian Council for Educational Research (ACER) to test the listening and reading comprehension skills in a number of languages of lower- to middle-year-level students in secondary school. The test is provided in six languages, four of which are offered at three levels, including the threshold level in listening only (Certificate 1) and an assessment of both listening and reading comprehension skills at Certificate 2 and 3 levels. The use of the target language in the listening comprehension test items was claimed to be unfair by some users of the test as it depressed scores, and this complaint was the motivation for the study.

This study consisted of two stages: (1) an analysis of data from a 2006 trial of listening comprehension tests in French and Japanese and (2) an analysis of the data from the final test in 2007, which included all six languages at Level 2 and five languages at Level 3, with a total of 25,000 test takers. In the 2006 trial there were two versions of each test. In one version, 15 of the questions were in the target language; in the other, the same questions were given in English (the L1 of the test takers). Rasch analysis enabled the comparison of difficulty estimates for the items written in both English and the target language. This involved separate calibrations of the two versions of the French and Japanese tests, and the subsequent use of common item anchoring to bring them onto a common scale (see Chapter 7 for more on item anchoring in Rasch measurement). In addition to Rasch analysis, a questionnaire survey was used to solicit test takers' views on the test in order to determine its face validity and test takers' perceptions of test difficulty.

Results of the Rasch analysis indicated that the trial data from each of the trial tests, as well as the data from the 2007 ALC tests, fitted the Rasch model well. The comparative difficulty analysis found an effect for the language of the 15 paired items: in general, they were easier when the question was in English than when it was in the target language. This finding accorded with the perceptions of the test takers, who found items written in the target language more difficult. Thus the complaint from test users was found to have substance. However, it was also found that the ability an item was designed to measure affected test takers' perceptions. Test takers found the items in the target language relatively easier where the questions involved listening for explicitly stated information. In questions that required test takers to listen for global meaning, language choice did not matter.

Reassuringly, each of the six tests that had some items in English and others in the target language showed a high level of reliability and fit to the single latent scale, indicating that items were functioning consistently, regardless of the language of the question; in other words, issues of difference in construct are not raised by the language of the items. These findings provide supportive evidence to test fairness. In view of the findings from this study, the author concluded that the teachers' comment that the ALC listening tests were not fair was more complex than it first appeared.

Another test format issue, which also touches on test constructs, is the increasing use of video in tests of listening on the grounds that it is a better representation of the way in which listening happens in the non-test setting. Batty (2015) investigated this issue in a foreign-language listening comprehension test in terms of the differences in difficulty between a test using audio only and an identical test that also incorporated video, as well as the interactions between the delivery format (i.e. audio or video) and text type, language proficiency level, and individual listening comprehension items. The participants in this study were 164 English-major university students in Japan, separated into four proficiency levels. The test in this study is a placement test, using three text types (monologue, conversation and lecture) and traditional four-option multiple-choice questions. MFRM was used in this study in order to: (a) compare the difficulties of the audio and video formats, (b) investigate interactions between format and text type and between format and proficiency level, and (c) identify specific items biased towards one or the other format.

Results showed that the difficulty estimates of the audio and video formats were almost the same, with a negligible difference of 0.08 logits. The index of separation was low for this facet, and the chi-square test yielded a non-significant result. The results confirmed the lack of significant difference in the levels of difficulty represented by the two formats. In addition, no significant interaction was found between delivery format and either text type or general proficiency level. The study concluded that the addition of nonverbal information via video to a traditional, multiple-choice listening test will have no appreciable effect, leaving the choice of whether to include it to test designer judgement, based on both construct and pragmatic factors.

With the increasing use of computer-delivered tests of speaking, such as TOEFL iBT, the question is often asked as to whether candidates are unfairly affected by this mode of testing compared with a face-to-face interview such as is used in IELTS. Kiddle and Kormos (2011) conducted a study to look into the effect of mode of response on test takers' performance in a speaking test delivered online. A face-to-face version of the test was designed and performances in the online test and the mocked-up face-to-face version were compared. Results of an MFRM analysis showed that the two modes of delivery did not differ significantly in terms of difficulty levels. A follow-up questionnaire indicated that while the majority of test takers believed that both versions were fair tests of their speaking ability, the face-to-face version received significantly higher ratings. The popularity of the face-to-face version is an aspect of the face validity of the test, but does not seem to have been a factor in actual performance.

A different issue, this time a listening test design issue, was the focus of a study by Papageorgiou, Stevens, and Goodwin (2012), who explored the relative difficulty of dialogic and monologic input in L2 listening comprehension assessment. Rasch measurement theory was used to analyse test takers' performance on listening items developed to accompany three pairs of stimuli, each consisting of a monologue and a dialogue with identical content and vocabulary. The findings of this study partially supported the hypothesis that items associated with dialogic input were easier for test takers than the same items associated with identical monologic input; that is, it seems easier for listeners to retrieve content successfully from conversational interaction than from monologues. This interesting study has implications for developing L2 listening assessments at the desired level of difficulty, and provides insight into the nature of second language listening.

Exploring the performance of different subgroups

A persistent concern in educational and other forms of testing is the possibility that test items, test content, and test tasks are biased in favour of one group of test takers over another, which constitutes another kind of potential unfairness. Differential item functioning (DIF) occurs in test items when two groups of test takers with equal ability on the construct being measured (for example, listening or writing) have unequal probabilities of answering an item correctly (see Chapter 7 for an extended discussion of DIF analysis). In other words, items display DIF when they function in favour of a subgroup of test takers without any basis in the construct being measured. If test items are found to display DIF, they are believed to be unfair to test takers because one subgroup of test takers will have a better chance of answering the items correctly than the other subgroup, despite their same ability on the underlying construct. DIF can also occur in relation to item bundles or to the entire test. Rasch analysis is one way of identifying the potential DIF in test items.

A study undertaken by Aryadoust, Goh, and Kim (2011) represents a typical example of using the Rasch model to investigate gender-based DIF in a high-stakes language assessment, the listening sub-test of the Michigan English Language Assessment Battery (MELAB). The study examined both uniform DIF (UDIF) and non-uniform DIF (NUDIF). Whereas UDIF occurs when a test item favours different subgroups with the same ability on the underlying construct, NUDIF occurs when a test item only favours subgroups at particular levels of trait ability. Take gender-related DIF as an example. If a test item functions in favour of male test takers over their female counterparts consistently, this item is considered as displaying UDIF; however, if the same trend is identified but only on certain subgroups of test takers (for example, those with higher ability on the trait that is being measured), this item can be considered as displaying NUDIF. (See Chapter 7 for a more detailed explanation of these terms.)

Whereas most previous studies only examined UDIF, Rasch-based DIF analysis enables one to detect both UDIF and NUDIF. The data set used in this study consisted of the performance of 852 test takers on 50 listening items in MELAB with 427 male test takers and 425 female test takers. The study focused on gender as a potential cause of DIF. UDIF analysis revealed eight items with significant DIF (five items favouring male test takers and three items favouring female test takers). Next, the subgroups were further divided into lower- and high-ability subclasses. The analyses revealed 24 instances of significant NUDIF. (In this case, the performance of male and female subgroups of differing ability levels were compared, thus allowing both cross-gender and cross-ability level comparisons to be made.)

Once DIF has been identified, researchers need to explain what might have caused the DIF and test developers need to decide whether anything is to be done to improve the fairness of the test instrument. One explanation was that low-ability male test takers were more ready than females to take risks by guessing answers and tended to make successful lucky guesses on difficult test items with unattractive distractors. Their chances of success were enhanced by one feature of the test design: the items were in multiple-choice format with only three choices, so that a guess has a reasonably high chance of being successful. This pattern of guessing was reinforced in the case of distractors with unusually long stems. The authors of the study recommended that 'Test designers should limit the possibility of guessing correctly on test items by increasing answer options to four or even five effectively performing distractors' (p. 381), and that distractor items should be carefully revised.

In a more recent study, Aryadoust (2016) explored the sources underlying biases that cause unfair and imprecise peer assessments in the context of oral presentations among science students in an Asian university. In particular, the study investigated gender and academic major bias in peer assessments. MFRM was utilized to examine the effect of multiple facets (for example, student presenters, their gender, their academic major, and raters) on the student and teacher ratings of oral presentations. In addition, MFRM was also used to adjust the ratings on oral presentations according to gender and academic major biases. The study found that the scores assigned by student raters exhibited good fit to the Rasch model. However, both gender and academic major biases were uncovered. For example, when evaluating the peers of the opposite gender, students' scores were overestimated. The study concluded that, after adjusting for biases, peer-assessment could be a reliable and useful form of alternative assessment, hence lending support to the Esfandiari and Myford (2013) study that we reviewed above.

Summary

In this chapter we have presented a survey of recent research using Rasch analysis in validation studies of language test data, updating an earlier survey (McNamara & Knoch, 2012). We used the survey to identify a range of fairness issues addressed in these studies. One focus, as in previous research, was on the role of raters in influencing estimates of ability in performance assessments, especially in tests of speaking and writing. Recent research has focused on background factors in raters that are associated with this variability, such as their degree of experience as raters, the languages that they know, and so on. If we understand the influence of these factors more clearly, we can perhaps intervene in the training of raters to improve test fairness. Can we improve rater training by giving raters feedback on their recent performance? Though research results appear quite disappointing, as we have seen in this chapter, future research is warranted to understand why giving feedback fails to achieve its intended outcomes. A second focus was found in studies directed at enhancing the technical quality of instruments and procedures used in assessment, in the interests of fairness—for example, by determining whether test items favour subgroups of test takers unfairly.

   In our presentation of a selection of these studies, we have illustrated the potential for Rasch analysis to enhance test fairness, to protect the right of test takers to be assessed fairly. The technical skills required to conduct studies such as these range from the simple and straightforward to the complex. What we hope is clear from our discussion, however, is that technical analysis of Rasch data is not primarily a technical matter at all, but a tool necessary for ensuring the reasonableness and meaningfulness of test scores.

7

Beyond the basics in Rasch measurement

Introduction

In this chapter we will explore some more advanced topics in Rasch measurement for readers who have an interest in gaining a deeper knowledge of the area. As was the case in previous chapters, we will attempt to discuss these topics in an accessible manner, without drawing too much on statistical theory. Topics in this chapter are discussed with two aims in mind: (1) to provide practitioners who use Rasch measurement in their assessment programs with the tools needed to understand and conduct more complicated procedures in Rasch measurement, such as equating and anchoring, and (2) to give readers an understanding of more advanced topics in the area of Rasch measurement. All topics we discuss in this chapter have an impact on fairness. The chapter is organized into four sections: (1) setting up data, (2) identifying initial problems, (3) further investigations and issues, and (4) reporting.

Setting up data

In this section we explore a number of topics relevant to preparing the analysis: (1) sample size, (2) missing data, (3) connectivity and subset connection (rating designs), and (4) anchoring.

Sample size

Sample size requirements in Rasch measurement are an important consideration, in particular, if we want to draw inferences about learners or make decisions about the quality of test items. It is therefore important to have some basic understanding of how sample size influences the outcomes of a Rasch analysis.

Let us start by considering a basic dichotomous analysis conducted in a software package such as Winsteps. Linacre (1994) lists three implications of analysing data with small sample sizes:

1 The estimates are less precise (i.e. there are bigger standard errors).
2 The fit analysis is less powerful.

3 The estimates are less robust (i.e. the estimates are more strongly influenced by unusual observations in the data).

In language assessment, large sample sizes are often not possible. This is particularly the case in classroom assessment contexts, or in the assessment of languages other than English, where fewer test takers may take a test. So what sample size is sufficient to ensure reasonable stable item and person calibration? Linacre (1994) argues that to arrive at reasonably stable values, sample sizes of 50 may be acceptable if the test takers are well targeted to the test. This number is calculated using a formula that ensures that the standard errors are within one logit value. He proposes higher minimum sample sizes for more high-stakes decision-making.

It is also important to remember that Rasch measurement programs such as Winsteps do not differentiate between items and test takers. It is therefore important to also have a sufficient number of items in a data set if stable person estimates are of interest. Based on Wright & Douglas (1975), Linacre recommends a minimum of 30 items in a test. A further important rule of thumb relating to sample size was proposed by Linacre in relation to polytomous data (Linacre, 2002b). He argues that for stable observations, 10 observations per category are required. If the Rasch-Andrich rating scale model is used, then this requirement is usually satisfied (as all items are modelled onto the same scale). However, the same is not the case for the partial credit model. (See Chapter 8 for further discussion of the difference between these models.)

Note that other authors indicate that the sample size estimates described above for both items and test takers may be insufficient and may have to be revised upwards. A number of authors (Draxler, 2010; Draxler & Alexandrowicz, 2015; Kubinger, Rasch, & Yanagida, 2009; Hobart et al., 2012; Smith et al., 2008) have provided more detailed technical discussions of the issue of sample size, which are beyond the scope of this chapter. However, in general, they are in favour of much higher minimum item and sample sizes than those described above.

When applying the many-facets Rasch model, it is also important to consider sample size in relation to the number of facets included in the analysis. Given the data requirements per facet, there is a need to limit the number of facets to be analysed in any single analysis, unless very large data sets are available (Linacre, 1994).

Missing data

The Rasch model is robust in the case of missing data (Bond & Fox, 2015), which is an advantage over techniques based on classical test theory, where data sets often cannot be analysed because of a small number of missing values, or because putative values need to be inferred into the gaps. The Rasch model, however, still requires adequate data density to allow for sufficiently precise calculations. Missing data can, of course, occur for different reasons, and may have different implications in Rasch analyses.

In objectively scored tests, Ludlow and O'Leary (2000) and Linacre (2016) state that it may be worth distinguishing between items that a test taker skipped and those that could not be reached in time. Linacre suggests that these two item types be entered with different missing data codes, and that when items are calibrated, the skipped items should be scored as wrong and the 'not reached' items ignored. When the test takers are calibrated, both item types are scored as wrong. Of course, knowing which items were skipped and which were not reached may not be possible. We recommend analysing the data set in both ways, once treating the missing values as missing and the other time treating them as wrong.

In the case of the many-facets Rasch model, the ability of the Rasch model to handle missing data is very useful as it allows us to create rating designs that do not require full matrices. This can be an advantage in terms of practicality. We discuss this issue in more detail in the following section.

Connectivity and subset connection: rating designs

Test administrators have a number of options when coordinating the rating of performance assessments. For example, they need to consider whether all raters will rate all candidate performances, which can of course be very expensive. In particular, in large-scale assessments, it is usually not practical to have all raters rate all examinees on all tasks. Such a rating design, also called a fully crossed design (see Table 7.1), is not only expensive but time-consuming and logistically complex in many cases.

If a fully crossed design is not possible, the test administrators need to decide which rating design to implement. There are two main issues to consider when choosing a rating design: (1) the amount of overlap between ratings and (2) subset connection. The Rasch model makes it possible to reduce the number of observations (indicated by Xs in Table 7.1). Fewer observations will mean slightly less precise estimation of parameters (for example, candidate ability measures) but this is usually acceptable if the error terms are not large. However, if the Xs are reduced too much, this can result

Rater	Test candidate									
	1	2	3	4	5	6	7	8	9	10
1	x	x	x	x	x	x	x	x	x	x
2	x	x	x	x	x	x	x	x	x	x
3	x	x	x	x	x	x	x	x	x	x
4	x	x	x	x	x	x	x	x	x	x
5	x	x	x	x	x	x	x	x	x	x
6	x	x	x	x	x	x	x	x	x	x

Table 7.1: Fully crossed rating design

in insufficient subset connection. A connected set of ratings is one where every element in a data set is either directly or indirectly linked to every other element (Eckes, 2011). Tables 7.2 to 7.4 set out a number of possible rating designs, each with varying implications for measurement. In Table 7.2, a connected rating design is shown, which saves nearly 50% of the ratings required when compared to a fully crossed design. In this design, each candidate is scored by three raters and each rater only scores a subset of the overall data set. While this rating set is much more efficient than a fully crossed design in terms of costs, the data set is still connected, as each element in each facet is linked to another element. For example, Rater 6 is linked to Rater 1 through common ratings of Candidates 5 and 6. Equally, Candidates 5 and 7 are linked through Rater 1, and so on. While this rating design is much more economical, it is still fairly uneconomical as three raters are rating each performance.

An even more efficient rating design is shown in Table 7.3 (Connected design 2). Around 67% of ratings are saved in comparison to the fully crossed design. There is, of course, also less data available to estimate the Rasch parameters, with a corresponding cost in terms of their precision. Therefore,

Rater	Test candidate									
	1	2	3	4	5	6	7	8	9	10
1	x				x	x	x			
2	x	x				x	x	x		
3	x	x	x				x	x	x	
4		x	x	x				x	x	x
5			x	x	x				x	x
6				x	x	x				x

Table 7.2: Connected design 1

Rater	Test candidate									
	1	2	3	4	5	6	7	8	9	10
1	x					x	x			
2	x	x					x	x		
3		x	x					x	x	
4			x	x					x	x
5				x	x					x
6					x	x				

Table 7.3: Connected design 2

depending on the stakes and purpose of the test, test administrators need to monitor the precision of the candidate measures.

A further reduction in rating is presented in Table 7.4 (Connected design 3). In this design, each candidate is rated by only one rater, except for one candidate, who is rated by all raters. The ratings on this candidate provide the connectivity of the subset. However, in terms of fairness, this design is a little problematic. The parameters for Candidate 10 are estimated with much more data, and therefore the results we get are more precise. This is not fair to Candidates 1 to 9, who are only evaluated by one rater each.

Linacre (1997b) has also proposed alternative rating designs, including a 'minimal effort judging plan', in which few rating points are required. How useful this rating design is in the context of language assessment is not clear—it requires three raters to judge a performance but using only one criterion each. This may not be a large cost-saving for test administrators.

Myford and Wolfe (2000) examined the utility of strengthening rating designs with fewer connections (such as the ones shown in Tables 7.2 and 7.4) by inserting a small number of previously rated benchmark samples into the rating design. (Benchmark samples are sample performances on which several raters have agreed on the scores.) They were able to show the benefit of such a practice and also showed that the highest-scoring benchmark samples produced the most stable link. Benchmarks that were in the middle scoring range and those that were low scoring provided the least stable link. The least consistent benchmark samples (i.e. those that were difficult to rate) provided more stable links than benchmark samples that were more consistent.

All rating designs presented thus far are considered connected designs. However, we can equally have a situation where the data set is not connected. Such data sets are flagged by the FACETS software as displaying disjointed subsets. Disjointed subsets are a problem as there are insufficient links between aspects of the subsets, which would make it impossible to report the parameters of these subsets on the same scale. We would also be unable to make any comparison between the subsets. Table 7.5 presents an example of such a rating design. There is no link between Candidates 1 to 5 and Candidates

Rater	Test candidate									
	1	2	3	4	5	6	7	8	9	10
1	x						x			x
2		x						x		x
3			x						x	x
4				x						x
5					x					x
6						x				x

Table 7.4: Connected design 3

Rater	Test candidate									
	1	2	3	4	5	6	7	8	9	10
1	x	x	x	x	x					
2	x	x	x	x	x					
3	x	x	x	x	x					
4						x	x	x	x	x
5						x	x	x	x	x
6						x	x	x	x	x

Table 7.5: Disjointed rating design

6 to 10. Equally, there is no link between Raters 1 to 3 and Raters 4 to 5. We therefore cannot estimate these subsets on the same logit scale. In other words, we could not compare the severity of Rater 1 with Rater 6 or the ability of Candidate 1 with Candidate 10, for example.

There are several ways to address disjointed subsets. First, as we can see in Connected design 3, it would be possible to add extra ratings by having one or more raters rate candidates across both subsets, or by having one or more candidates rated by raters across both subsets. This is not always possible, however, if no more money is available or if the raters have already finished their rating duties.

A further possibility, if issues with connectivity are diagnosed when no additional ratings are possible, is the use of a procedure called *group anchoring*. (Anchoring is described in more detail in the following section.) In our disjointed data set above, for instance, we would have to make some assumptions about the two groups of raters. We could make the assumption that our two groups of raters are sufficiently large (which is, of course, not the case for our small example data set), and that they have been allocated at random, allowing us to assume that they are rating with similar severity; alternatively, we could anchor the two groups of raters at the same severity measure (for example, at zero logits) and proceed with the analysis without a connected design. In this way, the raters within that group are allowed to float around the zero logit value, as we are not assuming that all raters rate at zero logit severity (just that each subgroup does).

We may also be in a situation where test candidates can choose a certain task to answer, or are provided with a certain task (with not all candidates getting the same task). This is the case in the Occupational English Test (OET), where doctors respond to a different writing task from the one nurses respond to, and so on. In such a situation, we can use *anchoring*, to anchor both tasks at zero difficulty, as we assume that both tasks are of equal difficulty.

Anchoring

At certain times, when setting up or conducting a Rasch analysis, we may want to use values from one analysis in another analysis, or use values from one aspect of our analysis for another aspect. Let us explain why we may want to do this with some examples.

Example 1

We may have data from a writing test in which test takers had the choice of two task types. None of our test takers have responded to both tasks. If we were to enter this data into a FACETS analysis, we would get a warning that we have disjointed subsets (one subset of students who responded to Task A and one group that responded to Task B). This problem impacts the relationship of the measures in the subsets (as discussed in the section on rating designs in this chapter). This means that we cannot compare the measures of the two subsets on the logit scale against each other. Thus, we cannot compare the ability of two students who responded to different tasks. One possible way of dealing with this is to make some assumptions about the data set. For example, we can take the decision that the two tasks are alike in difficulty[1] and specify this in the FACETS software by anchoring the two tasks at the same difficulty level, usually at zero logits. This then allows FACETS to interpret any score differences as differences in ability levels by the test takers. Anchoring is specified in the input file of a FACETS data set by stating next to a facet whether it is anchored, and specifying the anchor value. Figure 7.1 shows an example in which tasks used in a data set (Facet 3 is the task) are all anchored at zero.

A capital A (for 'anchoring') is specified after the facet in the control file, and a zero is specified after each element in the facet. In an analysis conducted in this manner, the tasks will all be shown to be of equal difficulty at logit zero and the other facets in the analysis will be comparable on the same logit scale. While group anchoring is not an ideal solution—because we need to make some assumptions about our data set that may not be warranted (in our case, that the two tasks are of equal difficulty)—it is at least a solution that allows us to continue with the analysis and place all elements onto the same logit scale. If the task types are, in fact, of varying difficulty, then this procedure is problematic, in particular for those test takers who responded to the more

```
3,Task,A

1=Task 1,0

2=Task 2,0

3=Task 3,0

4=Task 4,0
```

Figure 7.1: Control file instructions for anchoring

difficult prompt. A further analysis could examine whether they are of significantly different difficulty.

Example 2

Anchoring is also helpful if we want to make two data sets comparable. This is commonly used in the process of test equating, where two forms of the test are analysed and made statistically comparable to ensure that test takers' scores on one form of a test are comparable to scores on a second form of the test. This is an important fairness issue for test takers, and we take this up in more detail in the section on test equating on page 155. For now, we would like to explain how anchoring is helpful in the process of test equating. One method of test equating, called 'common item equating', requires the test developer to insert a set of common items into the two test forms, which can be taken by different groups of test takers. We can then analyse these common items to see how they have behaved in one test form, and compare them with the second analysis. If we then wanted to move the two test sets into the same frame of reference, we could anchor the item values from the common items in one analysis to the analysis of the second test form. This is described in more detail later in this chapter.

Identifying initial problems

Unidimensionality

Unidimensionality is an important assumption that needs to be addressed in a Rasch analysis. In Rasch measurement, a 'dimension' is an underlying individual attribute that is not directly observable. For example, in the assessment of language abilities, this may refer to 'listening ability' or 'pragmatic competence'. The principle of unidimensionality requires that one individual attribute be measured at a time (Bond & Fox, 2015). This principle might appear to run into conflict with the view espoused by many applied linguists that language ability is always multi-dimensional, thus making the Rasch model inappropriate for analysing language assessment data. The debate over dimensionality will be discussed in detail in Chapter 8. For the moment, we will focus on the psychometric (measurement) dimensionality in the data, which is a requirement of the analysis.

The Rasch model provides a powerful means of detecting psychometric multidimensionality in the data set. Residual-based statistics are routinely used in dimensionality analysis in Rasch measurement. Since the Rasch model is an idealized model that will never be reflected fully in empirical data, there are always discrepancies between the observed scores (i.e. the empirical data) and the values expected by the Rasch model. Such discrepancies are known as 'residuals'. For a unidimensional data set, the Rasch measure (i.e. the dimension extracted by Rasch analysis) should represent the only meaningful dimension; no subdimensions should emerge in the residuals that are substantively interpretable.

How shall we go about investigating whether meaningful dimensions exist in the residuals? Item- and person-fit statistics should be first examined, including infit and outfit mean squares (MnSq) and their associated Z values. Erratic fit statistics are symptomatic of the existence of subdimensions in the residuals. For example, if an item exhibits substantial underfit to the model, it is likely that the item taps into a different ability from the one that is explained by the Rasch model. Next, point-measure (PTMEA) biserial correlations should also be inspected. Items with negative PTMEA correlations suggest that they function in opposite ways to the underlying primary trait explained by the Rasch model, thereby suggesting the existence of competing dimensions.

In addition to fit statistics and PTMEA correlations, a procedure known as principal component analysis of Rasch residuals (PCAR) can assist an analyst in decomposing the residuals. The procedure involves a standard Rasch analysis, followed by a principal component analysis of the residuals that remain after the linear Rasch measure has been extracted. If PCAR results indicate that meaningful dimensions emerge from the residuals, we have reason to believe that the test is not unidimensional—it involves both a dimension extracted by the Rasch model and additional dimensions in the Rasch residuals.

If dimensionality analysis uncovers meaningful, competing dimensions in the data set, language test developers should consider administering the items that tap into different dimensions separately to test takers. It is also recommended that separate test scores be reported to relevant stakeholders (representing test takers' ability on different dimensions) to ensure valid interpretation and use of test scores (American Educational Research Association et al., 2014).

Despite the importance of dimensionality analysis, it does not seem to have been routinely included as an integral component of a Rasch analysis in language assessment research. In their survey of differential item functioning (DIF) research in language assessment, Ferne and Rupp (2007) observed that only eight out of 27 studies reported evidence as to data dimensionality in Rasch-based DIF studies. We recommend that language assessment researchers include dimensionality analysis when applying the Rasch model and report relevant evidence. Detailed instructions on how to investigate unidimensionality are available on our companion website (www.oup.com/elt/teacher/fjla).

Local independence

Local independence of test items is another important measurement property that needs to be addressed in a Rasch analysis. Local independence requires that test takers' responses to one item should not be affected by or hinge on their responses to other items in the test. In language assessment, however, this principle is sometimes violated. For example, it is not unusual for test designers to develop several items based on a single section of a text, or on one of a series of shorter texts, particularly in the assessment of listening and reading. Cloze procedure tests may also raise issues of local independence. Test takers' correct responses to one item may be closely dependent on whether they can get the previous item(s) correct. Violation of this principle may result in biased person-ability and item-difficulty estimate (Eckes, 2011).

No specific statistical test is recommended to examine local independence. Nonetheless, a number of empirical indicators are available. Fit statistics may be a useful indicator: if items exhibit overfit to the Rasch model, this suggests that there is less variability in responses to these items than the model expects. One explanation for this is that the content of the item may be dependent on the content of an earlier item.

An inspection of Pearson's correlations for the Rasch item residuals (provided as part of the output of Winsteps) may also be used to explore local independence. We would expect the residuals of pairs of items to differ from one another, and not be correlated. If the items' residuals are found to be substantially correlated with each other after the extraction of the Rasch measure through a standard Rasch analysis, it is reasonable to speculate that these item pairs may be related to each other, thus suggesting local dependence.

The violation of the principle of local independence may result in biased person-ability and item-difficulty estimates, which, in consequence, raise legitimate concerns over the fairness of the test, particularly when the results are used to make high-stakes decisions. So what measures should be taken if empirical indicators suggest the violation of this principle? First, test developers should take this principle into consideration when developing a language test and investigate any potential for dependence between and among items through content analysis and pilot studies. If, however, *post hoc* analyses indicate local dependence among items, and it is not possible to revise the items at this point, then the items that share the common stimulus could be combined into a polytomous super-item. Next, a polytomous Rasch model, such as the rating scale model or partial credit model, should be applied to rerun the analysis. It is worth noting that while such a procedure helps to tackle the problem of local item dependency within a testlet (i.e. items sharing a common stimulus), it also results in loss of measurement information at the item level (Baghaei, 2008). Therefore, the issue of local dependence is probably best addressed at the stage of test development and trialling.

Further investigations and issues

Test equating

Test equating is used when we want to link several tests or test forms. For example, it is used when we create a new test form for an already-existing test, and we want to know where the pass/fail points (or other decision-making points) are on the new form in relation to the existing form. Test equating addresses an important fairness issue, that is, that test takers taking two forms of the test (either in the same sitting of the test or on different days) and receiving the same score should have the same level of ability in the underlying trait. We need, therefore, to ensure that these two scores have the same meaning. Even if test forms are designed to be equivalent in terms of the underlying test specifications, it is only through a carefully designed process of trialling and test equating that we can ensure that test takers are not advantaged or disadvantaged by taking one of several possible test forms.

One way to understand test equating is through the analogy of thermometers (Linacre, 2011). We are all familiar with two well-known measuring systems to measure temperature: Celsius and Fahrenheit. They are both designed to measure the same underlying property (temperature), but they use different measurement scales. Fortunately, there are points that both scales have in common (i.e. they both have a specific boiling point and a specific ice-melting point), which we can use to compare the two measurement scales. These two points can serve as anchor points. With the use of these anchor points, we can compare the two scales to establish what each temperature point on one scale would be on the other.

When equating two test forms with each other, we also need something that is common to both tests, so we can peg the two test forms against each other. There are many different equating techniques available; however, in this chapter, we want to briefly mention two: (1) common item equating and (2) common person equating. In the case of common item equating, the two test forms are administered on two separate occasions to different groups of test takers. On each occasion, some test items are the same and these items, commonly referred to as anchor items or common items, provide the link between the two test forms, and help us peg one form against the other. In common person equating, two groups of test takers take the two different test forms on different occasions, with some test takers being the same. These test takers then provide the link when the two test forms are equated.

Common item equating is very commonly used and probably preferred over common person equating. It is practical in that extra items can easily be inserted (but possibly not counted) in operational administrations of tests, and it is cheaper, as test takers do not need to be asked to take a test twice, or to take two tests, as is the case with common person equating. Asking test takers to take two forms of the same test is problematic as they may become fatigued, which results in less stable candidate ability estimates. Item difficulty estimates used in common item equating are more stable.

A pre-condition for test equating is that the two tests that are equated to each other should be measuring the same underlying construct. This is important, as otherwise it is likely that test takers would be ordered differently by the test, making equating impossible. In language testing, if two test forms have been developed based on a common set of well-developed specifications, this should not be a problem.

Linacre (2016) recommends a minimum number of five common items to be used for common item equating. These items should be uniformly distributed across the item difficulties. More common items are preferable, as not enough items may be available if some misfit or change their item difficulties drastically in the two administrations. (This is known as 'item drift'.)

In equating, we commonly call the existing test form to which we want to equate a new test form the 'reference form'. We will now briefly describe the procedures for equating two test forms using common item equating. Full instructions on how to do this in Winsteps are available on the companion site (www.oup.com/elt/teacher/fjla).

The procedures for conducting a common item analysis are as follows. First, an analysis of the reference form is conducted. Let us assume it has 30 test items of which the first 13 are the common items that have also been used in the new test form. Once the analysis of the reference form in Winsteps is complete, an item file is requested from the output files menu. From this file, all items that are not common items are deleted. Table 7.6 (see page 158) shows the information about the common items included in the item file for our reference form.

The same procedure is then followed when the new test form is analysed. Then the statistics of how these 13 common items performed across the two test versions are compared using a scatterplot. In the scatterplot, the item measures of the two sets of anchor items from the two test versions are plotted (one test form on the y-axis and the other on the x-axis). We expect the trend line plotted through these data points to be parallel to the identity line (i.e. a line plotted through the zero point of the scatterplot). This provides us with information about whether any of the anchor items are outliers, that is, whether any the items functioned differently in the two instruments (and fall outside the confidence intervals in the scatterplot). Figure 7.2 (see page 159) shows the scatterplot for the anchor items in our two data sets.

It can be seen that almost all items fall within the confidence intervals (Item 2 is located slightly outside these lines—we could either live with this or delete it from further analysis). The results show that the anchor items are generally behaving similarly across the two test forms.

The next aspect to check is whether the items across the two test forms are equally discriminating. This can be checked by examining the empirical slope of the trend line in the scatterplot. If the slope is close to 45 degrees through zero, then the item discrimination is similar. In that case, equating procedures only need to adjust for item difficulty. Burga Leon (2008) presents a number of courses of action that can be taken if the trend line and the identity line are not parallel, suggesting that the anchor items in the two test forms may not be equally discriminating. On the one hand, if the trend line runs within the confidence intervals on the graph and we cannot reject the hypothesis that the trend line is statistically parallel to the identity line, Burga Leon then recommends using the item difficulties of the test form we are more confident in (usually the reference form) and using these values as anchor values for the other form. On the other hand, if the trend line is very different from the identity line, we could use equating to bring the items into the same frame of reference; however, we should be aware that this difference may indicate that the tests are measuring different constructs. If this is the case, we do not only need to adjust for item difficulty, but also for item discrimination in our item equating procedures. In other words, we need to convert the values from one

;ENTRY	MEASURE	ST	COUNT	SCORE	MODLSE	IN.MSQ	IN.ZST	OUT.MS	OUT.ZS	DISPL	PTMA	WEIGHT	OBSMA	EXPMA	PMA-E	RMSR	WMLE	G	M	R	NAME
1	-.72	1	79.0	63.0	.33	.72	-1.62	.50	-1.06	-.01	.61	1.00	89.9	83.5	.47	.29	-.70	1	R	.	A1
2	2.35	1	79.0	24.0	.29	1.30	2.01	1.55	1.48	.00	.31	1.00	73.4	77.6	.49	.45	2.33	1	R	.	A2
3	-.06	1	79.0	56.0	.29	.94	-.34	.75	-.65	.00	.55	1.00	75.9	78.8	.50	.37	-.05	1	R	.	A3
4	-2.73	1	79.0	75.0	.57	.83	-.26	.29	-.72	-.01	.42	1.00	96.2	95.5	.32	.18	-2.62	1	R	.	A4
5	.19	1	79.0	53.0	.28	.92	-.54	.87	-.31	.00	.55	1.00	81.0	77.0	.51	.38	.19	1	R	.	A5
6	2.03	1	79.0	28.0	.28	1.20	1.50	1.01	.14	.00	.43	1.00	63.3	75.6	.51	.44	2.02	1	R	.	A6
7	.79	1	79.0	45.0	.27	.88	-1.01	.87	-.44	.00	.58	1.00	78.5	74.4	.53	.39	.80	1	R	.	A7
8	-1.32	1	79.0	68.0	.37	1.08	.43	.89	.01	-.01	.40	1.00	84.8	87.5	.43	.32	-1.29	1	R	.	A8
9	.42	1	79.0	50.0	.28	.96	-.30	1.59	1.82	.00	.51	1.00	75.9	75.6	.52	.40	.43	1	R	.	A9
10	-.62	1	79.0	62.0	.32	1.34	1.81	1.82	1.55	-.01	.27	1.00	75.9	82.8	.48	.41	-.60	1	R	.	A10
11	-1.98	1	79.0	72.0	.44	1.28	.95	3.23	2.12	-.01	.14	1.00	92.4	92.0	.38	.29	-1.92	1	R	.	A11
12	.87	1	79.0	44.0	.27	1.17	1.40	1.19	.78	.00	.44	1.00	67.1	74.2	.53	.45	.87	1	R	.	A12
13	-3.60	1	79.0	77.0	.78	.77	-.18	.68	.09	-.01	.30	1.00	98.7	97.5	.26	.13	-3.38	1	R	.	A13

Table 7.6: Common item table

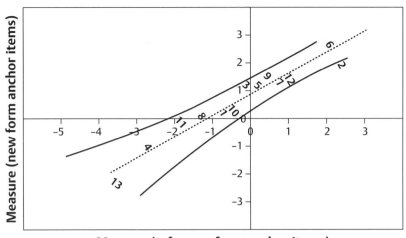

Figure 7.2: Scatterplot: item measures of anchor items in new and reference form

test form to more closely reflect those of the other. Once the conversion is complete, we can compare the two test forms because they are in the same frame of reference. On the companion website (www.oup.com/elt/teacher/fjla) we present detailed instructions on how to use common item equating in Winsteps using sample test materials.

Differential item functioning

Differential item functioning (DIF) analysis refers to a series of techniques for detecting potentially biased items in a language test. DIF occurs in an item when two subgroups of test takers with equal ability overall have unequal probabilities of correctly answering the item; that is, there is evidence from the differential performance of the two groups that the item represents a different level or perhaps a different kind of challenge for one group compared to the other, and is thus not contributing in an equal way to the measurement of test takers' ability. The existence of DIF may raise legitimate concerns over the validity and fairness of a language test, given that the purpose of a test is to ensure that fair decisions can be made about all test takers based on their performance on the test, irrespective of their backgrounds (for example, American Educational Research Association et al., 2014). Such an analysis can also be performed on several items together, known as differential bundle functioning (DBF), and on the entire test, known as differential test functioning (DTF).

In a typical DIF analysis, there is commonly a focal group, which is the group that is potentially unfairly disadvantaged on the items under analysis, and a reference group. Depending on the purpose of the test and the context where the test is developed and used, test takers are often grouped into focal and reference groups according to their gender, ethnicity, or academic discipline (see Ferne & Rupp, 2007). For example, a gender-based DIF analysis divides test takers into two subgroups, and then investigates whether male and female test takers with the same overall ability have the same probability of getting each item correct.

A useful distinction can be made between uniform DIF (UDIF) and non-uniform DIF (NUDIF). The former occurs when a test item favours different subgroups with the same overall ability on the trait being measured, whereas the latter occurs when a test item favours subgroups at different levels of trait ability (Linacre, 2012). For example, if a test item functions overall and uniformly in favour of male test takers over female test takers with the same ability, the item is considered as displaying UDIF; if an item favours only low-ability male test takers over low-ability female test takers, or if an item favours only high-ability male test takers over high-ability female test takers, but the DIF effect is restricted to these particular ability subgroups, the item can be considered to display NUDIF.

The existence of NUDIF suggests interactions between test takers' ability on the latent trait and their group membership. A failure to consider NUDIF, according to Ferne and Rupp (2007), can have serious practical implications. For example, without evidence about NUDIF, the development of cut scores may not be well-informed. As a consequence, this could lead to test fairness concerns, particularly when the results are used to make high-stakes decisions.

The Rasch model has often been used to detect DIF in language tests. The following procedures are often followed in a Rasch-based DIF analysis in Winsteps. The output from an analysis is inspected to check item fit, and checks for unidimensionality and local independence are carried out. DIF analysis follows. Winsteps output provides several kinds of information to assist an analyst in determining whether significant DIF occurs to a test item. Take a gender-based DIF analysis as an example. Winsteps provides difficulty measures of the items for males and females respectively, known as DIF measures, as well as their standard errors of measurement. It then compares the DIF measures between the two subgroups, yielding a DIF contrast that serves as a measure of DIF effect size. A small contrast indicates negligible difference between the focal and reference group in item difficulty measures, suggesting that significant DIF does not occur to this item. Conversely, a marked contrast is indicative of significant DIF.

The contrast should be at least 0.5 logits for DIF to have an impact (Linacre, 2012). A statistical procedure, known as the Rasch-Welch t-test, is used to ascertain whether the contrast represents a significant difference between the local difficulties for the two subgroups. A significant result (i.e. $p < 0.05$) indicates a noticeable DIF impact.

For UDIF and NUDIF, item characteristic curves (ICC) can be used as effective indicators. Recall that UDIF occurs when ability level and group membership do not show significant interactions. In other words, an item is considered as exhibiting UDIF if it functions uniformly in favour of one group over the other. As such, the ICCs of the subgroups should have similar slopes but different intercepts on the y-axis. However, when NUDIF occurs, ability level comes into interaction with group membership. For example, an item functions in favour of one group of test takers over the other in lower-ability test takers. The trend is reversed when it comes to higher-ability test takers. As a result, the ICCs of the subgroups will differ in slopes and intersect. The point of intersection is where both groups should have equal chance of getting the item correct.

Figure 7.3 displays the ICCs of an item displaying NUDIF. As shown in this figure, the ICCs of males and females have different slopes and intercepts on the y-axis, and they intersect at about 0.3 logits on the x-axis. For the lower-ability group (ability measures < 0.3 logits), males have a higher probability of getting this item correct than females. The trend is reversed for test takers with ability measures > 0.3 logits, where the item works in favour of females. On the companion website we present detailed instructions on how to perform DIF analysis in Winsteps (www.oup.com/elt/teacher/fjla).

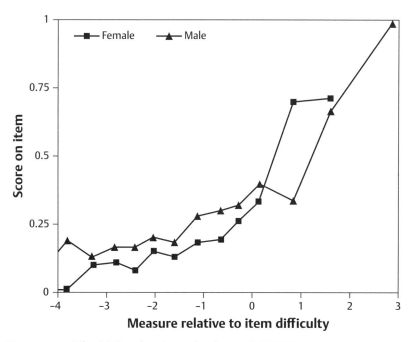

Figure 7.3: The ICCs of an item displaying NUDIF

Item banking and computer-adaptive testing

One of the advantages of Rasch approaches is that, via what is known as computer-adaptive testing, they enable the tailoring of test questions to the ability level of the candidate in objectively scored tests. This can be seen to contribute to fairness, as time is used more efficiently, and more precise estimates of candidate ability (particularly if the candidate is very strong or very weak) are produced. The fact that candidates will take different (but equivalent) versions of a test also contributes to test security, an issue of fairness.

Consider the situation that occurs in many language programs: at the beginning of the course, a relatively large number of students need to be sorted into classes, often at very differing levels of proficiency, and within a short time period. Such programs might use a multiple-choice test of grammar and vocabulary, but if there is only one form for the entire group of students, this means that lower-proficiency students will encounter a large number of questions that are too hard for them, and higher-proficiency students will encounter many questions they can answer easily, and which don't help in distinguishing finer levels of ability within this higher-proficiency group. A solution is to create a large number of items whose relative difficulties have been determined in trialling (possibly from multiple tests appropriate for each of the proficiency levels being targeted), which have subsequently been equated (linked to form a single scale of ability and difficulty). Such a large set of items is known as an 'item bank'. When a candidate takes a computer-adaptive test, the initial selection of a small number of items from across the range of proficiency levels allows the computer to determine roughly what level the student is at; it then selects items to be answered that are at that level. If the initial assumption about the ability level is wrong, so that the student has fewer or more correct answers than expected, the computer can again adjust its estimate and eventually home in on the relevant level, allowing a finer discrimination among students at that level. Eventually, when the estimate of the student's ability stabilizes, and adding further questions is unlikely to alter the estimate, the testing stops and the ability estimate is reported.

Computer-adaptive testing is expensive to develop initially, as it requires substantial investment in the development of the item bank, but this may be repaid in the efficiency of the testing that results as well as in the accuracy of ability estimates—if there are enough items of sufficiently different levels of difficulty to allow fine discrimination of ability levels.

Reporting

In this section we briefly cover a number of issues relating to reporting achievement using Rasch-based tests. Clearer and better score reporting is obviously fairer for all stakeholders.

Converting logits to meaningful units and rescaling

The logit scale, a scale reporting the probability of success on items of varying difficulty by candidates of varying ability, was introduced in Chapter 3. This scale can be confusing for non-experts, as zero on the logit scale usually represents the average difficulty of items, and abilities are expressed in terms of how likely it is that a person of a given ability would succeed on that item or at attaining a given score point from a judge. This means that some ability estimates will be negative (the individuals with those estimates will have a less than 50% chance of getting an item of average difficulty right), and, in general, logit scores will be difficult to interpret. Even if we convert probabilities expressed as logits into probabilities expressed in more familiar terms—percentage chance of success, as in Table 3.3 (see page 35)—this will still not meet normal expectations for score reporting.

We need a new reporting scale. There are a number of different approaches to this, but some are conceptually and computationally a bit tricky for the novice. A simplified approach is more transparent.[2] First, we multiply each logit score by a factor of 10, which means that 10 scale score points makes one logit, and one scale score point corresponds to 0.1 of a logit; this allows for sufficient detail in reporting differences in ability. In that way a person whose ability was estimated at, say, 1.3 logits would have this transformed into 13 scale points. But what about someone of below-average ability, say, −1.8 logits? They would have a scale score of −18. So, in order to avoid negative scores, we add a number to all the scores. The number we choose will represent average ability, so it is good to use a sufficiently large number so that an average ability will look reasonable —say, 120, as used in reporting scores on some of the Progressive Achievement Tests developed by ACER. Thus, an average score would be 120, someone at 1.3 logits would get 133, and someone at −1.8 would get 102.[3] More complicated equations using the mean ability of a population and its standard deviation are used in tests such as the PISA assessments of reading.[4] These are set out helpfully in Bond & Fox (2015), Smith (2000), and Wright & Stone (1979), and routinely calculated in Winsteps (see examples of output in Bond & Fox, 2015).

Mapping abilities and change over time

The output from a Rasch analysis defines a scale of ability, and the Wright map, introduced in Chapter 3, gives a visual representation of this: it indicates the location of tasks in terms of difficulty, and the location of individuals in terms of their likely mastery of each of the tasks. This leads to an intriguing possibility: by defining what is involved in tasks at various levels of difficulty, we can use the information to define ability in terms of the demands of those tasks that learners have mastered or have yet to master, and so have a sound empirical basis for qualitative descriptions of ability.

A version of this approach was used by Brian North in the creation of the scales of the Common European Framework of Reference (Council of Europe, 2001; North, 2000). In this study, he asked teachers to rank statements of ability ('can-do' statements) in terms of their relative difficulty for students typical of the ones they taught, and whose abilities in general they were familiar with. He then used Rasch analysis to scale these judgements. The items in the analysis were the can-do statements. He then identified groupings of can-do statements at various levels of difficulty, and used these to create the levels and associated definitions of the CEFR scale. He and his colleagues have used the same approach in a recent major elaboration and extension of the scale (North, Goodier, & Piccardo, 2017).

In an early use of Rasch scaling for the purpose of mapping ability, the authors of an Australian test of reading comprehension for L1 speakers, TORCH, identified what they claimed were the skills underlying successful performance on items at varying levels of difficulty:

> An important feature of TORCH is that all items have been analysed to identify the types of reading tasks required by students to complete each item. Eleven distinct tasks were identified:
>
> > Provide the subject of the story when given multiple references.
> > Complete sentences copied verbatim from the text.
> > Complete very simple rewordings.
> > Complete rephrased sentences.
> > Connect pronouns with previously mentioned nouns.
> > Connect ideas separated in the text.
> > Provide a detail in the presence of distracting ideas.
> > Provide a detail in the presence of competing answers.
> > Provide evidence of having understood the motive underlying a series of actions.
> > Reconstruct the writer's general message from specific statements.
> > Infer emotion from a few scattered clues and from the writer's tone.
>
> (Mossenson, Hill, & Masters, 1987, p. 2)

These skills were then used as the basis for a mapping of the growth of student abilities in reading (Mossenson et al., 1987, reproduced in McNamara, 1996). The process by which the skill demands of individual items was determined was not documented. It turns out, however, that applying this method to the development of second language reading skills was not straightforward. Alderson and Lukmani (1989) showed that judges had difficulty agreeing on the subskills involved in particular reading test items, and their judgements of the difficulty of the subskills underlying particular items bore little relationship to the empirical difficulty of the items when they were administered to learners. One problem subsequently identified in this study was that it involved the retrofitting of descriptions of subskills to already existing items, rather than items that had been written to a subskill specification. This latter approach was adopted by Kirsch and Mosenthal (1988) in a study exploring levels of adult literacy in the US. They defined a number of underlying variables, which, they proposed, explained the difficulty of document texts (timetables, forms, and the like) and wrote items to those specifications, thereby generating *a priori* predictions of item difficulty. Rasch analysis of performance on those items confirmed the predictions to a high degree. Kirsch implemented the approach in developing specifications for sub-tests of reading (Enright et al., 2000) and listening (Bejar, Douglas, Jamieson, Nissan, & Turner, 2000) in a large-scale test revision project for the Test of English as a

Foreign Language (TOEFL). The approach was found to work more success-fully for reading than for listening items. It seems that it remains difficult to know in advance what makes test items difficult for candidates, particularly in listening tests. This is unfortunate, and deserves more research, as the abil-ity to report criterion-referenced achievements from tests of these skills remains an attractive idea.

Scaling and change in ability over time

A further possibility for reporting combines the idea of test linking with the development of skills development maps. Tests of differing levels of difficulty can be linked through the processes of common person or common item equating, described above. Here, the techniques of equating are used not to determine the extent to which two forms of a test are equivalent to each other, so that candidates are not disadvantaged by taking one form over another, but to develop a scale of ability that can be used to measure progress over time. The TORCH reading tests mentioned above (Mossenson et al., 1987) consist of a series of reading tests suitable for children of different ages, rep-resenting increasing cognitive demands as the child's reading ability develops. Such tests are not intended to be equivalent in difficulty, but of increasing difficulty. Using common item or common person equating, the pairwise rela-tive difficulty of a series of tests can be established, with checks carried out to ensure the unidimensionality of the construct being measured across the tests. In this way, over the period of a learning program, for example, the years at school, the growth in ability can be tracked on a single scale. The potential for this kind of longitudinal mapping does not appear to have been exploited in second language assessment, but its potential usefulness in research on lan-guage development over time suggests it would be helpful if such longitudinal mapping were developed using Rasch techniques.

Summary

In this chapter we have introduced further measures that test developers can take using Rasch methods to improve test fairness. These include (1) quality assurance methods for setting up the data for the analysis and (2) detecting and remedying initial problems. It addresses how different forms of a test can be compared statistically with the intention of removing test form as a factor in the score that candidates get—an obvious source of unfairness. Test forms of overlapping but differing degrees of difficulty can be linked, and the existence of item banks (created in a similar way, covering a wide range of ability and difficulty, can lead to the automatic tailoring of test forms to individual candidate ability; this allows for more efficient and accurate measurement. We have also introduced methods for detecting unfair bias in test items that may adversely affect particular groups of test takers. Finally, we have discussed ways of interpreting and reporting test scores to make the outcomes of assessment more transparent to stakeholders. In the next chapter we will explore a number of more technical conceptual issues in Rasch measurement, which again have an impact on aspects of the fairness of tests.

Activities on the website

The data sets used in this chapter are provided on the companion website (www.oup.com/elt/teacher/fjla), with some activities for readers who are interested in exploring unidimensionality, test equating, and DIF analysis further.

Notes

1 Merely assuming that two writing tasks or speaking tasks are of equal difficulty is, of course, problematic. However, this is an assumption that many test developers in second language assessment make. This is often made on the basis of well-designed test specifications, which are designed to keep aspects of task design constant across prompts. Such performance assessments are, at times, not statistically equated (but see Muraki, Hombo, & Lee, 2000, for a review of some methods of statistical equating for performance assessments).

2 We are grateful to Andrew Stephanou of the Australian Council for Educational Research for suggesting this helpful approach.

3 https://www.acer.org/pat, retrieved 6 November, 2017.

4 http://www.oecd.org/pisa, retrieved 6 November, 2017.

8

Data, models, and dimensions

Introduction

In this chapter we explore a number of conceptual issues underlying the applications of Rasch modelling to language test data. We have found that understanding more deeply the thinking underlying Rasch measurement makes users more confident, and allows them to deal more independently with issues that arise in the analysis. We begin with a conceptual review of the family of Rasch models, introduced in earlier chapters. We then consider some debates about the appropriateness of Rasch modelling for the analysis of language test data. These are issues that surfaced particularly when Rasch analysis was first introduced to the field of language testing research: questions about the status of Rasch modelling versus the models available in other branches of item response theory; and the question of test dimensionality. In the last section of the chapter we offer a comparison of the Rasch model with some other statistical techniques that are used in the analysis of language test data: generalizability theory (G-theory) and structural equation modeling (SEM). This section is intended mainly for readers who have an interest in or curiosity about G-theory and/or SEM, and would like to compare the Rasch model with these two methods when analysing language test data. Rudimentary knowledge of G-theory and SEM should suffice to understand our discussions here.

The Rasch family of models

In this section we offer a conceptual overview of the family of Rasch models. Each of these models has been introduced separately in earlier chapters; the discussion is intended to present the whole family of models together, and to offer a more detailed discussion of the conceptual character of each.

Rasch analysis has developed considerably since Georg Rasch expounded its mathematical rationales in his seminal text in 1960 (Rasch, 1960/1980), laying the foundation for the basic Rasch model. As a result of the development over the years, several models have been developed and expanded on the basis of the basic Rasch model; these have been used to handle different types of test data yielded by different response formats in language assessments. Therefore, whenever we talk about Rasch measurement theory or the Rasch model, we are referring to it as a data analysis technique to distinguish it from non-Rasch techniques; we may also refer to the Rasch family of models, which consists of the following types:

(1) the basic Rasch model for dichotomous (right/wrong) data (see Chapter 3)
(2) three models for handling data from test items or tasks with multiple score points (for example, in scoring performances on speaking or writing tasks, or on polytomously scored objective item types). Two of these deal with the structure of the rating scales used—one relatively simple, the other more complex (see Chapter 4):

(i) the Andrich or rating scale model (simpler), which assumes that differences between scale points have been interpreted in the same way by judges or scorers
(ii) Masters' partial credit model (more complex), which makes fewer assumptions about the way in which the different scales and scale intervals have been interpreted

The third is Linacre's extended or many-facets Rasch model, where other factors likely to influence the score (in addition to the difficulty of items and the ability of the candidates) can be modelled. This is often used for handling data from rater-mediated performance assessment, where we are interested in rater variability (see Chapter 5).

Data types yielded by different response formats and/or scoring procedures in language assessment call for analysis using different Rasch models. These are summarized in Table 8.1. We have used some response formats or scoring procedures that are commonly employed in language assessment as examples to explain the appropriate analysis for the type of data yielded from them. Dichotomous data, yielded from response formats such as MCQ and True/ False (T/F) questions, are analysed using the basic Rasch model. For all polytomous data, we have a choice between a simpler analysis (using the so-called rating scale model developed by David Andrich) and a more fine-grained analysis (using the so-called partial credit model developed by Geoff Masters). We will review the rationale for using either of these models below (see also Chapter 4). For polytomous data yielded from test formats that take individual rater mediation or other additional facets of the rating context into consideration, Linacre's many-facets Rasch model (MFRM) is used; again, here we have a choice of a simpler or a more fine-grained analysis, depending on factors to be discussed below. While there are several computer programs now available to implement Rasch analysis, the programs Winsteps and FACETS, both developed by Linacre, have been most frequently used by language assessment researchers (see Chapter 6). These two programs have therefore been used throughout this book for illustrative purposes.

In the following section the Rasch family of models that were introduced in Chapters 3 to 5 will be reviewed as a whole, and in more depth. Note that while our discussion of these models is as non-technical as possible, the reader is introduced in the Appendix to some simplified formal statements of the models. For a journal article or research report featuring a Rasch analysis, it is good practice to report the formal statements of the Rasch model(s) selected

Data type	Response format/ Scoring procedure	Possible analysis	Recommended software
dichotomous	MCQ T/F question SAQ (dichotomous scoring)	basic Rasch model	Winsteps
polytomous (without or ignoring individual rater factors)	SAQ (with multiple score points) rating scale Likert scale semantic differential scale	polytomous form of Rasch model using either rating scale model (Andrich) or partial credit model (Masters)	Winsteps
polytomous (taking individual rater and/or other factors into account)	rating scale Likert scale semantic differential scale	many-facets Rasch model (Linacre) using either rating scale model (Andrich) or partial credit model (Masters)	FACETS

Note: MCQ = multiple-choice question; T/F = True or False; SAQ = short answer question.

Table 8.1: Data type, response formats/scoring procedures, possible analysis and recommended software

for analysis, together with the analysis software. Manuals for computer programs such as Winsteps and FACETS often make reference to these formal statements, so it is helpful for the reader to be able to recognize them. For quick reference we have also put them in the Appendix of this book.

The basic Rasch model

The basic Rasch model was originally developed by the Danish mathematician Georg Rasch (1960/1980). The American psychometrician Ben Wright invited Rasch to spend some time at the University of Chicago, and subsequently promoted the application of this model in the human sciences (see, for example, Bond & Fox, 2015). The basic Rasch model, also known as the dichotomous Rasch model, handles data from dichotomous items. In Chapter 3 we provided details of the model and showed how to apply it in language assessment. It should be noted that this model is the most fundamental of the Rasch models, and all other models in the family represent various extensions of it. For a more detailed explanation of the model see Wright & Stone (1979).

The rating scale model (Andrich)

The extension of the basic Rasch model to handle polytomous data occurred in two stages. The first is represented by the work of David Andrich. His work enabled the model to handle scores derived from rating scales in general, including those used in judging performances in speaking and writing in language assessment, for example, and Likert and semantic differential scales. Although we can conceive of the ability of test takers as varying along a continuum, rating scale categories represent sections of that continuum, and are given a category name, for example, 'excellent', 'very good', 'good', 'poor', and so on. The categories are typically represented visually on the score sheet or the response sheet with equal intervals between adjacent score categories, as in Figure 8.1.

The scoring categories are ordered visually as representing equal levels of increase in ability along the ability continuum. But we cannot be certain that movement along the continuum of ability is accurately represented in this way. The neat orderliness may not really reflect the actual increase in ability that is required in order for a candidate or a response to be classified as belonging to the next category up. And from the point of view of the test taker, movement along the continuum of the rating scale may actually be very uneven; it may take a very long time to move up a particular level on the scale, compared with movement between two other levels. This is familiar in scales, such as the Common European Framework of Reference for Languages (CEFR), which describes proficiency from that of a beginner to an expert user of the language in only six steps from lowest to highest: A1, A2; B1, B2; C1, C2, and is usually represented as involving equal steps, as in Figure 8.2.

Figure 8.1: Scoring categories (minus score labels) as they appear on a score sheet (giving the impression of a step structure with equal intervals)

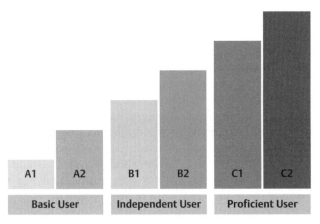

The Common European Framework of Reference for Languages (CEFR)

Figure 8.2: The scale of the Common European Framework of Reference for Languages (CEFR) (https://www.eaquals.org/our-expertise/cefr)

Language learners and language teachers know, however, that while it may not take many weeks of learning to move from A1 to A2, or from A2 to B1, it may take many more weeks to move from B1 to B2, or B2 to C1, and so on. The equal intervals of the scale may give the impression that the learning steps involved in moving along the scale are of equal size or difficulty. The same thing is true of the way in which raters may interpret the difference between score points along a scoring scale. While the visual layout of the scale suggests that movement from one scale step to another assumes equal increases in ability across the whole of the scale, raters may interpret the score points differently and unevenly. The reported step structure (as it is called) may then be visualized as involving unequal steps, as in, for example, Figure 8.3. Modelling this aspect of rater variability allows more accurate, and hence fairer, estimates of candidate ability.

Figure 8.3: Step structure reflecting actual rater behaviour (with unequal steps)

The rating scale model estimates for each step (each movement from one score category to an adjacent higher-score category) how much more ability is required. It determines at which ability point it becomes more likely that a score in the next-highest category will be given—always expressed in probabilities derived from examining the whole data set, as with the basic Rasch model. This allows us to show the actual relative level of challenge of each of the steps on the scale, and also to distinguish more finely among the abilities of test takers. It also allows us to establish, in general, how the judges/raters are interpreting each score point (i.e. each step) on the rating scale with which they are working, and how consistent this interpretation is at each step. We say 'in general' because the estimates of the step structure provided by the analysis—the ability points at which a score in a particular score category becomes more likely than a score in the adjacent score category—are the result of using the data across all scorers/judges/questionnaire respondents and across all items, without making distinctions among judges or items. Put another way, the step structure is considered to be the same for all judges/raters and items. In practice, this may not actually be the case. Not only may judges/raters interpret the rating scales in different ways, but the items or rating dimensions in a rating scale ('pronunciation', 'fluency', 'accuracy' in ratings of a speaking test, for example) may also have different step structures. In other words, the Andrich rating scale model involves a deliberate set of simplifying assumptions (that all judges will interpret the scale steps in the same way across all items and dimensions), similar to the way in which the basic Rasch model makes the simplifying assumption that item discriminations are the same, when they are unlikely to be so in practice. Sometimes, however, differences among judges or across items or rating dimensions are of interest, or a test has items with different scale steps; the partial credit model, to be explained below, represents a refinement in that it allows analysis of step structure for individual judges/raters and individual items.

Partial credit model (Masters)

The second extension of the basic Rasch model is represented by the work of Geoff Masters, who worked with Ben Wright at the University of Chicago. Masters found a way of estimating the step structure of particular items or score dimensions, rather than generalizing across them. Masters observed that, depending on how judges/raters interpret the rating scales with which they are working, even items with the same number of categories may also vary from each other in step structure. In the context of language assessment, judges may be asked to rate a number of aspects of performance. In the case of the Occupational English Test (OET), for example, raters are asked to provide ratings on dimensions such as 'intelligibility' and 'comprehension', among others. Obviously, the step difficulty of ratings on one of these aspects of the performance may be independent of the step difficulty of ratings on the other aspect. For example, it may be that judges are unwilling to give marks readily in the top-scoring category for 'intelligibility', whereas they may be more generous in scoring 'comprehension', if there are no obvious breakdowns in the communicative interaction. To accommodate the need for analysing data of this nature, Masters extended the basic Rasch model into the partial credit model. The most salient feature of this model lies in its ability to separate estimation of step difficulties for each item in a test or aspect in a rating scale, without averaging over items or generalizing over aspects. This is also important for analysing data from marking schemes involving different numbers of response categories for different items, as we saw in Chapter 4. Like the rating scale model, the partial credit model is also used in combination with the many-facets Rasch model in analysing data from rater-mediated performance assessment. The partial credit model is the most general of the three models we have examined so far; the basic Rasch model and the rating scale model may be seen as subsets of the partial credit model.

One final comment on the names 'rating scale model' and 'partial credit model': the names of these models are purely technical and potentially somewhat confusing, as they are not a guide as to which is the most appropriate to use with partial credit or rating scale data in general. Both the rating scale model and the partial credit model can analyse data from rating scales featuring items or aspects with the same number of categories, so which model should be selected for the analysis? The choice of model is determined by the kind of research question being asked of the data, or by the nature of the data itself. For example, sometimes, data sets have different rating scales for different tasks on a sub-test: only the partial credit model is suitable in this case. Similarly, an objectively scored test containing items with different steps requires the partial credit model.

Let us consider, by way of an example, the two aspects of performance in the OET mentioned earlier, i.e. 'intelligibility' and 'comprehension'. If there is a theoretical or empirically grounded reason that judges might have substantially different interpretations of the relative step difficulties on the two aspects, the partial credit model should be considered for analysis. The partial credit model is much more complex than the rating scale model, providing a more fine-grained analysis of each rating dimension separately; it may also require more data on each dimension to yield results with sufficiently small error terms in order to be readily interpretable. A rating scale analysis, which analyses data from all scale dimensions as a single large data set, is able to aggregate data across dimensions, and so is more efficient in data terms. A more parsimonious model (one requiring less data to yield stable results from the analysis) is usually preferred in data analysis if there is no clear evidence that the more fine-grained model can make much difference in the results. When speculation arises about whether the items have the same step difficulties, it is generally a good idea in practice to perform some exploratory analysis using the partial credit model first. If the step difficulties of the items are found to vary greatly from each other, the partial credit model should be retained; if, however the step difficulties of items are found to be similar, then a rating scale model analysis can be performed, as the greater size of the aggregated data set will allow more accurate parameter estimation. In Rasch computer programs such as Winsteps and FACETS, it is easy to specify an analysis using either the partial credit or rating scale models.

Many-facets Rasch model (Linacre)

The further extension of the basic Rasch model developed by Mike Linacre in the late 1980s in Chicago—the many-facets Rasch model (MFRM) (see Chapter 5)—can estimate the impact on score patterns of various factors in the assessment context (known as 'facets' in MFRM). These include, as we have seen, rater characteristics (the severity of particular raters, their consistency in awarding scores, and the way they interpret the scoring scheme), and thus, MFRM has the potential to improve the fairness of performance assessment. The MFRM is in fact now the most general Rasch model, and all other models can be derived from it. For example, the basic Rasch model can be considered as a special case of MFRM with two facets, i.e. person ability and item difficulty. As pointed out previously, a choice between the rating scale model and the partial credit model is required when analysing data with the MFRM.

Debates over Rasch measurement

Despite the numerous merits of Rasch measurement theory, the wide acceptance of the Rasch model by mainstream language assessment researchers as an important analysis method was not entirely smooth. Two debates surrounded the application of the Rasch model following the introduction of the concepts of Rasch measurement theory to the field of language assessment in the 1980s.

The first debate pertained to the relationship between the Rasch model and other item response theory (IRT) models, particularly the two- and three-parameter IRT models.[1] The need to model item discrimination and guessing behaviour lies at the heart of this debate. The second debate concerned the nature of language ability and the unidimensionality assumption that underlies Rasch measurement (Bond & Fox, 2015). As shown in Chapter 6, the application of the Rasch model has increased exponentially in the field of language assessment, notwithstanding these debates. Particularly with the increasing application of MFRM in language assessment, these debates have generally subsided and given way to an acceptance of the substantial practical benefits of applying MFRM to investigate the many issues involved in establishing the fairness of performance assessment (Bachman, 2000; McNamara & Knoch, 2012). However, the practicality of Rasch measurement does not simply dissolve or in itself adequately deal with the arguments of Rasch critics. Instead, as those criticisms are based on misconceptions of Rasch measurement, they need to be addressed theoretically and substantially so that we can feel confident about the appropriateness of applying the Rasch model to the analysis of language assessment data. As previously in this book, the approach we adopt for our discussions will be relatively non-technical and will assume no greater knowledge on the reader's part than in the previous chapters.

Rasch model vs other IRT models

While Rasch models constitute a family of models, as we have seen previously, they are themselves only one development within the broader field of item response theory (IRT). When Rasch models first began to appear, debates raged over the use of Rasch compared with other IRT models, both in the general measurement and the language testing literature; Rasch models had many powerful critics. In this section we will briefly consider the nature of the debate. It is helpful both as a reader of the research literature and as a test developer to have some understanding of the issues involved. As noted earlier, the debate has largely abated in language testing now. This is because the potential of MFRM (which is readily available and relatively easy to use) for the analysis of data from language performance tests is increasingly recognized and exploited in research papers and in the development of performance testing procedures (McNamara & Knoch, 2012; see also Chapter 6).

Item response theory

Item response theory (IRT) is a powerful general measurement theory that was developed in the 1950s and 1960s independently, it seems, in two different locations: by Alan Birnbaum in the United States and by Georg Rasch in Denmark. Rasch's work was promoted and extended by an American, Ben Wright, who attended a series of invitational lectures given by Rasch in Chicago in 1960, and who became his pupil and the advocate of his ideas in North America. Wright (1988) gives an account of the history of this relationship. Two main branches of item response theory (or latent trait theory, as it is sometimes still known), stemming from these two developmental traditions, are recognized: Thorndike (1982) gives a summary of the field. They differ theoretically and practically. The essential feature of both is that they attempt to model statistically patterns in data from performances by candidates on test items in order to draw conclusions about the underlying difficulty of items and the underlying ability of candidates. They differ mainly in the number of item parameters (characteristics of the interaction between a test taker and a test item) estimated in the analysis: Rasch analysis considers one item parameter (item difficulty), while other models consider one or more further parameters (item discrimination and a guessing factor). They also differ theoretically in relation to the question of 'specific objectivity'. Each of these points will now be briefly considered.

Parameters

The Rasch one-parameter model is concerned with defining a single variable or dimension on which to measure two variables: candidate ability and item difficulty. The 'one-parameter' label is thus misleading, as *two* aspects of the interaction between test taker and test item are estimated simultaneously in the analysis: person ability and item difficulty. However, by convention, IRT models are distinguished from each other by referring to how many characteristics of the item are being estimated. In traditional ('classical') analysis of item characteristics, the discrimination of items (the extent to which the item discriminates between higher- and lower-scoring candidates) is also calculated; this is (deliberately) not done directly in a Rasch analysis. It is a requirement of the Rasch model that items are equally discriminating. This is unlikely to be the case in most tests, and has caused some understandable consternation, even confusion, among language test developers and researchers, to the point where some have questioned the value of the Rasch model for the analysis of dichotomous data. In fact, the Rasch model can handle data from items that do not conform to this assumption (as most items will not have the same discrimination). Item-fit statistics, which are sensitive to departures from the mean discriminating power of items in the test, identify items whose discrimination is markedly different. Information on how well the data being analysed conforms (or otherwise) to the expectations of the model, and the consequences of such misfit, are thus routinely available as output from the analysis; in other words, there are built-in checks of the model's assumptions, the extent to which they are being violated, and the consequences of any such violation in relation to any data set. The Rasch assumption should not be regarded as just a blindness to the facts, but as a deliberate simplifying working assumption. We will consider this issue further below. One practical advantage of the one-parameter Rasch model is that Rasch analysis can be done with smaller data sets than those required for the two- and three-parameter models.

The two-parameter IRT model (Birnbaum, 1968; Hambleton, Swaminathan, & Rogers, 1991; Lord & Novick, 1968) includes an additional item parameter of *discrimination*. The three-parameter model (Hambleton, Swaminathan, & Rogers, 1991; Lord, 1980; Lord & Novick, 1968) incorporates a further parameter, this time for *guessing*. The fact that the Rasch model does not estimate item discrimination and guessing parameters (in the case of dichotomously scored items) may not, in practice, be as significant as it may seem at first sight. As has been pointed out above, although the Rasch model does not estimate item discrimination directly, information on discrimination is available indirectly from the results of the analysis in information on item fit, as was shown in Chapter 3. Additionally, although the three-parameter model is specifically designed to deal with guessing in multiple-choice format tests, the one-parameter model has been shown not to result in a high level of error, even when guessing is a significant factor in the performance of candidates; in other words, the Rasch model is robust (Choppin, 1982; Izard, 1981). On the other hand, Choi and Bachman (1992) have demonstrated that, for a particular set of dichotomous data, the two- and three-parameter models showed consistently greater model-data fit than the one-parameter model, and argue against the use of the Rasch model with such data on these grounds; they also strongly recommend that the issue of model-data fit should be addressed in any study in which a choice of models is possible (that is, in which dichotomous data are involved). It is not clear, nevertheless, what the practical consequences of this lack of fit might be, for example, on ability estimates; this was not done in the Choi & Bachman (1992) study, and also needs to be investigated.

Rasch models and objective measurement: the property of 'specific objectivity'

There are also theoretical arguments in favour of using Rasch models over other IRT models: these relate to the nature of 'objective measurement' (Wilson, 1991) and the property, unique to the Rasch model, of 'specific objectivity' (Rasch, 1966). Rasch (1961) himself defines the features of 'objective measurement' in the following way:

> The comparison between two stimuli should be independent of which particular individuals were instrumental for the comparison; and it should also be independent of which other stimuli within the considered class were or might also have been compared. Symmetrically, a comparison between two individuals should be independent of which particular stimuli within the class considered were instrumental for the comparison; and it should also be independent of which other individuals were also compared, on the same or on some other occasion.

(Rasch, 1961, pp. 331–332)

These features are subsumed under the technical term 'specific objectivity', which is explained by Wilson as follows:

> It should not matter who else is measured when you are measured, nor should it matter which particular measuring instruments are used to measure you, so long as they all belong to the relevant class. Rasch named this quality 'specific objectivity'.

(Wilson, 1991, p. 4)

Put more technically, 'specific objectivity' refers to the model's assumption of the separability of the parameters of person ability and item difficulty (Douglas, 1982; Griffin, 1985; Wright & Masters, 1982). This means that the probability of a candidate achieving a correct response (in the case of dichotomously scored items) or a certain level of score (in the case of polytomous items) is purely a question of the difference between the candidate's ability and the difficulty of the item or the difficulty of achieving a particular score level on an item. In other words, to take the simplest case, that is, one involving dichotomous items, the Rasch model proposes that it is only the difference between candidate ability and item difficulty that determines the chances of a correct score.

We are now in a position to understand a little more clearly why a 'discrimination parameter' is deliberately absent in the Rasch model. The inclusion of discrimination would mean that the property of specific objectivity would be lost. Thus, the apparently rather surprising position that the Rasch model adopts on the question of item discrimination has the great advantage that the relative difficulty of items (that is, the difficulty of items relative to each other for any pair of candidates) as estimated by the analysis remains invariant for all pairings of ability levels, and the relative abilities of individual candidates (that is, the abilities of candidates relative to each other for any pair of items) does not depend on which items we are considering. This means that for all candidates, we can map the order of difficulty of items, and a single order will result. Similarly, we can map the ability of candidates onto this single order. As we have seen, this mapping facility, which is characteristic of Rasch analysis, has many practical benefits. For a detailed discussion of the link between the assumption of equal item discrimination and the mapping of items and candidates onto a single ability/difficulty scale, see McNamara (1996, pp. 261–268).

Rasch analysis and the unidimensionality assumption

Another issue raised by Rasch models, and by implication all IRT models, is their assumption of what is known as 'unidimensionality' in the data, and the requirement that tests be carried out to ensure that this assumption is met as part of the analysis (see Chapter 7 for information on how this requirement is implemented). When Rasch first began to be used in language test development, a number of writers argued that, given the complexity of language proficiency models such as those of Canale and Swain (1980), Bachman (1990), Bachman and Palmer (1996), and others, Rasch modelling was inappropriate for the analysis of language test data (Buck, 1992, 1994; Hamp-Lyons, 1989; Nunan, 1988). As Skehan (1984) put it: 'The problem is, fundamentally, that any language performance that is worthy of interest will be complex and multidimensional' (p. 216).

What is unidimensionality? Let us consider the performance of children in a mathematics test that consists of items of two basic types: items where figures only are used ('naked number' problems) and items where the problem is presented in a real-world context, thus involving language ('worded' problems). Imagine that students taking the test come from two linguistic backgrounds: in the first group (Group A), children are native speakers of the language of the test (for example, English) and have few problems in understanding the language in which the worded problems are presented; in the second group (Group B), the children are recently arrived immigrants who have studied mathematics in their country of origin but who have varying degrees of difficulty with the language of the test. Performance in the test will be inconsistent for the latter group compared with the former. For example, assume that the ranking of four students from each group on the basis of the 'naked number' problems only is as shown in Table 8.2: it looks as if the students from Group B are more able. Now let us look at the way in which the rankings emerge when we include performance on the 'worded' problems as well as on the 'naked number' problems shown in Table 8.3. The picture is now different: it looks as if the native-speaker group (Group A) is the more able. Within that group, the relative positions of its four members have

Rank	Student #	Group
1	5	B
2	8	B
3	1	A
4	6	B
5	7	B
6	4	A
7	3	A
8	2	A

Table 8.2: The ranking of students on 'naked number' problems

Rank	Student #	Group
1	1	A
2	4	A
3	3	A
4	5	B
5	2	A
6	6	B
7	7	B
8	8	B

Table 8.3: The ranking of students on 'worded' and 'naked number' problems

remained constant across the two types of problem; that is, students who are better on one type tend also to be better on the other type. This is not so true for the non-native speaker group (Group B); their relative rankings across the two types of problem have changed.

Clearly, no single thing is being measured in this test as a whole: it is a test of language as much as it is a test of mathematical knowledge. Moreover, within the native-speaker student group, the two types of item seem to be measuring the same kind of ability, and so the rankings of the candidates across the two types of item remain constant. This is not so within the non-native speaker group, where differing degrees of proficiency in the language result in different outcomes on the worded problem items in the test compared with the other type of items. To the extent that this was unintended by the test constructors, the test is invalid as a test of mathematics; language skill is obscuring our picture of the ability of individual students to handle mathematical problems. For the native-speaker group considered separately, the test *is* unidimensional in terms of measurement, despite the existence of the two item types; a single pattern of ability emerges for this group across all the items in the test. Across the whole test-taking population (Groups A and B combined), and for the non-native-speaker group, however, the test is not unidimensional in a measurement sense (no single consistent pattern of item difficulty or person ability is emerging from the matrix of student responses to the test items), and this lack of measurement unidimensionality is indicative of a multi-dimensionality in what is being measured—both mathematical ability and language knowledge, which are not correlated.

The term 'unidimensionality' in the phrase 'unidimensionality assumption' in Rasch and other measurement refers to a statistical property of the data, and not the way in which the construct is conceptualized outside the measurement context. The confusion arises from the fact that the term 'unidimensionality' is used in two different ways (Henning, 1992; McNamara, 1991): it is used in psychology to refer to a single underlying (psychological) construct or trait and in measurement to refer to a single underlying pattern of scores observable in the data matrix. We saw such an emergent overriding single pattern in the data matrix in Table 3.2 on page 28; the pattern was sufficiently strong that it could be identified by a visual inspection of the matrix once it had been organized in a particular way. Rasch analysis assumes (or rather, looks for) unidimensionality in this latter measurement sense only, but there is nothing unusual about this. All analyses that involve the summing of scores across different items or different test parts make the same assumption. It should be pointed out, for example, that classical item analysis makes the 'assumption' of unidimensionality, but, unlike Rasch analysis, lacks tests of this assumption to signal violations of it (through fit statistics and other means). It will be argued here that this distinction between the two senses of unidimensionality is critical in understanding the question of the validity of Rasch models for the analysis of language test data. Choppin (1982) has pointed out that psychometric modelling of abilities that deliberately ignores dimensions of complexity known from experience may be compared to the creation of two-dimensional maps to represent distances and areas on the earth's surface. Even when it is known that the assumption of flatness is incorrect, that is, the model is at variance with what is known of the reality being modelled, such maps are useful and adequate for most purposes. It is not a question either of it being necessary to know to what extent our measurement model involves a simplification or distortion; all scientific models are approximate representations of reality, wittingly or unwittingly. As we pointed out in Chapter 4, the famous map of the London Underground shows the direction and stops on various underground lines, but is no guide to the actual physical distances between stations, whether the stations have escalators, and so on. Despite these evident deviations from reality, the simplifying assumptions have yielded a map of great usefulness.

Henning (1992) presents data in support of the view taken here. As we have done, he distinguishes psychological from psychometric unidimensionality. The former he defines in the following way:

> Psychological unidimensionality in a test implies that the test scores are intended to be interpreted as reflective of the extent of the presence of some known unitary psychological construct or trait. ... Inferences may be drawn about the extent of the presence of the intended construct from item performance.

(Henning, 1992, p. 2)

Psychometric unidimensionality, on the other hand (Henning, 1992), 'can be present when the test measures a variety of correlated underlying psychological dimensions ... even when there is no explicit interpretation possible of the primary dimension said to be measured, apart from the operational definitions provided by the items themselves' (p. 3).

Henning produces artificially constructed data sets in which he shows that psychological unidimensionality may be present in the context of psychometric multidimensionality and, more importantly for the present discussion, that psychometric unidimensionality may be present in the context of psychological multidimensionality. He concludes that 'since test modelling procedures involving item response theory assume psychometric unidimensionality rather than psychological unidimensionality, it is apparent that such procedures need not be restricted from application to most language testing data that may be psychologically multidimensional in character' (p. 9).

We can consider the role of each of these meanings in relation to the mathematics example just given. At the test design and construction stage, the test developers formulate an idea of what the test is measuring (the test construct). It is presumably something like 'mathematical ability' or 'mathematical ability in relation to a particular domain of mathematical knowledge and skill'. They may not be aware of the fact that they have also designed a language test. The analysis of the data then attempts to find psychometric (measurement) unidimensionality in the data—a single clear emergent pattern of scores on the items—but fails to find it; instead, multidimensionality is discovered in the data. This search for unidimensionality and the failure to find it is then fed back to the test designers, who can then interpret the failure to establish statistical unidimensionality in the light of their understanding of what is involved in answering the test items; they presumably then become aware of the fact that the items causing the problem are ones where a certain level of language proficiency is required. They are then faced with a difficult decision, which again can only be made in the light of the theory and principles of the teaching of mathematics, about whether the ability to handle worded problems in the language of the local educational system is a necessary part of the mathematical skill being developed in that system. If it is, they may decide to retain the worded problems, but they will need to report the scores on the two item types separately, as they do not go together, at least for the whole group of test takers. The two types of item are apples and oranges, so to speak, and scores on the items cannot simply be added together from a measurement point of view, at least for the non-native speakers, and therefore for the test-taking group as a whole.

We have, then, a kind of interplay between two sources of insight into what the test is measuring: (1) the professional and theoretical knowledge and skill of the test developers, who will have *a priori* theories of the construct(s) underlying their tests at the test design stage, and who will interpret the output of the data analysis in the light of their understanding of these constructs; and (2) the empirical evidence from data analysis (*a posteriori* evidence) which may confirm or disconfirm the claims for the construct validity of the test made by the test constructors.

In designing a test, we hypothesize that the items and persons can be arranged along a single measurement dimension. If items or individuals are found to be misfitting, that is, not measurable along the same dimension, this fact may be interpreted in a number of ways. In relation to items, it may indicate (1) that the item is poorly constructed or (2) that if the item is well-constructed, it does not form part of the same dimension as defined by other items in the test, and is therefore measuring a different construct or trait. In relation to persons, it may indicate (1) that the performance on a particular item was not indicative of the candidate's ability in general, and may have been the result of irrelevant factors such as fatigue, inattention, or failure to take the test item seriously, factors that Henning (1987) groups under the heading of 'response validity'; (2) that the ability of the candidates involved cannot be measured appropriately by the test instrument, that the pattern of responses cannot be explained in the same terms as applied to other candidates, that is, there is a heterogeneous test population in terms of the hypothesis under consideration; or (3) that there may be surprising gaps in the candidate's knowledge of the areas covered by the test. This information can then be used for diagnostic and remedial purposes.

A further issue arises when the data analysis establishes a single measurement dimension where it is proposed that multiple psychological constructs are involved. This is likely to happen where performances of test takers on the separate constructs are correlated, as in most models of language proficiency.

In this case we cannot, of course, argue that the test developers or theorists are wrong about the multiplicity of constructs involved, but that the multiplicity of constructs has not prevented a single, orderly measurement process being achieved. After all, every human activity is bound to be made up of countless different subskills, not all of which it is desirable to measure separately (indeed, it may not be possible even to conceptualize them). Given, then, that psychometric and psychological unidimensionality do not map onto one another in any simple, one-to-one fashion, the question arises as to how sensitive the Rasch measurement model is to departures from unidimensionality in the data, which may perhaps be open to interpretation in terms of test constructs. This is both a theoretical and an empirical question: it has to do with the robustness of the measurement model, and can be addressed empirically: under what circumstances is multidimensionality in the data signalled in practice?

A study that addressed this issue in the context of the 50-minute listening sub-test of the Occupational English Test (OET) is reported in McNamara (1991). Part A required candidates to follow an abstract monologic discourse, whereas Part B involved understanding details of concrete events and personal circumstances in a case history, within the context of a dialogue. Given that different kinds of listening tasks were represented in the two parts of the sub-test, that is, the test was multidimensional from a construct point of view, was it possible to construct a single measurement dimension of 'listening ability within professional contexts' from the data from the sub-test as a whole? Did it make sense to add the scores from the two parts of the listening sub-test? That is, was the listening sub-test psychometrically unidimensional?

Two sorts of evidence were available in relation to these questions. Data from candidates' performances in the test were analysed twice. In the first analysis, data from Parts A and B were combined, and all the items except two were found to form a single measurement dimension, and the overwhelming majority of candidates were able to be measured meaningfully in terms of the dimension of ability so constructed. On the basis of this standard analysis, then, our questions have been answered in the affirmative. A second analysis was carried out in which Part A and Part B were treated as separate tests, and estimates of item difficulty and person ability were made on the basis of each test separately. Following Wright and Masters (1982), if a test as a whole is unidimensional, then it should be possible to produce estimates of person ability using items from different parts of the test, and the estimates should be identical (allowing for the inevitable measurement error in each case). Two different types of statistical test were carried out on the two sets of person ability estimates, and were reassuringly found to provide further strong support for the assumption of psychometric unidimensionality in the test as a whole. Details of the study and of the statistical tests used are provided in McNamara (1991).

More recently, the same procedures were used to check the unidimensionality of a revised scoring rubric for the speaking subsection of the Occupational English Test (O'Hagan, Pill, & Zhang, 2016). Following a study of the criteria used by health professionals in their judgements of the communication skills of trainees in interaction with patients, two additional criteria focusing on engagement with the patient and management of the interaction were added to the existing linguistically oriented criteria. The question arose as to whether there was a single dimension being measured by the new rating scale, or whether performance against the linguistic criteria constituted a separate measurement dimension from that being measured by the two new criteria. The analysis in this case found that the data was not unidimensional, a finding which led to the need for difficult decisions about what would be lost or gained by reporting the two dimensions of communicative ability separately.

As this example shows, the tension between the dimensions of an ability as conceptualized in applied linguistic theory and the unidimensional assumptions of Rasch and other forms of measurement can be put to good use in test validation. An earlier example is a study by O'Loughlin (1992), who designed a comprehension-based writing task and scored the following as separate items: (1) comprehension of the stimulus texts, (2) organization, (3) appropriateness, (4) resources of grammar and expression, and (5) spelling and punctuation. When the items were analysed together, responses to the item 'comprehension of the stimulus texts' were found not to fit the dimension of ability, which could be constructed from responses to the other items. Productive writing skills and comprehension skills, in other words, appeared to represent different dimensions in the analysis; psychometric multidimensionality was found in the data, and this could readily be interpreted in terms of multidimensionality of construct. O'Loughlin therefore decided to report comprehension scores separately from writing ability scores. When the items focusing on productive skills in writing were analysed without the inclusion of the responses on the comprehension item, responses on the item 'spelling and punctuation' were found to be mildly misfitting, that is, another level of multidimensionality was revealed in the data. Again, it was easy to interpret this in the light of our understanding of the components of the writing skill, as this item focuses on mechanical aspects involved in the surface-editing of text, rather than in the expressive aspects of writing. It may be wondered why this item was not misfitting in the original analysis. The answer is that this subtler degree of multidimensionality was masked by the grosser level of multidimensionality apparent in the first analysis. In other words, scores on the item 'spelling and punctuation' were more closely correlated with performance on the other items involving productive writing skills than on the comprehension item. So, scores on 'spelling and punctuation' clustered more with the other writing skill scores rather than with the comprehension score. When the comprehension scores were removed, the diversity within the 'writing' cluster became clearer.

Multidimensionality in a data set such as in O'Loughlin's study is shown to be a relative matter. The more we throw disparate things together in the analysis, the more the analysis will try to fit all the elements together, and the harder it will be to get any clear view of detail. It is a bit like trying to take a photograph in which you want to include a family group in the left middle ground and a church in the background to the right. You can fit them in only by standing back a long way, and in this case it may be hard to recognize detail on the faces of the family members. But if we abandon the attempt to take in the church, and focus just on the family group, then a lot more detail will be revealed.

It seems, then, that the Rasch model, for all its robustness, is capable of detecting psychometric multidimensionality in the data, which can then be interpreted in the light of views on the nature of the skills and abilities involved, thus clarifying the reasons for the observed multidimensionality. As a further check on dimensionality, current practice suggests that in addition to fit analysis, a principal components analysis be carried out on the residuals from the Rasch analysis, to see if a further dimension can be found in the residuals. Methods for carrying out such an analysis can be found in Chapter 7 and on the companion website (www.oup.com/elt/teacher/fjla).

To sum up the argument being made in this section: it is crucial to the discussion of unidimensionality to distinguish consistently between two types of model: a measurement model and a model of the various skills and abilities potentially underlying test performance. The measurement model posited and tested by Rasch analysis deals with the questions: 'Does it make sense in measurement terms to sum scores on different parts of the test? Can all items be summed meaningfully? Are all candidates being measured in the same terms?' This is the 'unidimensionality' assumption (made also within classical test theory analysis). The alternative position requires us to say that separate, qualitative statements about performance on each test item, and of each candidate, are the only valid basis for reporting test performance. As for the interpretation of test scores, this must be done in the light of our best understanding of the nature of language abilities, that is, in the light of current models of the constructs underlying test performance. *A priori* models of this latter type are in a kind of critical tension with the findings of empirical analysis based on measurement models such as the Rasch model, and both kinds of analysis have the potential to illuminate the nature of what is being measured in a particular language test.

The Rasch model and other data analytic methods

In this section we will compare Rasch analysis with two alternative or complementary methods of analysis of language test data that are used in the validation of language tests: generalizability theory (G-theory) and structural equation modelling (SEM). Each will be introduced in a straightforward way, and their relation to Rasch methods will be presented and discussed.

G-theory and the Rasch model

Generalizability theory is an extension of classical test theory, which takes into account multiple sources of variability. It offers a conceptual framework and a set of statistical procedures for identifying and estimating the effect of different factors (known in G-theory as 'facets') in the measurement process (Brennan, 1992). We can use an L2 writing assessment as an example to explain how G-theory works. In a writing assessment, the facets might refer to tasks that test takers are required to complete and the raters who rate their performances. An investigator of a writing assessment might be interested in understanding to what extent task difficulty and rater severity affect test takers' scores. G-theory can help us answer this question by estimating the variability of each facet (i.e. task, rater) and its effect on test score variance.

In the case of this L2 writing assessment, we would expect the variability of test takers' writing ability to be the most important factor in accounting for the variance in test takers' scores. This would give us confidence that the test is really measuring test takers' writing ability. However, as illustrated in previous chapters, factors such as task difficulty and rater severity can affect test takers' scores to a considerable extent. There may also be interaction among the facets: for example, tasks could have differential difficulty on only certain subgroups of test takers, and raters may exercise differential severity when rating different subgroups of test takers. G-theory can estimate the effect of these facets as well as their interactions through a generalizability study (or G-study).

A G-study can distinguish the effects of each facet through partitioning the total variance into variance components, and estimating the magnitude of the effect of each facet and their interactions on test scores. In the case of an L2 writing assessment, a G-study can partition the total variances into: 1) systematic variability of test takers, 2) variability between tasks, 3) variability between raters, and 4) the interactions between test takers, tasks, and raters (i.e. test taker * task; test taker * rater; test taker * task * rater) if task and rater are of interest to the investigator. By so doing, G-theory enables us to pinpoint which sources of variation are particularly problematic and may need to be addressed in assessment procedures in the interest of fairness in assessment. For example, if a G-study indicates that rater variability contributes significantly to the total variance of test scores, the assessment developer should consider providing raters with more rigorous training before they embark on rating, or adding more raters.

On the basis of a G-study, a decision-study (D-study) can be subsequently performed, using the same data as the G-study. The purpose of a G-study, as explained previously, is to pinpoint the sources of variation and estimate the effect of each facet through breaking down the total variance into variance components. In a D-study we can see what it would take to deal with this variance in terms of tasks and raters: we specify a set of conditions for each facet of interest, and then investigate whether and to what extent changing the conditions of the facet affects the dependability or reliability of measuring the target construct. In this example, we can specify the number of tasks and raters, and investigate to what extent dependability of measurement would be altered if, for example, we increased (or decreased) the number of tasks candidates take, or if we increased (or reduced) the number of ratings for each performance. This special feature of D-study is particularly useful to test designers who intend to optimize the design of their assessment instruments. Results from a D-study can help test designers make informed decisions about how to strike an opportune balance between the desired qualities of measurement and practicality. For example, test designers can decide which level of score dependability is achievable, based on an understanding of what resources are required to achieve that desired level.

G-theory differs from Rasch measurement theory in several important aspects. First, G-theory specifies and estimates the effect of different facets through breaking down the total variance into variance components, whereas the Rasch model transforms each raw score into a linear measure and places each measurement facet (for example, person, task, rater) onto an interval (logit) scale so that they can be directly comparable. Second, G-theory provides statistics at the group or aggregate level for each facet. The Rasch model, in comparison, provides estimates for each individual in each measurement facet. In the L2 writing assessment example, G-theory treats test takers, tasks, and raters each as a group, and then provides statistics at group level for each facet. In the case of Rasch analysis, a three-facet Rasch model can be applied to analyse the same data set. The Rasch model then generates a measure (in logits) for each facet (i.e. test taker, task and rater), accompanied by an estimate of the precision of this measure and diagnostic fit statistics (see Chapter 5). Thirdly, while estimating the effect of each facet on test scores, G-theory does not adjust the scores based on the analysis. The Rasch model, on the other hand, adjusts the scores, taking into consideration the variability of the measurement facets such as task difficulty and rater severity. In FACETS, a statistic called 'fair average' represents test takers' adjusted scores (in logits) (see page 102). Perhaps most importantly of all, Rasch measurement is more flexible in rating designs, and can cope with missing data if the analysis is properly designed (see Chapter 7). G-theory analyses require complete data sets, i.e. each rater must assess each candidate on each task of interest. Its tolerance for missing data is limited.

Despite the differences between the two methods, both G-theory and the Rasch model can play a significant role in designing, evaluating and researching language assessments in the interest of fairness. While G-theory can give us a more general picture of the different facets in the measurement process, the Rasch model presents more fine-grained information about each of them. Contingent on the nature of inquiry, assessment developers may use either or both of them to investigate the assessment procedures. For example, if the assessment developer intends to understand whether rater variability affects test takers' scores as a whole, G-theory is a proper choice; on the other hand, if the assessment developer wants to investigate the performance of individual raters, the Rasch model is more useful. The two methods are not antithetical; rather, they are complementary in nature. As Lynch and McNamara pointed out:

> Using the microscope as an analogy, FACETS [the Rasch model] turns the magnification up quite high and reveals every potential blemish on

the measurement surface. GENOVA [G-theory], on the other hand, sets the magnification lower and tends to show us only the net effect of the blemishes at the aggregated level.

(Lynch & McNamara, 1998, p. 176)

Drawing on the complementary roles of G-theory and the Rasch model, researchers in language assessment have employed these two methods collaboratively in designing and evaluating performance assessments (for example, Bachman, Lynch, & Mason, 1995; Kozaki, 2004; Lynch & McNamara, 1998; Sudweeks, Reeve, & Bradshaw, 2004). Because of the unique strengths that each method boasts, it is our view that they can be used collaboratively, in combination, to investigate and reveal the quality of measurement instruments, thus enhancing the fairness of language assessment.

Structural equation modelling and the Rasch model

Structural equation modelling (SEM) is a comprehensive statistical methodology that can analyse whether a theoretical model is supported by empirical data (for example, Byrne, 2010). Differing from traditional statistical methods which can only investigate the relationships between observed variables, SEM is capable of analysing the complex relationships between and among observed and latent variables. Unlike observed variables, which are directly measurable, latent variables are measured indirectly and inferred from other variables that are observable. Latent variables are very useful because they are often aggregated from several or a large number of observed variables, hence making a large data set much more manageable. SEM is a family of statistical techniques, among which the most commonly used include path analysis, confirmatory factor analysis, and structural regression analysis.

The purpose of SEM analysis is to verify whether hypothesized relationships among variables (observed and latent) are supported by empirical data. The following steps are usually followed in a typical SEM analysis. First, a theoretical model is specified *a priori*, based on substantial theory or a hypothesis to be tested. This is a crucial step in SEM analysis, known as 'model specification' or 'model proposal'. Next, SEM is applied to estimate the discrepancy between the variance–covariance matrix as implied by the model and the observed variance–covariance matrix of the empirical data. The discrepancy is indicated by chi-square statistics. The smaller the chi-square statistic, the closer the data fits the model. This step is known as 'model identification'. In addition to chi-square statistics, a host of indices have been made available to assess the fit between the proposed model and the empirical data. A comprehensive introduction to SEM is beyond this chapter. Readers can refer to Kunnan (1998), In'nami & Koizumi (2011), and Ockey & Choi (2015) for a systematic review of SEM as well as its application in language assessment research.

As a powerful statistical analysis method, SEM can be used to address a variety of research questions in language assessment. A typical application of

SEM in language assessment is the investigation of the internal structure of a language test, as an important component of test validation (American Educational Research Association et al., 2014). Based on the theory of language ability underpinning its design, hypothetical relationships can be specified between the different components of the test, each of which is designed to tap into a different aspect of language ability. Next, SEM can be applied to examine whether the hypothesized relationships are supported by the data from the language test, through the model identification procedure explained earlier. It should be noted that in an SEM analysis, several competing models can be specified, assessed against the test data, and compared with each other in terms of model fit. Subsequently, a multi-sample SEM analysis can be performed to investigate the equivalency of a model on different test populations. The analysis is aimed at examining whether the selected model has the same configuration in different groups of test takers. Such evidence can shed light on the interpretations of test scores and, by extension, test fairness.

So how does SEM differ from the Rasch model? As with G-theory, can researchers use SEM and the Rasch model in combination in language assessment research? First, SEM and the Rasch model approach a research question or phenomenon from different methodological perspectives. As explained earlier, SEM takes a confirmatory approach through specifying a model first and then assessing the fit between the model and empirical data. Rasch measurement theory similarly proposes a model (the Rasch model, with its attendant advantages) and sees to what extent the data fits the model. Theoretical models are also important in a further way in Rasch measurement. Nonetheless, because of the different approaches adopted by SEM and the Rasch model, interpretations of fit are different. In SEM, model-data fit is indicated by the chi-square statistic and a host of indices indicating the extent to which the hypothesized relationships in the model are supported by empirical data; in Rasch measurement, fit statistics, indicated by infit and outfit statistics, provide diagnostic information about the functioning of a particular test taker, item, or rater in the measurement process.

Secondly, like G-theory, SEM models data at the group level, whereas the Rasch model provides estimates for each individual in each measurement facet. Importantly, SEM uses raw data to model the hypothesized relationships, specified *a priori*. The Rasch model, however, transforms these data from a non-linear scale to a linear, logit scale that is truly interval. Take a five-point Likert scale used to evaluate test takers' writing performances as an example. SEM treats the data collected with such scales as interval; this data is then used in the SEM analysis. In a Rasch analysis, such scales are considered as ordinal in nature, and the analysis of the data allows the construction of an interval scale onto which item difficulty, person ability, rater severity, and so on can be mapped. SEM is still largely descriptive, despite the complexity of analysis it entails. Given the different features of the two analysis methods, one may ask whether they can be used together in one study. Bond and Fox gave the following advice to those who would like to use SEM and the Rasch model collaboratively:

> For those who are more thoughtfully wedded to SEM, our advice would be spread over two steps: First, that Rasch analysis should be adopted to guide the construction and quality control of measurement scales for *each* of the variables that feature in the research. Second, that the interval-level person Rasch measures and their standard errors *(SEs)* that derive from each of those instruments should be *imputed* into the SEM software for the calculation of the relationships between those variable measures.

(Bond & Fox, 2015, p. 240)

In other words, a Rasch analysis should be performed first with two purposes in mind: 1) to ensure the quality of measurement instruments through such indices as item- and person-fit statistics, and 2) to transform the raw, ordinal measurement scale into an interval one. Next, person ability estimates and their standard errors from the Rasch analysis should be used for a subsequent SEM analysis. In this way, the data in SEM analysis is not raw, that is, it is not from measurement scales that are ordinal; rather, it is derived from a Rasch analysis that prioritizes objective measurement.

Although (as mentioned earlier) SEM has already been used quite extensively in language assessment, we have not seen studies in language assessment employ the two methods, following the advice of Bond and Fox, shown in the quote above. Those who are familiar with both methods may consider leveraging their full potential through applying them sequentially (first Rasch, then SEM) and collaboratively in language assessment research.

Summary

In this chapter we provided an extended summary of the conceptual basis of the family of Rasch models. We examined two of the debates relating to the usefulness of Rasch measurement for the analysis of language testing data; these are debates that appeared in the years immediately following the adoption of Rasch methods in language testing research. The first is about the virtues of Rasch compared with other item response theory models, and the second about the appropriateness of Rasch analysis with its assumption of unidimensionality in the data for the analysis of data from tests of language proficiency, for which complex, multidimensional models have been advanced. We offered an explanation of the potential of different Rasch models for the analysis of dichotomous, polytomous and judge-mediated data, and showed that a proper understanding of the nature of Rasch measurement supports the use of Rasch measurement in language testing research. In the last part of the chapter we briefly compared Rasch measurement with two frequently used classical measurement approaches to the analysis of language testing data— generalizability theory and structural equation modelling—and suggested that the methods, while differing from Rasch measurement in fundamental respects, can be used in a complementary fashion with Rasch methods in the design of studies intended to promote test fairness.

Note

1 The Rasch model is sometimes regarded as roughly equivalent to the one-parameter IRT model, although there are differences (Boone, Staver, & Yale, 2014) that are not relevant to the present discussion.

9

Conclusion: reconciling fairness and justice

This book has attempted to bring two things together that are often kept apart: an introduction to the expertise in measurement techniques necessary for the development and validation of language tests, and the question of the defensibility of the use of tests. We have argued that there are two main issues in arguing for the defensibility of the inferences about individuals drawn from tests and the decisions that result from them. The first is the quality of the inferences themselves: does the test accurately reflect the abilities of the candidate that it claims to be measuring? We have argued that expertise in measurement is crucial for investigating and understanding the potential of tests to draw misleading conclusions about candidates; this is particularly important in borderline cases, and when there is a lot at stake for candidates (access to employment or study opportunities, for example). The second is the use of the test itself, even when the quality of the inferences about candidates that it yields can be guaranteed. Is the use of the test justified? Whose interests is it serving? What values and ideologies does it represent? This takes us away from measurement, although research involving measurement may play a part in clarifying what is at stake and what is feasible in this context. The justification for test use is thus complex, as Messick (1989) in his famous discussion of validity makes us aware. Tests do not exist in a social and policy vacuum but always serve social goals and embody values that are often not made fully explicit. The values that tests embody and the policies that they serve are often not within the control of test developers and researchers; however, even if we cannot alter them, we do have a responsibility to understand them.

In this concluding chapter we will consider the issue of balancing the need for fairness with the need for justice in language testing, as defined in the opening chapters of this book. These two things often go together, but sometimes they do not. Tests can be *just* (i.e. their use is justified) but not *fair* (i.e. their quality is poor), and that is what this book is mainly about: we have focused on ways in which measurement expertise, specifically in Rasch measurement, can act as a lens through which to understand the potential unfairness of tests, and through which to ameliorate factors associated with unfairness.

But what about the opposite case, when tests are of good quality, and hence fair, but their use in the first place is not justified (that is, they are not *just*)? What values are at stake in such cases, and how, as language testers, are we to recognize the values in test constructs, and to reconcile the need for fairness with the need for justice?

A recent example may clarify what is at stake. In 2017 the Australian Minister for Immigration, Peter Dutton, announced proposed changes involving higher English language proficiency requirements in order to be eligible for citizenship. Prior to the announcement, there was no separate test of English proficiency; instead, the required 'knowledge of society' test, which was offered only in English, acted as a *de facto* English test (McNamara & Ryan, 2011). Applicants would now be required to demonstrate a pass at Band 6 on the IELTS test (General Training module) in all four skills (speaking, listening, reading, and writing). IELTS Band 6 is the equivalent of B2 on the Common European Framework of Reference (CEFR) and is sometimes used for university entrance. This proposed new requirement represented a higher level than that currently required in any country in Europe, which itself has seen a progressive tightening of language requirements for citizenship over the last 20 years (Extra et al., 2009; Hogan-Brun et al., 2009; Shohamy & McNamara, 2009; Extramiana et al., 2014). (The highest level required in any country in Europe is B1, and many countries require less.) Moreover, the requirement that applicants demonstrate proficiency in all four language skills imposed a stringent literacy requirement. The UK, for example, requires demonstration of proficiency only in the skills of speaking and listening, at B1 level.

What is the role of the expertise that is the subject of this book in such a context? A number of Australian language-testing specialists, including two of the authors of this book, commented publicly on the proposal, both in the media and in Senate hearings. We were able to point out the inappropriateness of the use of IELTS for this purpose, and questioned the need for such high levels of proficiency and literacy, particularly in the light of the European comparison. If the government had decided to use a test specifically developed for the purpose (instead of IELTS), we would have faced a dilemma regarding whether to be involved in such a development project. On the one hand, an argument could be made in favour of it on grounds of *fairness*— it would be a more appropriate test than IELTS—that is, one more suited to measuring the communicative readiness to participate in the daily tasks of a citizen, and the need to set a standard not arbitrarily but as the result of established standard-setting practice. In each case the expertise that has been discussed in this book would be relevant—in establishing the quality of the test instrument, and in underpinning the standard-setting activity. On the other hand, cooperation in developing such a test would force us to question the *justice* of the test, given the political background to the proposal. A number of researchers have pointed out an ambivalence in the rhetoric of politicians favouring enhanced language proficiency requirements for citizenship. On the surface, the focus of the politicians' arguments is a functionalist one, based on the need for citizens to have sufficient communicative ability in the main language of the country in order to integrate successfully. Shohamy (2009) rejects this argument on a number of grounds: that the use of one's own language is a right and that the acquisition of a language to the required level later in life is both an unreasonable burden and unnecessary. McNamara and Shohamy (2008, p. 93) argue that 'immigrants are ... capable of acquiring aspects of the host language as and when the need arises, and of using other languages to fulfil all the duties and obligations of societal participation (voting, expressing opinions, managing tasks in the workplace and so on)'. Some years previous to the recent proposals for tightening requirements, a senior Australian conservative politician whose parents had emigrated from Greece opposed an earlier proposed tightening of the language proficiency requirements on the grounds that his parents would never have gained citizenship if they had been in force at the time they had applied for citizenship. They had gained citizenship, and they had proven to be upright, productive citizens, using their multilingual networks to communicate effectively, and raising a son who demonstrated evidence of their successful integration. But is the functionalist argument, whatever its merits, the only issue in these debates anyway? Studies of the rhetoric accompanying proposals for tighter language requirements have identified a further underlying theme in the arguments for the proposals which has nothing to do with the functionalist argument. Blackledge (2009) and Horner (2009) analysed speeches of politicians in the UK and Luxembourg respectively favouring tougher language requirements and identified a theme of contested social values: what kind of society will there be in an era of immigration, multiculturalism, and social change? The national language in this context, Blackledge and Horner argued, was a proxy for conservative political values, particularly in relation to immigration, diversity, and multilingualism. In the Australian context, the political background to the proposed changes appeared to indicate something similar. The centre-right government in which Peter Dutton was a Minister was under electoral pressure from a right-wing populist party in the state of Queensland in the north of the country, a state that was likely to prove crucial to the outcome of the next national election. In addition, Minister Dutton belonged to the socially conservative wing of the party, and the proposed changes could be seen as demonstrating his conservative credentials. In the end, the Minister's proposals were defeated in Parliament, but the public debate surrounding the proposals, even the involvement of academic experts who were critical of the government's proposal, effectively publicized the government's intention of getting 'tough' on immigration and citizenship.

Discussions of values in language assessment (McNamara, 2013), central to the conception of validity in Messick's work, are surprisingly absent in language testing research, with the notable exception of work within Critical Language Testing (Shohamy, 2001). There are, perhaps, two reasons for this. The first is the liberal ideology of the educational research tradition in the United States within which Messick and successors like Kane have worked, with its belief that the amelioration of the educational system is in the hands of educators and educational researchers. This tradition assumes the good-will of educational institutions, and takes it as given that the values within assessments can be established and supported by the creators and developers of tests, rather than seeing tests as the servant of policies determined else-where. Perhaps language testing is a particular case, as language is so central to cultural, social, and political life, and can never be divorced from its social context. The structuralist tradition, which still dominates applied linguistics and the training of language testers, also pushes social context and values into the background. Psychometrics and measurement, with their armory of sophisticated techniques that tend to paralyse critique from those not initi-ated in their mysteries, are also cognitive and asocial in orientation.

The second reason is the elusive nature of values in test constructs. We examined the case of the International Civil Aviation Organization (ICAO) language proficiency requirements in Chapter 2. Presumably the native speak-ers who dominated the policy committee that established the requirements were not conscious ideologues of native-speaker privilege. (Remember that native speakers are exempt from the communication requirements, even though studies of communication between pilots and air traffic controllers show that the problems in communication are caused by native speakers in many cases.) Another example is the total absence of tests of English as a lingua franca (ELF), even though much of the world's business, including international education, and activity within multicultural immigrant socie-ties such as the US, Australia, and increasingly the UK, is conducted via English as a lingua franca communication, defined as 'the communicative use of linguistic resources, by native as well as non-native speakers of English, when no other shared means of communication are available or appropriate' (Widdowson, 2013, p. 190). This is because the expert user is enshrined as the benchmark for communicative expertise. But if we take a broader view of communication, not all native speakers are equal by any means. Communication involves the whole personality of the speaker, as Hymes (1972) pointed out, and this includes both non-cognitive and other non-lin-guistic cognitive aspects of communicative ability. Tests of English as a lingua franca communication ability would make no distinction between native and non-native speakers. This seems increasingly appropriate in many work-places, for example in the health service in multicultural societies such as the UK, the US, Australia, Canada, and New Zealand, where those involved in communication in English need to communicate successfully with other speakers whose English might be better or worse than their own. The con-struct in an ELF test would still include language proficiency, but also a range of other things, including communication strategies, willingness to communi-cate, sensitivity to misunderstanding and communication, and the personality characteristics that underlie such abilities. There seems to be little appetite for such a revolutionary change: the inertia of the native-speaker institutions that dominate English language assessment, and the enormous commercial enter-prise which is English language teaching and testing, militate against change. The nature of these issues is rarely articulated within language testing, though they are well canvassed in the literature on English as a lingua franca (Seidlhofer, 2011; Mauranen, 2012; Jenkins, Baker, & Dewey, 2018).

We have described a number of scenarios in which the measurement expertise, which is the principal subject matter of this book, may play a role in relation to broader questions of justice. In the case of the development of a test of English as a lingua franca communication ability, the measurement expertise would become highly relevant to ensure that the test is fair. There are many conceptual and practical issues in the development of such a test that could be investigated using Rasch measurement techniques. For example, the pairing of students of potentially unequal language proficiency in tests of speaking in ELF contexts is likely to involve a variety of differences in proficiency. Would the same impression of ability emerge if the candidate were paired with another candidate of lower ability, or of higher ability, or of equal ability? Should each of these possibilities be sampled in the test design, to see how candidates manage with each other, or can a stable estimate be reached with a single interlocutor, regardless of the proficiency differences? Can stable judgements be made of motivational factors in this communication setting, such as preparedness to negotiate meaning and to notice and resolve miscommunication? What is the role of language proficiency in performance on such a test?

The same palette of measurement techniques can, however, be used to support the use of a test serving an *unjust* policy. As mentioned in Chapter 2, the International Language Testing Association has offered its measurement skills to the International Civil Aviation Organization (ICAO) to improve the quality of the language proficiency tests used in various jurisdictions around the world, many of which are clearly unfair in the measurement sense (i.e. they provide unreliable and uninformative information about the candidate's ability to communicate successfully in the aviation context). But if the policy is misguided, what is the point of this effort? Clearly, as discussed previously, many national jurisdictions have no faith in the reasonableness of the policy, and are using various means to subvert it, for example by disclosing test content, allowing multiple attempts, or choosing a test that everyone can pass. Language testers are usually shocked at this behaviour, but it can be seen as reasonable from the point of view of achieving a more just testing regime to avoid situations in which older, more experienced pilots and air traffic controllers are unreasonably forced out of professional employment because they cannot pass a language proficiency test at the required standard (even though there is evidence that they are actually safe because of their experience and insight into potentially dangerous situations as they begin to unfold).

A similar case of the prioritizing of fairness over justice occurred some twenty years ago when a group of leading American language testers was asked to develop a test of proficiency in English to be used as part of the procedure for gaining American citizenship. The law requires that a person seeking citizenship must have a knowledge of the English language:

> No person [...] shall [...] be naturalized as a citizen of the United
> States upon his own application who cannot demonstrate—an

understanding of the English language, including an ability to read, write and speak words in ordinary usage in the English language.

(United States Code, 2011 edition, title 8 para. 1423 (a) (1))

Typically, implementation of this requirement was rather informal and haphazard. Listening and speaking were assessed informally in the course of the citizenship interview, reading involved reading two sentences aloud, and writing involved writing down two sentences from a known list dictated by the interviewing officer. This clearly did not constitute a valid test of language proficiency. However, when a 'fairer' test was developed along orthodox language testing lines, it was vigorously opposed by immigrant organizations and was never implemented, on the grounds that the modern, 'rational' test was harder, and people were more likely to fail it. The language testers had missed the point of the test. The test functioned as a ritual acknowledgement of the role of English as an aspect of American life, an acknowledgement that people were encouraged and helped to make, rather than an assessment of communicative capacity. Here, the values in the test, and its symbolic function, were misunderstood by the language testers, and their efforts were rightly resisted by those subject to their test and their advocates.

The confusion of fairness and justice in language testing in the context of citizenship is sometimes expressed in other ways. In some countries (for example, previously in the UK, and currently in Australia, although this may change, as we have seen), language is not assessed separately in the citizenship procedure; instead, it is assessed by giving a so-called 'knowledge of society' test in the language concerned, so that the language test is subsumed within the content knowledge test. This has two consequences. First, it disguises the language demands of the test, which remain implicit, so that ordinary citizens, particularly native speakers or fluent users of the language, can't see what all the fuss is about, given that the substantive knowledge of society required of the test consists of ordinary general knowledge of the society's institutions and values. Second, it focuses discussion on oddities in the content. For example, one version of the Australian citizenship test contained questions about a famous cricketer, a favourite of the prime minister who introduced the test. There is an implication that if the content were rectified, the test would become acceptable. This also seems to be the weakness in the critique by Piller (2001) of a citizenship test introduced in Germany. Her target is the policy, a question of justice, but her critique focuses on fairness issues, that is, technical inadequacies in the test.

The overall aim of this book, then, has been to clarify the distinction between fairness and justice in language assessment, and to evaluate the role of measurement expertise in relation to that distinction. It has been necessary to do so for two reasons. First, for those working in language testing, it has attempted to demonstrate that language testing has to be seen in its social context, as necessarily involving values, and that most language testing research has the aim of guaranteeing the fairness of the test, and not addressing its justice, except tangentially. The issue of the justice of language tests, particularly the way in which language tests embody social values and ideologies, is still seriously neglected in language testing research. It requires other kinds of knowledge and skill in addition to psychometric knowledge: awareness of policy and of political processes, insights from social theory, from socially informed philosophy and ethics, and from history. The training of language testers needs to broadened to enable language testing researchers to better understand the deeper meaning of their work.

Second, the book has attempted to show that the apparently arcane, even barren, technical skills required to develop valid tests are in fact skills in the service of another kind of justice—the fairness of language tests. The leading American psychometrician Robert Mislevy once said that he would feel his professional life were worthwhile if he devoted himself exclusively to ensuring the quality of measurement instruments, given the negative consequences for individuals and society of unfair tests; that the task of ensuring test fairness was a life's work, regardless of the broader issues of justice involved in testing (Mislevy, personal communication with Tim McNamara, 2002). We have tried in this book to humanize the technical aspect of language assessment by demonstrating what is at stake for individuals subject to tests when the tests are of poor quality and have been insufficiently validated.

In summary, then, this book has argued that the defensibility of language tests, the justification for their use, must be pursued on two fronts. On the one hand (and this has been the main focus of the book), the quality of test instruments must be established to guarantee their fairness to the greatest extent possible, and this requires the sort of measurement expertise that Rasch measurement represents, given its suitability for the kinds of language tests that are needed today. On the other hand, the values implicit in test constructs, and the policies and ideologies that language tests serve, must be investigated and, if necessary, exposed: this will usually involve another kind of skill, another kind of thinking, though psychometric analysis can sometimes clarify possibilities for alternatives when existing practice is found wanting. Language testing, in other words, as Messick (1989) insisted was true of educational assessment in general, is a thoroughly social, even political activity, and responsible language testing research and practice must be fully cognizant of this reality.

Appendix

Formal statements of Rasch models

In this Appendix we will give a brief introduction to some formal statements of Rasch models. The reader who is not involved in actually using programs such as Winsteps and FACETS may wish to skip this section, which is intended for those needing to make sense of the accompanying program manuals.

Basic Rasch model

We saw that the basic, simplest model is the one that can handle data from dichotomous (right/wrong) items. In this model, the probability that a person will get a score of 1 (as against a score of 0) on a given item is the difference between the ability of the person taking the item and the difficulty of that item. In very simple terms we may express this formally as follows:

$P = Bn - Di$

where:

P = a mathematical expression of the probability of a correct response
Bn = the ability (B) of a particular person (n)
Di = the difficulty (D) of a particular item (i).

Rating scale model (Andrich)

The next two members of the Rasch family of models involve data either from rating scales, or items where partial credit is given for answers; for example, the scores available for a particular question are a range of scores, say 3, 2, 1, or 0, depending on the quality of the answer. (In a comprehension question where the candidate is asked to express his/her understanding freely, points may be allocated according to the amount and relevance of the information provided in the answer.) In this case, a new term is introduced into the model statement: the model statement expresses not only the overall difficulty of any particular item (Di), but the difficulty of gaining a score in each of the available scoring categories for any item, that is, the *step difficulty*.

We can express this as:

P = Bn – Di – Fk

where:

P = a mathematical expression of the probability of achieving a score within a particular score category on a particular item
Bn = the ability (B) of a particular person (n)
Di = the overall difficulty (D) of a particular item (i)
Fk = the difficulty (F) of achieving a score within a particular score category (k) on any item

This is known as Andrich's rating scale model. An important feature of this model is that the step difficulty of an item is assumed to be the same for all items containing a given number of steps; the step difficulty is an average across all items. The possibility of differences in step difficulty between individual items is not considered, or is ignored.

Partial credit model (Masters)

A refinement of the previous model, an expression of a more general case, is Masters' partial credit model. In this model, the step difficulty of the available scoring categories in each item is calculated independently of the step difficulty of each other item—there is no averaging out. We can express this symbolically as follows:

P = Bn – Di – Fik

where:

P = a mathematical expression of the probability of achieving a score within a particular score category on a particular item
Bn = the ability (B) of a particular person (n)
Di = the difficulty (D) of a particular item (i)
Fik = the difficulty (F) of scoring within a particular score category (k) on a particular item (i).

Many-facets or extended Rasch model (Linacre)

Linacre's contribution was to show that it was possible to extend the model to add a further term (or terms) to this sequence, as required. For example, it was possible to add a term for judges (raters) and another for task difficulty; it was also possible to add terms for the interaction between particular judges, particular items and particular rating categories. Each of the aspects of the rating situation—item, ability, task, judge, etc.—is termed a *facet*.

There is no limit in principle to the number of facets that may be specified—the number of aspects of the rating situation considered relevant to the chances of a candidate achieving a particular score on a particular item—but we will restrict ourselves to the common three-facet situation, where the facets are *candidate*, *item*, and *judge*. Analyses at varying levels of delicacy are possible, depending on the extent of complexity with which we wish to model the way judges are interpreting step difficulty: for each item separately, or averaged across all items? For each judge separately, or averaged across all judges? McNamara and Adams (1994) demonstrated the different kinds of information that can be obtained in practice by specifying each of these levels in an analysis of data from four judges scoring performances on the writing sub-test of IELTS, a British/Australian test of English for Academic Purposes. What follows may appear dauntingly abstract and complex, but the possibilities for specification are in fact limited, and represent simple combinations of types of analysis already discussed. It is important to have some understanding of these possibilities in order to carry out a multi-faceted analysis, as you are required to specify which level of delicacy you require. Four commonly used model statements are given below. It is not important to try to be able to reproduce these statements from memory, simply to appreciate that choices of analysis are possible and, in fact, necessary.

(1) Assuming a common step structure across all items and for all judges (i.e. the rating scale is assumed to have the same structure for each observation, regardless of the examinee, item or judge concerned—Andrich's model), we have the *common step* model:

$$P = Bn - Di - Cj - Fk$$

where:

P = a mathematical expression of the probability of achieving a score within a particular score category on a particular item from a particular judge
Bn = the ability of person (n)
Di = the difficulty of item (i)
Cj = the severity of judge (j)
Fk = the difficulty (F) of achieving a score within a particular score category (k) averaged across all judges and all items.[1]

(2) We may wish to continue to ignore differences among *judges* in the way they are interpreting the internal structure (the step difficulties) of the rating scale, but incorporate the refinement of considering the scale structure separately for each *item*. In this case, we get the *item-step* model:

$$P = Bn - Di - Cj - Fik$$

where:

Fik = the difficulty (F) of achieving a score within a particular score category (k) averaged across all judges, but for each item (i) separately. In this case, each *item* is acknowledged to have its own separate step structure, but differences between *judges* are ignored; in other words, we will use the partial credit model for items, but the rating scale model for judges.[2]

(3) In the *judge-step* model, on the other hand, the situation is reversed. Differences in step difficulty among items are ignored, but we model how each individual judge is interpreting these step difficulties:

P = Bn – Di – Cj – Fjk

where:

Fjk = the difficulty (F) of achieving a score within a particular score category (k) averaged across all items but for each judge (j) separately. In this case, we specify the partial credit model for *judges*, but the rating scale model for *items*.[3]

(4) The most delicate level of analysis involves modelling the way each individual judge interprets the scoring categories for each item separately. This is the *judge-item-step* model:

P = Bn – Di – Cj – Fijk

where:

Fijk = the difficulty (F) of achieving a score within a particular score category (k) modelled separately for each item/judge (ij) combination. In this case, we specify the partial credit model for both judges and items.[4]

Table Appendix 1 summarizes the possible model specifications in a multi-faceted analysis involving the facets candidate, item, and judge, and the relevant coding for the FACETS program (the rating scale model is currently coded as '?'; the partial credit model is coded as '#').

Model name	Item	Judge	Model statement	FACETS code (person, item, judge)
common step	rating scale (Andrich)	rating scale (Andrich)	P = Bn - Di - Cj - Fk	?,?,?
item-step	partial credit (Masters)	rating scale (Andrich)	P = Bn - Di - Cj - Fik	?,#,?
judge-step	rating scale (Andrich)	partial credit (Masters)	P = Bn - Di - Cj - Fjk	?,?,#
judge-item-step	partial credit (Masters)	partial credit (Masters)	P = Bn - Di - Cj - Fijk	?,#,#

Table Appendix 1: Model specifications in multi-faceted measurement (example using three facets: person, item, judge)

Notes

1 In the program FACETS, this model corresponds to the selection of the code '?' for each facet in the 'model statement' (a line of commands required in the control file). Thus, where the facets are in the order 'candidate, item, judge', the model statement would contain the string '?,?,?'. For further information, consult the FACETS program manual.

2 The relevant string in the model statement is '?,#,?'.

3 The relevant string in the model statement is '?, ?, #'.

4 The relevant string in the model statement is '?, #, #'.

References

Adams, R. J., & Khoo, S. T. (1993). *Quest: The interactive test analysis system*. Hawthorn, Victoria: Australian Council for Educational Research.

Adams, R., Wu, M., & Wilson, M. (2012). The Rasch rating model and the disordered threshold controversy. *Educational and Psychological Measurement*, 72(4), 547–573.

Alderson, C. (2010). A survey of aviation English tests. *Language Testing*, 27(1), 51–72.

Alderson, C., & Lukmani, Y. (1989). Cognition and reading: Cognitive levels as embodied in test questions. *Reading in a Foreign Language*, 5(2), 253–270.

American Educational Research Association, American Psychological Association, & National Council on Measurement in Education. (2014). *Standards for educational and psychological testing*. Washington, DC: AERA.

Andrich, D. A. (1978). A rating scale formulation for ordered response categories. *Psychometrika*, 43, 561–573.

Aryadoust, V. (2016). Gender and academic major bias in peer assessment of oral presentations. *Language Assessment Quarterly*, 13(1), 1–24.

Aryadoust, V., Goh, C. C., & Kim, L. O. (2011). An investigation of differential item functioning in the MELAB listening test. *Language Assessment Quarterly*, 8(4), 361–385.

Bachman, L. F. (1990). *Fundamental considerations in language testing*. Oxford: Oxford University Press.

Bachman, L. F. (2000). Modern language testing at the turn of the century: Assuring that what we count counts. *Language Testing*, 17(1), 1–42.

Bachman, L. F., Lynch, B. K., & Mason, M. (1995). Investigating variability in tasks and rater judgments in a performance test of foreign language speaking. *Language Testing*, 12(2), 238–257.

Bachman, L. F., & Palmer, A. S. (1996). *Language testing in practice: Designing and developing useful language tests*. Oxford: Oxford University Press.

Bachman, L. F., & Palmer, A. S. (2010). *Language assessment in practice: Developing language assessments and justifying their use in the real world*. Oxford: Oxford University Press.

Baghaei, P. (2008). The Rasch model as a construct validation tool. *Rasch Measurement Transactions*, 22(1), 1145–1146.

Batty, A. O. (2015). A comparison of video- and audio-mediated listening tests with many-facet Rasch modeling and differential distractor functioning. *Language Testing*, 32(1), 3–20.

Beglar, D. (2010). A Rasch-based validation of the Vocabulary Size Test. *Language Testing*, 27(1), 101–118.

Bejar, I., Douglas, D., Jamieson, J., Nissan, S., & Turner, J. (2000). *TOEFL® 2000 listening framework: A working paper. TOEFL Report MS-19*. Princeton, NJ: Educational Testing Service.

Birnbaum, A. (1968). Some latent train models and their use in inferring an examinee's ability. In F. M. Lord, & M. R. Novick (Eds.), *Statistical theories of mental test scores* (pp. 397–472). Reading, MA: Addison-Wesley.

Blackledge, A. (2009). "As a country we do expect": The further extension of language testing regimes in the United Kingdom. *Language Assessment Quarterly*, 6(1), 6–16.

Bond, T., & Fox, C. M. (2015). *Applying the Rasch model: Fundamental measurement in the human sciences* (3rd ed.). New York: Routledge.

Boone, W. J., Staver, J. R., & Yale, M. S. (2014). *Rasch analysis in the human sciences*. New York & London: Springer.

Brennan, R. L. (1992). Generalizability theory. *Educational Measurement: Issues and Practice*, 11(4), 27–34.

Brown, J. D. (2001). *Using surveys in language programs*. New York: Cambridge University Press.

Buck, G. (1992, February–March). *The construction of multidimensional data sets*. Paper presented at the 14th Language Testing Research Colloquium, Vancouver.

Buck, G. (1994). The appropriacy of psychometric measurement models for testing second language listening comprehension. *Language Testing, 11*(2), 145–170.

Burga Leon, A. (2008). Common-item (or Common-person) equating with different test discriminations. *Rasch Measurement Transactions, 22*(3), 1172.

Byrne, B. M. (2010). *Structure equation modeling with AMOS: Basic concepts, applications, and programming* (2nd ed.). Mahwah, NJ: Lawrence Erlbaum Associates.

Cameron, R., & Williams, J. (1997). Senténce to ten cents: A case study of relevance and communicative success in nonnative–native speaker interactions in a medical setting. *Applied Linguistics, 18*(4), 415–445.

Canagarajah, S. (2018). Translingual practice as spatial repertoires: Expanding the paradigm beyond structuralist orientations. *Applied Linguistics, 39*(1), 31–54.

Canale, M., & Swain, M. (1980). Theoretical bases of communicative approaches to second language teaching and testing. *Applied Linguistics, 1*(1), 1–47.

Chapelle, C. A. (2008). The TOEFL validity argument. In C. A. Chapelle, M. Enright, & J. Jamieson (Eds.), *Building a validity argument for the Test of English as a Foreign Language* (pp. 319–352). London: Routledge.

Choi, I. C., & Bachman, L. F. (1992). An investigation into the adequacy of three IRT models for data from two EFL reading tests. *Language Testing, 9*(1), 51–78.

Choppin, B. (1982). The use of latent trait models in the measurement of cognitive abilities and skills. In D. Spearritt (Ed.), *The improvement of measurement in education and psychology: Contributions of latent trait theories* (pp. 41–63). Hawthorn, Victoria: Australian Council of Educational Research.

Council of Europe. (2001). *Common European framework of reference for languages: Learning, teaching, assessment*. Cambridge: Cambridge University Press.

Davies, A. (Guest Ed.) (1997). Ethics in language testing. Special issue. *Language Testing, 14*(3).

Davies, A. (Guest Ed.) (2004). The ethics of language assessment. Special issue. *Language Assessment Quarterly, 1*(2 & 3).

Dörnyei, Z. (2003). *Questionnaires in second language research: Construction, administration, and processing*. Mahwah, NJ: Lawrence Erlbaum Associates.

Douglas, G. A. (1982). Conditional inference in a generic Rasch model. In D. Spearritt (Ed.), *The improvement of measurement in education and psychology: Contributions of latent trait theories* (pp. 129–157). Hawthorn, Victoria: Australian Council of Educational Measurement.

Draxler, C. (2010). Sample size determination for Rasch model tests. *Psychometrika 75*, 708–24.

Draxler, C., & Alexandrowicz, R. W. (2015). Sample size determination within the scope of Conditional Maximum Likelihood estimation with special focus on testing the Rasch Model. *Psychometrika, 80*, 897–919.

Eckes, T. (2011). *Introduction to many-facet Rasch measurement: Analyzing and evaluating rater-mediated assessments*. Frankfurt: Peter Lang.

Elder, C. (Ed.). (2016). Special issue: Authenticity in LSP testing. *Language Testing, 33*(2).

Elder, C., Knoch, U., Barkhuizen, G., & von Randow, J. (2005). Individual feedback to enhance rater training: Does it work? *Language Assessment Quarterly, 2*(3), 175–196.

Elder, C., McNamara, T., Kim, H., Pill., J., & Sato, T. (2017). Interrogating the construct of communicative competence in language assessment contexts: What the non-language specialist can tell us. *Language and Communication, 57*, 14–21.

Enright, M. K., Grabe, W., Koda, K., Mosenthal, P., Mulcahy-Ernt, P., & Schedl, M. (2000). TOEFL® 2000 reading framework: A working paper. *TOEFL report MS-17*. Princeton, NJ: Educational Testing Service.

Esfandiari, R., & Myford, C. M. (2013). Severity differences among self-assessors, peer-assessors, and teacher assessors rating EFL essays. *Assessing Writing, 18*(2), 111–131.

Extra, G., Spotti, M., & Van Avermaet, P. (Eds.). (2009). *Language testing, migration and citizenship: Cross-national perspectives on integration regimes*. London: Continuum.

Extramiana, C., Pulinx, R., & Van Avermaet, P. (2014). *Linguistic integration of adult migrants: Policy and practice. Report on the 3rd Council of Europe survey*. Strasbourg: Council of Europe.

Fédération Internationale de Natation. (2017). FINA diving rules [PDF]. Retrieved from http://www.fina.org/sites/default/files/2017-2021_diving_16032018.pdf

Ferne, T., & Rupp, A. A. (2007). A synthesis of 15 years of research on DIF in language testing: Methodological advances, challenges, and recommendations. *Language Assessment Quarterly, 4*(2), 113–148.

Filipi, A. (2012). Do questions written in the target language make foreign language listening comprehension tests more difficult? *Language Testing, 29*(4), 511–532.

Fisher, W. P. (1992). Reliability statistics. *Rasch measurement: Transactions of the Rasch measurement SIG, 6*, 238.

Frost, K. (2018). *Test impact as dynamic process: Individual experiences of the English test requirements for permanent skilled migration in Australia*. (Unpublished doctoral dissertation), The University of Melbourne.

Fulcher, G. (2003). *Testing second language speaking*. London: Pearson Longman.

Goodwin, A. P., Huggins, A. C., Carlo, M., Malabonga, V., Kenyon, D., Louguit, M., & August, D. (2012). Development and validation of extract the base: An English derivational morphology test for third through fifth grade monolingual students and Spanish-speaking English language learners. *Language Testing, 29*(2), 265–289.

Griffin, P. E. (1985). The use of latent trait models in the calibration of tests of spoken language in large-scale selection-placement programs. In Y. P. Lee, A. C. Y. Y. Fok, R. Lord, & G. Low (Eds.), *New directions in language testing* (pp. 149–161). Oxford: Pergamon.

Hambleton, R. K., Swaminathan, H., & Rogers, H. J. (1991). *Fundamentals of item response theory*. Newbury Park, CA: Sage.

Hamp-Lyons, L. (1989). Applying the partial credit method of Rasch analysis: Language testing and accountability. *Language Testing, 6*(1), 109–118.

Henning, G. (1987). *A guide to language testing: Development, evaluation, research*. Cambridge, MA: Newbury House.

Henning, G. (1992). Dimensionality and construct validity of language tests. *Language Testing, 9*(1), 1–11.

Hirai, A., & Koizumi, R. (2013). Validation of empirically derived rating scales for a story retelling speaking test. *Language Assessment Quarterly, 10*(4), 398–422.

Hobart, J. C., Cano, S. J., Warner, T. T., Thompson, A. J. (2012). What sample sizes for reliability and validity studies in neurology? *Journal of Neurology, 259*(12), 2681–2694.

Hogan-Brun, G., Mar-Molinero, C., Stevenson, P. (Eds.). (2009). *Discourses on language and integration: Critical perspectives on language testing regimes in Europe*. Amsterdam: John Benjamins.

Horner, K. (2009). Language, citizenship and Europeanization: Unpacking the discourse of integration. In G. Hogan-Brun, C. Mar-Molinero, & P. Stevenson (Eds.), *Discourses on language and integration: Critical perspectives on language testing regimes in Europe*. Amsterdam: John Benjamins.

Hsieh, M. (2013). An application of multifaceted Rasch measurement in the Yes/No Angoff standard setting procedure. *Language Testing, 30*(4), 491–512.

Hymes. D. H. (1972). On communicative competence. In J. B. Pride, & J. Holmes (Eds.), *Sociolinguistics* (pp. 269–293). Harmondsworth: Penguin.

IELTS. (2018). How IELTS is scored. Retrieved from https://www.ielts.org/about-the-test/how-ielts-is-scored

In'nami, Y., & Koizumi, R. (2011). Structural equation modeling in language testing and learning research: A review. *Language Assessment Quarterly, 3*, 250–276.

Izard, J. (1981). *The robustness of Rasch analysis procedures*. Hawthorn, Victoria: Australian Council for Educational Research.

Jenkins, J., Baker, W., & Dewey, M. (2018). *The Routledge handbook of English as a lingua franca*. London and New York: Routledge.

Johnson, J. S. (2003). *Michigan English language assessment battery technical manual 2003*. Ann Arbor, MI: University of Michigan, Testing and Certification Division, English Language Institute.

Kane, M. T. (2006). Validation. In R. L. Brennan (Ed.), *Educational measurement* (4th ed., pp. 17–64). Westport, CT: American Council on Education/Praeger.

Kane, M. (2010). Validity and fairness. *Language Testing, 27(2)*, 177–182.

Kiddle, T., & Kormos, J. (2011). The effect of mode of response on a semidirect test of oral proficiency. *Language Assessment Quarterly, 8(4)*, 342–360.

Kim, H. (2012). *Exploring the construct of aviation communication: A critique of the ICAO language proficiency policy* (Unpublished doctoral dissertation), The University of Melbourne.

Kim, H., & Elder, C. (2015). Interrogating the construct of aviation English: Feedback from test takers in Korea. *Language Testing, 32(2)*, 129–149.

Kirsch, I. S., & Mosenthal, P. B. (1988). Understanding document literacy: Variables underlying the performance of young adults. *ETS Research Report Series, 1988(2)*, i–67.

Knoch, U. (2009). *Diagnostic assessment of writing: The development and validation of a rating scale*. Frankfurt: Peter Lang.

Knoch, U. (2011). Investigating the effectiveness of individualized feedback to rating behaviour – a longitudinal study. *Language Testing, 28(2)*, 179–200.

Kozaki, Y. (2004). Using GENOVA and FACETS to set multiple standards on performance assessment for certification in medical translation from Japanese into English. *Language Testing, 21(1)*, 1–27.

Kubinger, K. D., Rasch, D. & Yanagida, T. (2009). On designing data-sampling for Rasch model calibrating an achievement test. *Psychology Science Quarterly, 51*, 370–384.

Kunnan, A. J. (1998). An introduction to structural equation modeling for language assessment research. *Language Testing, 15(3)*, 295–332.

Kunnan, A. J. (Ed.) (2000). *Fairness and validation in language assessment*. Cambridge: Cambridge University Press.

Kunnan, A. J. (2004). Test fairness. In M. Milanovic, & C. Weir (Eds.), *European year of languages conference papers, Barcelona* (pp. 27–48). Cambridge: Cambridge University Press.

Kunnan, A. J. (2010). Test fairness and Toulmin's argument structure. *Language Testing, 27(2)*, 183–189.

Likert, R. (1932). A technique for the measurement of attitudes. *Archives of Psychology, 22*, 5–53.

Lim, G. S. (2011). The development and maintenance of rating quality in performance writing assessment: A longitudinal study of new and experienced raters. *Language Testing, 28(4)*, 543–560.

Linacre, J. M. (1989). *Many-faceted Rasch measurement*. Chicago, IL: MESA Press.

Linacre, J. M. (1994). Sample size and item calibration stability. *Rasch Measurement Transactions, 7(4)*, 328.

Linacre, J. M. (1997a). KR-20/Cronbach Alpha or Rasch Person Reliability: Which tells the 'truth'? *Rasch Measurement Transactions, 11(3)*, 580–581.

Linacre, J. M. (1997b). *Judging plans and facets (Research Note No. 3)*. Chicago: University of Chicago, MESA Psychometric Laboratory. Retrieved from http://www.rasch.org/rn3.htm

Linacre, J. M. (1999). Investigating rating scale category utility. *Journal of Outcome Measurement, 3(2)*, 103–122.

Linacre, J. M. (2002a). What do infit and outfit, mean-square and standardized mean? *Rasch Measurement Transactions, 16*, 878.

Linacre, J. M. (2002b). Optimizing rating scale category effectiveness. *Journal of Applied Measurement, 3*(1), 85–106.

Linacre, J. M. (2004). Optimizing rating scale effectiveness. In E. V. Smith, & R. M. Smith (Eds.), *Introduction to Rasch measurement* (pp. 257–278). Maple Grove, MN: JAM Press.

Linacre, J. M. (2011). *Winsteps tutorial further topics 4*. Retrieved from http://winsteps.com/a/winsteps-tutorial-further-4.pdf

Linacre, J. M. (2012). *Winsteps tutorial*. Retrieved from http://www.winsteps.com/tutorials.htm

Linacre, J. M. (2015). Facets computer program for many-facet Rasch measurement, version 3.71.4. Beaverton, Oregon: Winsteps.com.

Linacre, J. M. (2016). *Winsteps® Rasch measurement computer program User's Guide*. Beaverton, Oregon: Winsteps.com.

Linacre, J. M., & Wright, B. D. (1994). Dichotomous infit and outfit mean-square fit statistics. *Rasch Measurement Transactions, 8*(2), 360.

Lord, F. M. (1980). *Applications of item response theory to practical testing problems*. Hillsdale, NJ: Lawrence Erlbaum Associates.

Lord, F. M., & Novick, M. R. (1968). *Statistical theories of mental test scores*. Reading, MA: Addison-Wesley.

Ludlow, L. & O'Leary, M. (2000). What to do about missing data? *Rasch Measurement Transactions, 14*(2), 751.

Lumley, T., Lynch, B. K., & McNamara, T. (1994). A new approach to standard-setting in language assessment. *Melbourne Papers in Language Testing, 3*, 19–39.

Lynch, B. K., & McNamara, T. (1998). Using G-theory and many-facet Rasch measurement in the development of performance assessments of the ESL speaking skills of immigrants. *Language Testing, 15*(2), 158–180.

Marefat, F., & Heydari, M. (2016). Native and Iranian teachers' perceptions and evaluation of Iranian students' English essays. *Assessing Writing, 27*, 24–36.

Masters, G. N. (1982). A Rasch model for partial credit scoring. *Psychometrica, 47*, 149–174.

Mauranen, A. (2012). *Exploring ELF: Academic English shaped by non-native speakers*. Cambridge: Cambridge University Press.

McNamara, T. (1991). Test dimensionality: IRT analysis of an ESP listening test. *Language Testing, 8*(2), 139–159.

McNamara, T. (1996). *Measuring second language performance*. London & New York: Longman.

McNamara, T. (2013). Values in language assessment. In C. A. Chapelle (Ed.), *The Encyclopedia of Applied Linguistics*. Volume 10 (pp. 6027–6032). Oxford: Wiley-Blackwell.

McNamara, T. (2014). 30 years on – evolution or revolution? *Language Assessment Quarterly, 11*(2), 226–232.

McNamara, T., & Adams, R. (1994). Exploring rater behaviour with Rasch techniques. *Selected Papers of the 13th Annual Language Testing Research Colloquium (LTRC)*. Princeton, NJ: Educational Testing Service, International Testing and Training Program Office (also available as ERIC Document Reproduction Service No. ED 345 498).

McNamara, T., Khan, K., & Frost, K. (2014). Language tests for residency and citizenship and the conferring of individuality. In B. Spolsky, O. Inbar-Lourie, & M. Tannenbaum (Eds.), *Challenges for language education and policy: Making space for people* (pp. 11–22). New York: Routledge.

McNamara, T., & Knoch, U. (2012). The Rasch wars: The emergence of Rasch measurement in language testing. *Language Testing, 29*(4), 555–576.

McNamara, T., Morton, J., Storch, N., & Thompson, C. (2018). Students' accounts of their first-year undergraduate academic writing experience: Implications for the use of the CEFR. *Language Assessment Quarterly, 15*(1), 16–28.

McNamara, T., & Roever, C. (2006). *Language testing: The social dimension*. Malden, MA: Blackwell.

McNamara, T., & Ryan, K. (2011). Fairness vs justice in language testing: The place of English literacy in the Australian Citizenship Test. *Language Assessment Quarterly, 8*(2), 161–178.

McNamara, T., & Shohamy, E. (2008). Language tests and human rights. *International Journal of Applied Linguistics, 18*(1), 89–95.

Messick, S. (1989). Validity. In R. L. Linn (Ed.), *Educational Measurement* (3rd ed., pp. 13–103). New York: American Council on Education & Macmillan.

Moore, T., & Morton, J. (2005). Dimensions of difference: A comparison of university writing and IELTS writing. *Journal of English for Academic Purposes, 4*, 43–66.

Moore, T., Morton, J., Hall, D., & Wallis, C. (2015). Literacy practices in the professional workplace: Implications for the IELTS reading and writing tests. *IELTS Research Reports Online Series 2015/1.* Retrieved from https://www.ielts.org/-/media/research-reports/ielts_online_rr_2015-1.ashx

Mossenson, L., Hill, P., & Masters, G. (1987). *TORCH: Test of reading comprehension. Manual.* Hawthorn, Victoria: Australian Council for Educational Research.

Muraki, E., Hombo, C. M., & Lee, Y. W. (2000). Equating and linking of performance assessments. *Applied Psychological Measurement* 24, 325–337.

Myford, C. M., & Wolfe, E. W. (2000). Strengthening the ties that bind: improving the linking network in sparsely connected rating designs. *TOEFL technical report TR-15.* Princeton, NJ: Educational Testing Service.

Myford, C. M., & Wolfe, E. W. (2003). Detecting and measuring rater effects using many-facet Rasch measurement: Part 1. *Journal of Applied Measurement, 4*(4), 386–422.

Myford, C. M., & Wolfe, E. W. (2004). Detecting and measuring rater effects using many-facet Rasch measurement: Part 2. *Journal of Applied Measurement, 5*(2), 189–227.

North, B. (2000). *The development of a common framework scale of language proficiency.* New York: Peter Lang.

North, B., Goodier, T., & Piccardo, E. (2017). *Common European framework of reference for languages: Learning, teaching, assessment. Companion volume with new descriptors* (Provisional Edition). Strasbourg: Council of Europe, Language Policy Programme, Education Policy Division, Education Department. Retrieved from https://rm.coe.int/common-european-framework-of-reference-for-languages-learning-teaching/168074a4e2

Nunan, D. (1988). Commentary on the Griffin paper. *Australian Review of Applied Linguistics, 11*(2), 54–65.

Ockey, G. J., & Choi, I. (2015). Structural equation modeling reporting practices for language assessment. *Language Assessment Quarterly, 12*(3), 305–319.

O'Hagan, S., Pill, J., & Zhang, Y. (2016). Extending the scope of speaking assessment criteria in a specific-purpose language test: Operationalizing a health professional perspective. *Language Testing, 33*(2), 195–216.

O'Loughlin, K. J. (1992). *Final report of the University of Melbourne Trial English Selection Test.* Language Testing Research Centre, The University of Melbourne.

Pae, H. K., Greenberg, D., & Morris, R. D. (2012). Construct validity and measurement invariance of the Peabody Picture Vocabulary Test–III Form A. *Language Assessment Quarterly, 9*(2), 152–171.

Papageorgiou, S., Stevens, R., & Goodwin, S. (2012). The relative difficulty of dialogic and monologic input in a second-language listening comprehension test. *Language Assessment Quarterly, 9*(4), 375–397.

Pill, J., & McNamara, T. (2016). How much is enough? Involving occupational experts in setting standards on a specific-purpose English language test for health professionals. *Language Testing, 33*(2), 217–234.

Piller, I. (2001). Naturalisation language testing and its basis in ideologies of national identity and citizenship. *International Journal of Bilingualism 5*(3), 259–278.

Rasch, G. (1960/1980). Probabilistic models for some intelligence and attainment tests. (Copenhagen, Danish Institute for Educational Research), expanded edition (1980) with foreword and afterword by B. D. Wright. Chicago: University of Chicago Press.

Rasch, G. (1961). On general laws and the meaning of measurement in psychology. In *Proceedings of the fourth Berkeley symposium on mathematical statistics and probability* (pp. 321–333). Berkeley, CA: University of California Press.

Rasch, G. (1966). An individualistic approach to item analysis. In P. F. Lazarsfeld, & N. W. Henry (Eds.), *Readings in mathematical social science* (pp. 89–107). Chicago: Science Research Associates.

Read, J., & Knoch, U. (2009). Clearing the air: Applied linguistic perspectives on aviation communication. *Australian Review of Applied Linguistics, 32*(3), 21.1–21.11.

Seidlhofer, B. (2011). *Understanding English as a lingua franca.* Oxford: Oxford University Press.

Shohamy, E. (2000). Fairness in language testing. In A. J. Kunnan (Ed.), *Fairness and validation in language assessment* (pp. 15–19). Cambridge: Cambridge University Press.

Shohamy, E. (2001). *The power of tests: A critical perspective on the uses of language tests.* London: Pearson.

Shohamy, E. (2006). *Language policy: Hidden agendas and new approaches.* Abingdon & New York: Routledge.

Shohamy, E. (2009). Language tests for immigrants: Why language? Why tests? Why citizenship? In G. Hogan-Brun, C. Mar-Molinero, & P. Stevenson (Eds.), *Discourses on language and integration: Critical perspectives on language testing regimes in Europe.* Amsterdam: John Benjamins.

Shohamy, E. & McNamara, T. (2009). Language tests for citizenship, immigration, and asylum. *Language Assessment Quarterly 6*(1), 1–5.

Skehan, P. (1984). Issues in the testing of English for specific purposes. *Language Testing, 1*(2), 202–220.

Skehan, P. (1998). *A cognitive approach to language learning.* Oxford: Oxford University Press.

Smith, A. B., Rush, R., Fallowfield, L., Velikova, G., & Sharpe, M. (2008). Rasch fit statistics and sample size considerations for polytomous data. *BMC Medical Research Methodology, 8*(1), 33.

Smith, E. V., Jr. (2000). Understanding Rasch measurement: Metric development and score reporting in Rasch measurement. *Journal of Applied Measurement, 1*(3), 303–326.

Smith, R. M. (1996). Polytomous mean-square fit statistics. *Rasch Measurement Transactions, 10*(3), 516–517.

Spolsky, B. (1981). Some ethical questions about language testing. In C. Klein-Braley & D. K. Stevenson (Eds.), *Practice and problems in language testing* (pp. 5–21). Frankfurt: Peter Lang.

Stemler, S. E. (2004). A comparison of consensus, consistency, and measurement approaches to estimating interrater reliability. *Practical Assessment, Research and Evaluation, 9*(4), 1–20.

Stemler, S. E., & Tsai, J. (2008). Best practices in interrater reliability. Three common approaches. In J. W. Osborne (Ed.), *Best practices in quantitative methods* (pp. 29–49). Los Angeles: Sage.

Sudweeks, R. R., Reeve, S., & Bradshaw, W. S. (2004). A comparison of generalizability theory and many-facet Rasch measurement in an analysis of college sophomore writing. *Assessing Writing, 9*(3), 239–261.

Thorndike, R. L. (1982). Educational measurement-theory and practice. In D. Spearritt (Ed.), *The improvement of measurement in education and psychology: Contributions of latent trait theories* (pp. 3–13). Hawthorn, Victoria: Australian Council for Educational Research.

United States Code, 2011 Edition, Title 8 – Aliens and Nationality. Retrieved from https://www.gpo.gov/fdsys/pkg/USCODE-2011-title8/html/USCODE-2011-title8.htm

Wei, J., & Llosa, L. (2015). Investigating differences between American and Indian raters in assessing TOEFL iBT speaking tasks. *Language Assessment Quarterly, 12*(3), 283–304.

Widdowson, H. G. (2013). ELF and EFL: what's the difference? Comments on Michael Swan. *Journal of English as a Lingua Franca 2*(1), 187–193.

Wigglesworth, G. (1993). Exploring bias analysis as a tool for improving rater consistency in assessing oral interaction. *Language Testing, 10*(3), 305–319.

Wilson, M. (Ed.). (1991). *Objective measurement: Theory into practice.* Norwood, NJ: Ablex.

Winke, P., Gass, S., & Myford, C. (2013). Raters' L2 background as a potential source of bias in rating oral performance. *Language Testing, 30*(2), 231–252.

Wright, B. D. (1988, April). *George Rasch and measurement.* Informal remarks at the Inaugural Meeting of the American Educational Research Association Rasch Measurement SIG. New Orleans, April.

Wright, B. D. (1991). Diagnosing misfit. *Rasch Measurement Transactions, 5*(2), 156.

Wright, B. D. (1992). Point-biserials and item fits. *Rasch Measurement Transactions, 5*(2), 174.

Wright, B. D., & Douglas, G. (1975). *Best test design and self-tailored testing. MESA Memorandum No. 19.* Department of Education, The University of Chicago.

Wright, B. D., Linacre, J. M., Gustafsson, J. E., & Martin-Loff, P. (1994). Reasonable mean-square fit values. *Rasch Measurement Transactions, 8*(3), 370.

Wright, B. D., & Masters, G. N. (1982). *Rating scale analysis.* Chicago, IL: MESA Press.

Wright, B. D., & Stone, M. H. (1979). *Best test design.* Chicago, IL: MESA Press.

Xi, X. (2010). How do we go about investigating test fairness? *Language Testing, 27,* 147–170.

Yan, X. (2014). An examination of rater performance on a local oral English proficiency test: A mixed-methods approach. *Language Testing, 31*(4), 501–527.

Zhang, J. (2016). Same text different processing? Exploring how raters' cognitive and meta-cognitive strategies influence rating accuracy in essay scoring. *Assessing Writing, 27,* 37–53.

Zhang, Y., & Elder, C. (2011). Judgments of oral proficiency by non-native and native English speaking teacher raters: Competing or complementary construct? *Language Testing, 28*(1), 31–50.

Index